W9-BHZ-532

CARIBBEAN STORY
Book One: Foundations

CARIBBEAN STORY
Book One: Foundations

William Claypole PhD (UWI)
John Robottom BA

Assignments provided by Coleridge Barnett
Principal, Wolmers Boys' School, Kingston, Jamaica

Editorial adviser Dr Bridget Brereton
Department of History, UWI, St Augustine, Trinidad

Longman Caribbean

Longman Caribbean
Longman Group UK Limited
Longman House, Burnt Mill, Harlow,
Essex CM20 2JE, England
and Associated Companies throughout the world.

Carlong Publishers (Caribbean) Limited
P.O. Box 489
43 Second Street, Newport West,
Kingston 10, Jamaica

Longman Trinidad Limited,
Boundary Road, San Juan, Trinidad

© Longman Group Ltd 1980
This edition © Longman Group UK Ltd 1989

All rights reserved. No part of this publication may be reproduced,
stored in a retrieval system or transmitted in any form or
by any means, electronic, mechanical, photocopying, recording,
or otherwise, without the prior written permission of the Publishers.

First edition 1980
Second edition 1989
Seventh impression 1993

Set in 10/12pt Plantin, Linotron 202
Printed in Malaysia by PA

Claypole, William
  Caribbean story. – (New ed)
  Bk. 1, Foundations
  1. Caribbean region, history
  I. Title II. Robottom, John
  909' .0982 1

ISBN 0 582 03984 3

Acknowledgements

The authors are grateful to the many people who
advised on the manuscript. In particular they would
like to thank Dr Sahadeo Basdeo, Dr Bridget
Brereton, Anne Hickling-Hudson, Professor Keith
Laurence, and Constance Morgan.

The Publishers are grateful to the following for their
permission to reproduce photographs:

American History Picture Library for figs. 1.4, 14.2,
17.1 and 15.2; Barbados Tourist Board for fig. 19.2;
British Museum for figs. 1.1, 2.1, 2.2, 2.5, 3.1; 10.3;
Camera Press for fig. 22.2; Church Missionary Society
for fig. 20.3; Adrian Deere-Jones for fig. 1.3; Mary
Evans Picture Library for figs. 3.3, 3.4, 4.2, 4.3, 5.1,
5.2, 6.3, 7.3, 7.4, 8.2, 8.3, 8.4, 12.4, 18.1, 19.1, 20.1,
20.2, 20.5 and 21.2; Fotomas Index for figs. 11.3 and
18.2; Hoa-Qui for fig. 10.2; Hulton Deutsch Collection
for figs. 3.2, 6.2, 6.4, 9.1, 9.2, 11.2, 17.3 and 20.4;
Mansell Collection for figs. 1.2, 2.4, 6.1, 8.1, 12.1,
16.1, 16.2 and 22.1; National Maritime Museum for
figs. 7.2 and 15.1; National Museum, Lagos for
fig. 10.4; RIDA Photo Library for fig. 10.1; Royal
Commonwealth Society Library for figs. 8.5, 13.2, 13.3,
13.4, 14.3 and 15.3; U.S.P.G. for fig. 8.7; Werner
Forman Archive for fig. 11.1 and West India
Committee for figs. 2.3, 4.1, 7.1, 8.6, 12.2, 12.3, 14.1,
17.2, 19.3, 21.1 and 21.3

The cover photograph was kindly supplied by the
British Museum.

Introduction

To the student

This book has been written to help with your studies for the CXC examination. To encourage you to study in the way which the examiners expect there are assignments at the end of each chapter. Some will help you to be sure of understanding the main points and the most important ideas in the chapter. Some raise issues which you might like to discuss and others give ideas for further investigation.

The assignments have been chosen so that you can become familiar with the types of question, and the way that they written, in Paper 2 of the examination. You will see that some questions set a topic for an essay and others start with a piece of stimulus material – which means a picture or quotation which you are asked to explain and give the background to. You will need to practise writing answers so that they deal with the question you are asked and so that you do not just copy information in the book.

Thirty per cent of the marks for the final result are given for school-based assessment which can be done as nine assignments (three per term for three terms), or one term's assignments may be replaced by a longer project. Many of the assignments in this book could be used for school-based assessment, although your teacher may give you different ones.

At the end of the book you will find the guidelines for the examination papers and the course work you will need to complete for the CXC.

CONTENTS

PART FOUR: SLAVE COLONIES: CULTURE and CONTROL

PART FIVE: TOWARDS EMANCIPATION

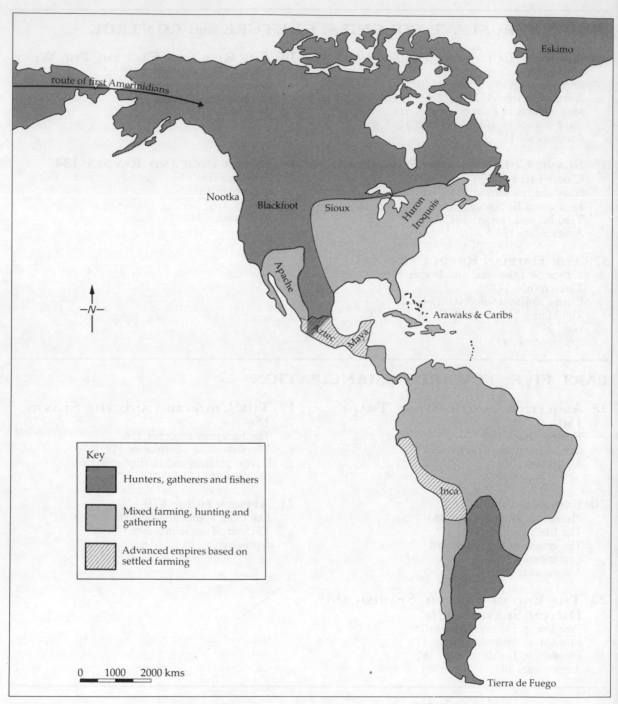

Map 1 *The American continent before Columbus.*

1 THE FIRST AMERICANS

Hunters and farmers

The story of the peoples of the American islands and continents begins in pre-historic times, long before any written records. It is thought that hunters first entered America over 50,000 years ago. They followed animals across the land or ice bridge which then joined Alaska to Asia. Before the bridge disappeared many other groups of hunters followed and pushed those who had come before them further south. 12,000 years ago they were crossing the isthmus of Panama into South America. 5,000 years later their descendants were building the first fires on the frozen tip of the continent at Tierra del Fuego, the land of fire.

These hunters of pre-historic times were the forefathers of the people living in the Americas at the time of the European explorer, Columbus. He called them 'Indians', for he believed he had discovered India in Asia. But, of course, he had discovered a continent whose people had developed in completely different ways from those of India, so today they are given the name of Amerindians.

The first Amerindians followed herds of caribou, buffalo and seals as they moved from one feeding ground to the next. They could not have a permanent camp or many bulky possessions. Numbers had to be kept small, as too many people in one area would lead to the death of too many animals and then the Amerindians would starve. So they lived in small groups. Larger numbers were not possible until a settled way of life based on farming was developed.

Farming for subsistence

The first small beginnings of agriculture came about 7000 B.C. when people living in the Mexican highlands found a wild grass with tiny ears of grain which they could eat. For centuries the wild grass was carefully cultivated until it produced the first kernels of Indian maize. One discovery led to another. By 5000 B.C. the Mexican Amerindians were eating a diet of maize, squash, beans and chilis. At the same time, the people of the Caribbean shores were learning to cultivate yams, cacao and tobacco. The Amerindians of the rainforests of South America discovered how to remove the poisonous liquid from bitter cassava by grating and straining the pulp through a wicker basket. All Amerindians kept and ate small dogs, but the Mexicans also had flocks of turkeys and ducks. Amerindians in Peru kept llamas, alpacas and vicunas, which they used as beasts of burden and for meat and wool.

Where the climate was too harsh for farming Amerindians were forced to remain hunters and gatherers; Eskimos in the Arctic had no choice but to hunt seal and fish. Where game was still plentiful there was no need to change from hunting. The plains' Amerindians had their needs supplied by enormous herds of buffalo. Other groups combined hunting and gathering with farming. Among them were the Huron and Iroquois people in North America and the Arawaks and Caribs in the West Indies. They grew only enough in one season to meet their needs and, when supplies ran out, they turned to fishing, hunting and gathering wild fruits. Most of the Amerindian peoples grew food only for their own needs as subsistence farmers.

Surplus farming

In some societies farmers produced more crops than they needed. This happened among the Incas, Aztecs and Maya. The surplus crops meant that their lands could feed large numbers of people and there were still some crops left to trade for other goods or to pay as taxes. Their societies became very complex and divided into different groups and occupations. Kings and nobles rose to power and organised the yearly round of work according to calendars worked

Fig. 1.1 *A pottery figure of a god with a feathered headdress. Made in the first century A.D., it was found in Mexico.*

Fig. 1.2 *Machu Picchu, a fortified city in the Andes which was used by local governors of the Inca Empire. The highest building to the left is a sun temple. The city could be approached only from one side.*

out by priests, whose task was to take charge of religious ceremonies. Next in rank were the warriors who conquered neighbouring peoples and created large empires. Towns grew up where craftsmen cut building blocks, wove cloth and made fine jewelry and ornaments. At the bottom of the society were the common people and slaves, who grew the food and toiled to build magnificent stone cities, fine bridges, aqueducts and roads.

The Aztecs ruled an empire of over seven million people from their beautiful stone city, Tenochtitlan, built on islands in the centre of Lake Texcoco. The empire of the Incas in Peru was paid for by taxes collected from people they had conquered on the western coast of South America. Both the Incas and Aztecs had learned much from the older society of the Maya who lived in Central America.

The Maya

At the height of their civilisation the Maya occupied 324,000 square kilometres, which included the modern Mexican states of Yucatan, Campeche and Tobasco, as well as all of Belize, Guatemala and the western edge of Honduras. Unlike the Incas, the Maya never tried to build a centralised empire ruled from one capital. Instead, their lands were divided between many independent city-states, Each one was ruled by a 'priest-king'. This office was hereditary and each priest-king took power when his father died. His capital was a temple-city and from there he ruled the countryside around with the aid of priests and nobles.

Remains of the temple-cities show that they were a collection of temples and monuments. The most usual arrangement was a courtyard with pyramids on three sides and public meeting rooms on the fourth. Steps up the sides of each pyramid led to a temple on its flat top. The larger cities had several of these sets of buildings and the spaces in between were filled with stone blocks or pillars, put up to mark the passing of every twenty years. All the buildings were decorated with carvings and wall paintings.

The temple-cities are proof of the power and importance of Maya priests. This power came from their skill in working out the calendars, so necessary to growing crops. As time went on the measurement of time became completely

Fig. 1.3 *The remains of a Mayan step-pyramid with its temple at the summit (Chichén Itzá, Yucatan, Mexico).*

Fig. 1.4 *Maya noblemen playing their ball game at Chichén Itzá. The game was like a violent form of basketball in which the players tried to pass a solid rubber ball through a stone ring. Notice the sloping heads of the players.*

mingled with worship of the gods. Each day was under the protection of one god and each night of another. The will of these gods could be worked out by observing sunrise and sunset and the position of the sun, moon and planets. Some of the temples were built for priests to use as observatories. There were also other gods who watched over corn, wind, water, war, human sacrifice and violent death. Goddesses controlled floods, childbirth and weaving. There was a god for every number and symbol in the Maya alphabet. When displeased, Chac, the raingod, refused to send rain; the corn did not grow and the Maya faced famine. Only the priests might then save the people.

Peasants

The peasants lived in small villages where each family group had its houses around an open space. There was one of these mud and wattle homes, with a thatched roof, for every man and wife and their unmarried children. The men worked at clearing fields and growing the crops. Most important of all was maize but they also grew beans, chilis, and cotton. The women and their daughters spent most of their time in domestic work, especially cooking and grinding the maize. Ground maize was made into tortillas which were eaten with vegetables and sometimes with the meat from a small animal caught by the men.

The whole success of the Maya civilisation depended on the peasants' crops. They grew enough to be able to support the many priests and the nobles who were the state's fighting men. These warriors were easy to recognise by their long narrow skulls which were forced into that shape by fixing boards to their heads when they were young babies.

Every twenty days, peasants brought gifts to be offered to the gods in the city-temples. Once a year they came with a percentage of their crops which they handed over as taxes to the priest-king, the priests and the warriors. At these times, the courtyards in front of the temples were used for dancing, music and religious ceremonies. Only the priests entered these temples. Yet the peasants had to spend time

3

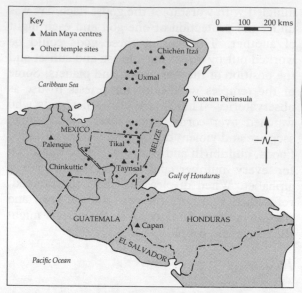

Map 2 *The main sites of the Maya. The sites in the centre and south were used between A.D. 300 and 900. They were then replaced by those in the Yucatan.*

each year working on them. The many remains show that these were always being added to with more and more elaborate stone decorations.

The second Maya

This way of life went on for hundreds of years from the second century A.D. to the seventh or eighth. Then, in one city after another, the temples were abandoned. Buildings were left unfinished and cornfields went unplanted. Fierce-looking stone gods fell from their bases. No one has fully explained why. Some archaeologists think it was caused by a shortage of corn due to soil exhaustion; others believe that a series of deadly diseases swept through the city-states. In some places there may have been wars between states or a peasant revolt against the priests and nobles.

Whatever happened, the Maya civilisation reappeared in the tenth century but only in northern Yucatan. This second Maya civilisation was never as fine as the first. Wars were common and made peaceful farming difficult. The temples and monuments were less grand and sculpture and painting less beautiful. Yet

the Maya only collapsed altogether in the face of Europeans. The first Spanish arrived in 1511. Soon the new conquerors were destroying one city after another. The Maya retreated to their last stronghold at the city of Tayasal deep in the jungle. This finally fell to the Spaniards in 1597. The stone of its temples was used to build Christian churches, and the Maya books were burnt.

Other circum-Caribbean people

Many other people lived in the lands around the Caribbean but none had the same skills in farming, building and science as the Maya. In the Colombian highlands the Chibchas were skilled workers with gold but they built no great cities. Other Amerindian people who spoke a Chibcha language were the Chocho and Cuna in Panama, and the Mosquito-coast Indians in Belize. Their numbers remained small and they had no need for temples or other monuments. Their agriculture was purely for subsistence, with cassava as the main crop. The rest of their food was gathered from the forests and seas. Tools were simply made from stones and shell.

Fig. 1.5 *A Chibcha gold ornament. The upper part shows a human head with a royal head-dress.*

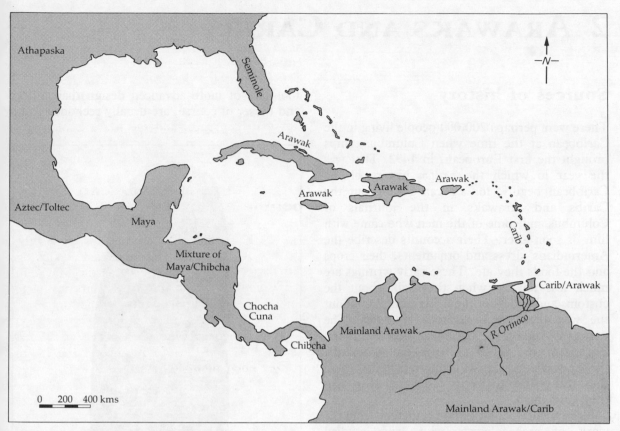

Map 3 *Peoples of the circum-Caribbean.*

They had no system of writing or mathematics, although they were skilled at making dugout canoes, hammocks and clay pottery. Their homes were made from flimsy sticks and thatch and grouped together in small villages. Two other peoples living at these levels were the Arawaks and Caribs. Some of them made permanent homes on the South American mainland and were the ancestors of people such as the Warraws and Wapisians who live in present-day Guyana and Venezuela. Other Arawaks and Caribs left the mainland and made the Caribbean their home.

Assignments

1 *Draw your own map to show where the Aztecs, Incas and Maya lived. What are the names of the present-day countries which made up their territory?*

2 *What are the similarities between the ways that Aztecs, Incas and the Maya organised their societies?*

3 *How did growing surplus crops make the Aztec, Inca and Maya societies different from those of the hunters, gatherers and subsistence farmers?*

4 *Explain as fully as possible how we have been able to learn so much about the way of life of the first Americans.*

2 ARAWAKS AND CARIBS

Sources of history

There were perhaps 200,000 people living in the Caribbean at the time when Columbus' ships brought the first Europeans in 1492. That was the year in which the *written* history of the Caribbean begins, for we can read about the Caribs and Arawaks in the journals of Columbus and some of the men who came with him or soon after. Their accounts describe the Amerindians' dress and ornaments, their crops and the foods they ate. These early writings are much less reliable when they talk about the customs and beliefs of the Amerindians or about the way they organised their societies. The writers looked on the Caribbean people through European eyes. They also needed to describe the Arawaks and Caribs as more primitive than they really were to justify the harsh treatment they gave them.

More accurate information can come from the work of archaeologists who have studied remains of settlements before written history. Archaeologists working in the Caribbean are less fortunate than those who have studied the Maya and can look at the ruins of cities and stone carvings or even books and calenders made by priests. In the islands they have to begin with sites of villages which have been covered with earth and vegetation for many years. If they remove the soil carefully, the archaeologists may find the kitchen middens, which were heaps of rubbish piled up outside villages. By sifting through the middens, it is possible to find pieces of pottery, stone axe-heads or celts, weights for fishnets and ornaments.

Archaeologists then record the distribution of all the remains which have a similar design. This tells them how far the people who made objects in that way were spread over the Caribbean islands. If they can date the objects, they will know the order in which different groups of Arawaks or Caribs came to an area. Some tools are of more advanced design than others and these, of course, are usually reckoned to be

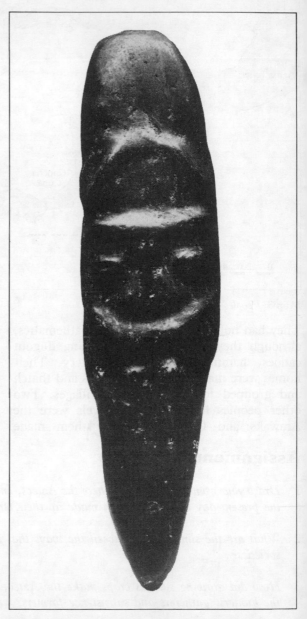

Fig. 2.1 *A stone axe-head, 26 cm long, found in the Dominican Republic. It bears a simple carving of a human face.*

the most recent. Sometimes the differences in date can tell a story. If archaeologists find earlier tools in one area, and nearby come across remains which include later spears and swords, they may be able to reconstruct the history of a settlement whose people were conquered by invaders. On some islands it is possible to see that the earlier people were forced to move inland, or into the mountains, to avoid being destroyed altogether by new arrivals who settled near the coast. Trade and raiding routes can be understood by noting whether sites are on the leeward or windward sides of islands and whether the currents would take canoes from land to land.

Some Arawak people buried their dead in caves, along with items used in life. Archaeologists lucky enough to find a burial cave may see the remains of canoe paddles, or a *duho*, the chief's ceremonial stool, or *zemis*, the figures which represented Arawak gods. If a cave was dry enough, examples of Amerindian weaving and basket-making may have survived for many hundred years to give us a better understanding of the Caribbean's first inhabitants.

Three Caribbean peoples

Archaeologists tell us that some of the earliest settlers came to the Caribbean islands more than a thousand years before Columbus. They were the Ciboneys or Sibonays. In 1492 a few of these people may have lived in parts of the Bahamas and Jamaica. Everywhere else in the western Caribbean was occupied by the Arawaks and the eastern Caribbean was shared between Caribs and Arawaks.

The first home of the Arawaks was probably in the forests between the Orinoco and Amazon rivers. About a thousand years before Columbus they began to move north. Some settled along the coast of Guyana. Others moved on across the Caribbean. They usually settled on each island they came to. After a few years some would move on to the next island. In this way they had occupied the whole of the Caribbean. No one knows for sure why the Arawaks spread out in this way. It may have been because the coast and the islands gave an easier life than the

jungle. The climate and soil were more suitable for growing food and there were no dangerous animals. It may have been that their population was growing and they needed more lands and places where it was easier to farm, hunt and fish. Whatever the reason, by about A.D. 1000 almost every island had Arawak villages along the coast and beside the rivers. Then the pattern of settlement began to change.

The Arawaks were followed into the islands by the Caribs. They were a more warrior-like people whose first home had also been in the jungles around the Orinoco. They moved from island to island in the Lesser Antilles. At each one they fought the Arawak men and usually defeated them. Arawak women were captured and taken as wives. In this way the whole of the eastern Antilles, apart from Barbados and most of Trinidad, was resettled by Caribs.

Barbados lies to the windward of the rest of the Lesser Antilles and it it may have been difficult for Carib canoes to return there after a hunting or raiding expedition. Even so, remains of bones and shells tell us many Caribs did visit Barbados. Caribs also settled the northwest of Trinidad but the Arawaks were still the strongest group in most of the island.

The island Arawaks of Columbus' time were divided into groups. In the west there were the Lucayanos in the Bahamas, the Tainos in Cuba, Jamaica and Haiti and the Borequinos who had occupied Puerto Rico. In the east the Ignerian Arawaks lived in Barbados and Trinidad. They traded with the Caribs peacefully but further north the Caribs were threatening the Arawak settlements in Puerto Rico.

Arawak and Carib livelihood

Farming and food

Both Arawaks and Caribs were subsistence farmers, growing food mainly for their own needs and with a little left over for trade. They carried out 'slash and burn agriculture', cutting branches from trees and setting fire to them. Crops were then planted in the ashes among the blackened tree stumps. After about five to ten

Fig. 2.2 *Two stone pestles used for grinding food. The right-hand one comes from the Dominican Republic and the left-hand one may have come from Jamaica. How are they similar?*

years the soil was exhausted and the village people cleared fresh land. Some Arawaks used slightly more advanced methods. In Cuba and Hispaniola, irrigation ditches were dug and fields were fertilised with a mixture of ash and urine. Arawaks in Hispaniola also blocked inland rivers to make artificial fish ponds.

These simple farming methods produced a variety of crops. Maize was widely grown in the Greater Antilles. Cassava was produced in all the islands and on the Guyana coast along with sweet potatoes and hot pepper (chili). Cotton and tobacco were also grown. Yet Arawaks and Caribs did not rely on field crops for all their food. The islands and the surrounding seas were rich in foods which needed little effort or skill to gather: snails, shellfish, barnacles, grubs, gull and turtle eggs. Huge piles of shells have been found among the remains of camp sites. There were no large wild animals to hunt but the Amerindians trapped many small animals including snakes, bats, lizards, iguanas, conies and rabbits and agoutis. Birds were snared or trapped in finely woven nets strung between trees. As well as parrots, doves and wild ducks there were other birds which are now extinct or very rare. The only domestic animal known to Arawaks and Caribs was a small dog which was fattened on corn meal and then eaten as a great delicacy.

Large numbers of fish were eaten. Fishermen used nets, hooks, spears and the remora. The remora is a fish with suction cups on the back of its head which it uses to cling to larger fish. A cotton line was tied tightly to the remora's tail and was gently let out until the remora attached itself to a fish or turtle. The remora and its captive were then carefully pulled back to the canoe. The Caribs relied more on seafood than the Arawaks. As well as hooks and nets they used long arrows and a type of poisoned bark which stunned the fish when it was thrown into the water. Manatee and pedro seal, now extinct, were also hunted.

The simplest Arawak and Carib dish was 'pepper-pot'. A large clay pot was set close to the fire and filled with any bits and pieces from the fields and the day's hunting. The mixture was heavily seasoned with red pepper and left to stew. A good pepper-pot lasted for weeks, its flavour changing each day as some new lizard, fish or bat was added. Bread and cakes were prepared from maize and cassava. The green maize was pounded with stone pestles into a watery pulp which was wrapped in green leaves and baked over the fire. Cassava flour was mixed with a little water and cooked into nearly rock-hard cakes on a hot clay griddle.

There were very few wild fruits to add to the diet. Coconuts, bananas and citrus fruits were all brought to the Caribbean by Europeans. But the Amerindians did eat guava and occasionally avocados and pineapples. Both Arawaks and Caribs feared to eat certain foods. The Arawaks would not touch mammy apples which they believed were food for the souls of the dead; Caribs refused to eat turtles and manatee for fear of becoming slow and stupid like the animals.

Crafts

Pottery was made from the local red, brown and grey clays. The potter's wheel was unknown. Pots were not glazed but were decorated with markings different for each village. They were often made in fanciful shapes of frogs, birds, or heads with wide eyes and large ears to serve as handles. The Caribs were better potters than the Arawaks and gave their pots a rim at the top

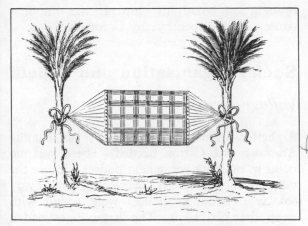

Fig. 2.3 *A drawing of a Carib hammock taken from a book written by Oviedo, a Spaniard who wrote one of the first European accounts of the Americas.*

to add strength and make pouring easier. They also made pots from several layers of clays and then cut patterns through the layers to give their designs different colours. The most elaborate pots were used as funeral urns for holding ancestors' bones or placing food in the grave.

Tools were made from wood, stone, bone and shell. To make baskets, fish traps and lobster pots, wood was soaked and split into supple strips. The Arawaks were excellent basket-weavers. A basket for carrying water was made by double-weaving wood and leaves.

Seamanship

Dugout canoes were made with great skill without the aid of any metal tools. A wide silk-cotton tree was first ringed and burnt off at the base. The trunk was hollowed by chipping the upper side and slowly burning out the interior. The canoe was shaped by wetting the hollowed trunk and inserting wooden wedges of different lengths to widen it in the middle and slightly taper it at each end. It was then buried in damp sand to cure before being dried in the sun. Some Arawak canoes were large enough to carry seventy or eighty people or a tonne of trading goods. The Caribs built several different kinds of boats and rafts. Their war canoes, *piraguas*, were narrow with high prows at the front. They were easy to manoeuvre and could cover great distances. On very long voyages several piraguas were lashed together under a platform on which a shelter was built.

The canoes made it possible for the Arawaks to carry out some trade between the islands in cloth, tools, weapons, furniture, tobacco, certain fruits and gold. Puerto Rico and Haiti exported gold to Cuba, Jamaica and the Bahamas. The small island, Petit Goave, was famous for its fine duhos, the ceremonial stool used by Arawak chieftains. Some groups in Puerto Rico grew pineapples and exported them to other islands. The first European explorers used Arawak traders as guides and pilots. Some archaeologists think that Maya carvings found in Cuba show that the Arawaks also traded with the mainland; but it is likely that they were brought by Maya slaves carried there by the Spanish in the sixteenth century. The Caribs nearest to Trinidad and Guyana kept a busy trade with the Arawaks. In other places the Caribs used their seamanship to make lightning raids on the Arawaks and steal food, clothing and slaves.

Weapons

Flint, obsidian (a volcanic rock) and other hard stones were shaped and smoothed with great patience to make tools and weapons. Fishing arrows and spears were tipped with shell and bone. Fishhooks were cut from turtle shell with sisal string, moistened and dipped in sand to make a simple saw. The Arawaks' war weapons were much simpler than the Caribs'. Columbus noticed that the Lucayanos on the Bahamas were armed with only wooden javelins. On Hispaniola the Tainos had darts with reed shafts and wooden points hardened with fire which were thrown with spear-throwers. The Tainos often used a stout wooden 'sword club', the *macana*, which the Spaniards soon came to fear, as a well-aimed blow could crush even a skull protected by thick armour plating. The Arawaks in the Bahamas, Cuba and Jamaica seldom used bows and arrows, but those in Puerto Rico and Hispaniola used them to defend themselves from Carib attacks.

Carib weapons were altogether more deadly.

They used fire- and poison-tipped arrows. The poison was almost always fatal to someone hit by the arrow. An early English explorer warned his readers that the 'person shot endures the most insufferable torment in the world, and suffers a most ugly and lamentable death, sometimes dying stark mad'. The Caribs also had a variety of clubs and spears. One club, the *butu*, had sharpened flints fixed in its head.

Dress

Columbus described the Arawaks and Caribs 'as a people in their original simplicity . . . stark naked as they were born, men and women'. Yet although they wore hardly any clothing, they spent a lot of time adorning their bodies. Newly born babies had their skulls bound between two boards so that they grew up with high elongated heads. This may have been to thicken the skull so that it could stand up to heavy blows: tales were told of Spaniards who broke their swords on Arawak heads. Clay and fat mixed with bright coloured dyes were smeared in patterns all over the body: 'some of them . . . with black, others white and others red, most of them on their bodies, and some on their faces, and eyes, or only the nose'. Besides being colourful, the clay and grease kept off insects and rain. Small amulets, or charms, were carried in sacks round the neck, and others made from clay, shell and cotton were woven into the hair.

Caribs were more decorative than Arawaks. They applied down, flower petals and gold dust to their body paint before it dried. They also wore chains of stone and coral around their arms, wrists and legs. They pierced their noses, lips and ears to hold ornaments made from fish spines and plates of turtle shell. Caribs greatly respected crescents of gold and copper which were worn round the neck of chiefs and warriors as a badge of rank. Neither the Caribs nor Arawaks saw gold as anything more than a form of decoration, and were quite ready to trade it to the Europeans. They were bewildered at Columbus' excitement when he saw a woman with 'a little plate of gold hanging at her nose' and immediately ordered her to be brought on board his ship. It was the first American gold seen by any European.

Social organisation and beliefs

Village society

A shelter to keep off the rain was all that the Arawaks and Caribs needed. There was no point in building permanent houses because the villagers moved to fresh gardening plots every few years. Arawak houses were round with steep thatched roofs. The larger ones had a covered porch before the door. The village chieftain's house was rectangular and held several rooms. Arawak villages also had a separate dwelling for the tribal gods. Large villages had a ball court at the centre. Here men and youths played ball games, which may have been copied from the Maya, while spectators watched from a bank.

Carib villages were similar, but their houses were made of woven thatch reaching almost to the ground, looking like large beehives. The woven thatch made a strong flexible house which could stand up to hurricanes. The villages were open and not protected by stockades or other defences.

Each Arawak village was the home of related people who obeyed a hereditary headman or chieftain. Often several of these family villages in a district were grouped into a clan headed by a clan chieftain, sometimes called a *cacique*. In Puerto Rico and Hispaniola several such clans were united under a paramount chieftain; there were seven chieftains in Hispaniola. These alliances probably came about as a way of defending the Arawaks against Carib raids. Where the risk was less as in the Bahamas, Cuba and Jamaica, the Arawaks seldom organised anything larger than a family village or clan.

The family idea was reflected in daily village life. Property, land, food, canoes and tools belonged to everyone in common. Like any family, the village group shared what was available. Columbus wrote: 'I could not clearly understand whether this people possess any

Fig. 2.4 *Carib carvings on a rock in Grenada. Suggest what their purpose might have been.*

private property, for I observed that one man had the charge of distributing various things to the rest but especially meat provisions and the like'. Arawak law supported the importance of working together for the good of the tribe. The greatest crime was theft since the whole tribe shared in the loss. A convicted thief suffered a horrible death; impaled on a sharpened stick. A murderer was treated more mercifully, by being banished or executed quickly by strangling.

There were divisions between the work of women and men, as there were with the Maya. The women and girls of the village worked together to plant the crops. They did the cooking. Meals were eaten first by the men and then by the women and young children. The women also did the spinning and weaving of cotton and made the hammocks.

Men cleared the fields for the women's gardening plots, made the houses and the canoes. They did not farm but they caught the village's fish and meat. These trades were learned by boys.

Leadership

Caciques were treated with great respect and looked on as the father of all the people. The cacique was important as a religious leader, but he was also an all-powerful ruler. He decided who should hunt, fish or work in the fields and was the final judge in all disputes. He did not demand regular tax payments from the people but received the best food brought in by hunters, fishers and farmers. When a cacique became sick or injured so that he could no longer carry out his duties, he was strangled and replaced by his eldest son. If there was no son, his sister's eldest male child became cacique. As a final mark of respect the cacique was buried with his most valuable articles and a few favourite wives.

In a large village or clan the cacique was helped by a number of nobles or *nitayanos*. Nitayanos were usually the oldest males who were expected to know the borders of their people's land and remember agreements reached with other groups. When the cacique was considering a new treaty with neighbouring groups he would discuss it with the nitayanos in a council meeting. Some nitayanos were also priests and sorcerers; they cared for the clan's gods, supervised religious rites and trained medicine men. Their songs and dances were a way of teaching the younger people about the history and laws of their people.

The Caribs had a more complicated organisation to give them the best leadership in their warlike society. As with the Arawaks, they had hereditary chiefs, nobles and priests, but military leaders were elected. The village commander was the *obutu*. Anyone who wished to stand for election as obutu had to have killed several Arawak warriors or at least one cacique with his own hands. The obutu was assisted by a lieutenant or *ubutu maliarici*. Each clan also elected a *naharlene* or commander of the canoes as well as a captain, or *tiubutuli canaoa*, of each crew.

A Carib group's strength was reckoned on the number of male warriors and it was common for it to keep a number of Arawak slave women to produce male children who could be raised as fighters. Before a child could become a warrior he had to undergo a painful initation in which he fasted and had his flesh scarred. If the child went through the test without flinching he was allowed to enter the *carbet*, a meeting house where only warriors were allowed.

Religion

Amerindian religion was a colourful mixture of nature worship, ancestor worship and protective magic. The Arawaks believed their land had been created by a male sky-god and a female earth-goddess. Both were too far away to affect their daily lives, but there were many nature gods and ancestral spirits who controlled wind, rain, sickness, luck and misfortune. Each of

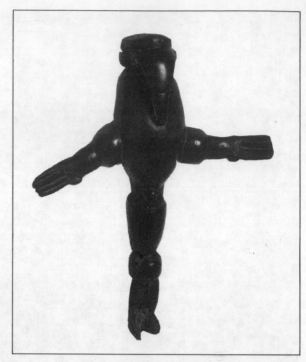

Fig. 2.5 *An Arawak carving of a bird-faced figure found in Jamaica. It is made from an extremely hard wood and stands 88 cm tall.*

these gods could be represented by a zemi. Zemis were made from wood, bone or shell in the shape of a human or animal. Cotton zemis held the bones of a respected ancestor. The skulls and bones of ancestors could also be neatly packed in a zemi basket and kept in the household. Arawaks believed that trees, rivers and rocks were the homes of evil spirits. To protect themselves they wore amulets, painted their bodies with sacred designs and took specially prepared medicines.

Each village had its zemi house, set aside from the other buildings. It was a shadowy place where the priests and caciques offered food and clothing to the spirits and asked for their help. Powdered tobacco was burnt before the zemis. Sometimes it was taken by the priests to send them into a trance in which the spirits would speak to them. A Y-shaped pipe was placed deeply in the nostrils and the priest breathed the fumes until he fainted. The Arawak word for powdered tobacco, *coyiaba*, also meant 'prayer'.

Arawaks believed that the soul left the body, after death and wandered for a while at night feeding on mammy apples. This unhappy time ended when the soul was miraculously carried to magical islands in the south to join other souls. Death was something to look forward to and not to be dreaded. Columbus found this belief very strong and persuaded several Arawaks to come on board his ship by making the false promise to sail them south to the magical islands.

The Caribs shared the belief that death led to a life in another form. From this arose the belief that their live bodies could become homes for the souls of dead enemies, so eating the flesh of a brave warrior would give them his strength and courage. Enemies killed in a raid were cut up and favourite portions were eaten on the spot. Yet Caribs preferred to take captives live and test their courage before the rest of the warriors. Prisoners were kept tied in a hammock near the roof of the carbet. After several days of fasting they were brought down and horribly tortured. Brave prisoners were expected to take the pain without flinching and to mock at their torturers. Those who did so with the greatest courage were the most valued. They were killed quickly and eaten with great reverence as the central part of a ceremonial feast. The rest of the body was boiled; the fat was skimmed off and rubbed into the bodies of young male children to give them additional strength. Of course, flesh eating was not an everyday practice, and people with whom the Caribs traded did not become victims. Yet among Europeans a myth grew up that anyone sailing to the 'Caribbees' was in danger of being eaten, and such tales appeared in European books for 300 years.

Caribs also worshipped ancestor spirits. However, they spent more time in trying to please the evil god Maboya and the many sea spirits they believed in. Death for the Carib meant a journey to either a heaven or a hell. The souls of brave warriors went to the 'fortunate' islands where they were waited on by Arawak slaves; cowardly souls went to a dreary desert where they became the slaves of Arawak masters.

Assignments

1   *Imagine that you are an Arawak or Carib youth (male or female). Describe a day in your life – where you live, how you dress, what you eat, your activities on that particular day. Illustrations may be included.*

2   *What were the main similarities and the main differences between Arawak and Carib societies?*

3   *In what ways were the Arawak and Carib societies different from the Aztecs, Incas and Maya? Were there any similarities?*

4   *What would the Arawaks and Caribs teach their children?*

5   *Which Amerindian group lived in your area? Find out and document as much as you can about them.*
    Or
    If there are any Amerindian sites which you can visit describe as fully as possible:
    a)   *What remains today.*
    b)   *What it looked like at the time of use by the American group.*
    c)   *How it was used.*
    d)   *What materials and equipment were found at the site and how these were obtained.*
    Supply illustrations if possible.

3 THE SPANISH

Land! Land!

It was 2 a.m. on Friday 12 October 1492 when a seaman, high in the crow's nest of the *Pinta*, saw a dark line of land edged with sand gleaming silver in the moonlight. His cry of *Tierra! Tierra!* – land! land! – carried back to the two following ships, the *Nina* and the *Santa Maria*. All three dropped anchor and the fleet's admiral, Christopher Columbus, slept. In the morning he would be, he believed, the first European to put ashore in the East Indies after a voyage entirely by sea. Only many years later was it known for certain that the fleet was rocking gently off the reefs outside the tiny Watling Island on the other side of the world from the Indies.

On that night five centuries ago, Europeans 'discovered' the Americas. Not for the first time. The Vikings, from modern Norway, and the Irish, had sailed the north Atlantic six hundred years before Columbus, but all records of their journeys had been lost. Columbus' voyage was different. It was the start of regular contact between Europe and America because it took place at a time of great developments in ship-building, navigation and map-making. His fleet had sailed from Spain, in a part of Europe which had been eagerly seeking overseas trade and colonies throughout the fifteenth century.

Christianity and Islam

Columbus' ships had been provided by Isabella, Queen of Castile. She had married King Ferdinand of Aragon. The marriage had united the two kingdoms which became one state, known as Spain. The unification made Spain a strong European country, for very few other areas were united under one ruler; France was, and so were England and Wales, but Scotland was still a separate kingdom. Across the middle of Europe were hundreds of separate states, some with only one main city. The Holy Roman Empire claimed to rule most of these states but their princes and kings often resisted interference.

The Christians

In 1492 most countries in Europe accepted the Roman Catholic faith. The Roman Catholic Church was an international organisation with the Pope in Rome at its head. Almost every village had its church and parish priest. Above them in the cities there was a bishop and above the bishops were the archbishops. Archbishops were often wealthy and very powerful in the government of a kingdom or state. Everywhere the Church was wealthy and in most countries it was the largest single landowner. Much of its wealth was held by the monasteries. As well as the monks and nuns in the monasteries, there were other organisations of holy men, especially the friars who were important as teachers and doctors and who often became missionaries.

The Muslims in Spain

For centuries, Christianity and the Roman Catholic Church had been threatened by Muslim followers of the faith of Islam, which had been expanding ever since the time of its prophet, Muhammad, in the seventh century A.D. Muslims had conquered and settled a huge area of land across north India, the Middle East and north Africa. As early as 711 they had crossed to Spain and occupied almost the whole area.

For seven hundred years there was warfare in Spain between Christians and the descendants of the Muslim invaders who were known as 'Moors'. The struggles had led to the rise of the *hidalgos*, a class of Spanish knights who became known for their eagerness to take part in campaigns against the Moors. As reward, hidalgos were free of taxes and each could wear his own coat of arms. An even greater reward

Map 4 *Europe in the lifetime of Columbus.*

was to be granted an *encomienda* by the king or queen. The holder of the encomienda had almost compete control over the people and their land in a district which had been reconquered from the Moors.

Defeating the Moors was seen as a religious struggle. Rulers such as Isabella and Ferdinand and the powerful bishops who advised them were convinced that it was their duty to convert non-believers to Christianity. This often led to great hardship and cruelty. For instance, about 150,000 Jews were expelled from Spain in the early 1490s. A few years later there was a revolt among the reconquered Moors, who were being forced to give up their Islamic faith and accept Christianity. Some Church leaders believed that more gentle methods should be used but almost all Europeans believed that it was God's work to convert everyone who did not accept the Christian faith.

The reconquest was completed in 1492 when Spanish forces took Granada, the last stronghold of the Moors. The end of the struggle left a large gap in many Spanish people's lives. There were no more battles for adventurous fighting men, no more encomiendas to be won in Spain and no more non-believers for friars to convert to Christianity. In Chapters 4 and 5 you will see how all these groups saw new opportunities in the Americas.

Trade with the East

Many European traders made their biggest profits on goods they bought from Arab merchants in the towns on the south and east shores of the Mediterranean Sea. These Arabs were Muslims and could move freely across the vast areas of land ruled by people of their faith. This meant that they controlled trade routes into parts of the world which were quite unknown to Europeans. One set of routes went into the interior of Africa. From the coastal towns of Tunis, Tripoli and Ceuta, Arab trading caravans of loaded camels made the slow trek to Gao, Kano and Timbuctu bringing back gold, ivory and ebony goods.

Even more important were the Arab routes to the East or 'the Indies' as Europeans sometimes called the lands from India itself on to the spice islands which are now part of Indonesia. Two routes left from Constantinople and went overland into Persia and India or into China. The third route began with a land journey to the Red Sea. From there traders sailed in Arab or Chinese ships. They might cross to India or go on further to the spice islands.

Few Europeans risked their lives by travelling across the Muslim lands. But many grew

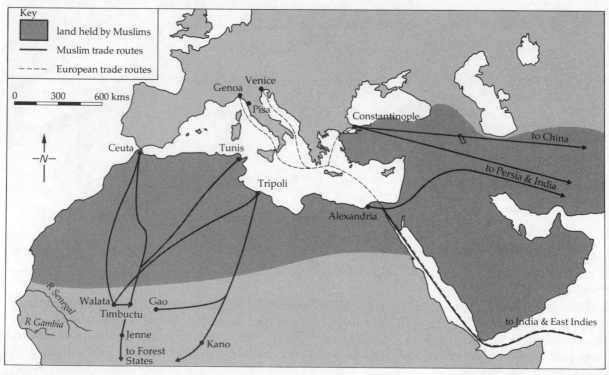

Map 5 *Arab trade routes.*

wealthy by purchasing goods from Arab merchants and bringing them into Europe. Europeans learned to enjoy food seasoned with pepper, nutmeg, ginger and other spices. For the first time they could drink coffee, sweetened with cane sugar. Fine eastern textiles were used by the wealthy for ladies' dresses, cloaks and costly church vestments. Europeans came to want more and more of the wonderful perfumes, gems, gold, ivory and ebony carvings and leather goods.

All these goods were expensive, especially because of the taxes placed on them by the rulers of the Arab states, who were generally unfriendly to the Christian Europeans.

Because of the high prices, European merchants began to consider ways of finding their own sea route to the Indies. It had been estimated that one ship alone could carry half the amount of all the pepper brought into Europe by land each year. Yet no one in Europe knew if it was possible to sail to the Far East. Seamen feared to go far west of Gibraltar or south of the northern curve of Africa. They told each other fantastic stories of ship-eating monsters, boiling seas and reaching the edge of the world. Most sailors did not trust those men who told them that the world was round. It took most of the fifteenth century to overcome these fears.

The explorations

Renaissance geography and technology

The best chance of finding a sea route to the Indies was by sailing round Africa. The country in the best position to explore this route was Portugal. The man who did most to see that Portuguese sailors succeeded was Prince Henry who was called the 'Navigator'. In fact he did little navigating or sailing himself, but made it his business to see that Portuguese sailors knew all the most up-to-date geographical ideas. Henry lived at a time when there were so many new inventions and theories that Europeans later called it the *Renaissance*, an age of the rebirth of knowledge. The new knowledge of the Renaissance gave Prince Henry the chance to develop techniques and technology which made possible exploration into the unknown.

Navigation

In 1450 a German, Johann Gutenburg, invented the first European printing press with movable type. It was now possible to produce many copies of books, and accounts of travellers and explorers could be printed and read by large numbers. Map-making too was mechanised. Instead of expensive hand-drawn maps, known as *portolani*, cheaper printed maps were produced. These showed coastlines, currents, winds and the position of dangerous shoals and banks. Henry the Navigator collected the newest studies in geography, mathematics, astronomy and map-making into a library at Sagres. The town stands on the south-west tip of Portugal, jutting into the Atlantic Ocean, and Henry made it the headquarters for his country's seamen.

Early sailors kept close to the shores so they could use landmarks to check their position. Sailors going to Africa could not do this. They needed to let the winds take them out into the Atlantic and then make their way back to the coast using other winds or currents. That meant they needed instruments to check their position. Renaissance times had provided three new inventions to do this: the astrolabe, the cross-staff and the quadrant. Henry had them all improved so that seamen could use them to check their angle from the Pole Star at night or the sun at noon. With this information they could work out their ship's position.

Henry also ordered improvements to the compass. The old one was a magnetised needle floating on a cork in a bowl of water. It was replaced by a compass set in a glass box which was far more accurate.

Ship-building

There would have been no new discoveries without Henry's ship-builders. They were ordered to produce a new type of ship which needed a smaller crew than the old vessels that sailed along the coast and had to call in to ports for new food supplies. The ship-builders' solution was the type of ship known as the 'caravel'. This ship usually had three movable sails which made much lighter work of tacking against the wind. Pulleys, wrenches and pivots were used to aid work on the sails, so fewer sailors were needed for each caravel. This increased the space for cargo and provisions and made possible longer voyages without putting into land.

Weapons

Henry's sailors and ships were equipped with the latest European weapons. Gunpowder was a Chinese invention which came to Europe in the fourteenth century. The knowledge of gunpowder had been combined with skill in iron work so that ships of Henry's time could be armed with cannon. More important, sailors and explorers could carry muskets and pistols. By today's standards they were clumsy and slow to fire but they were more deadly weapons than any others in the world at the time. This gave Europeans great confidence as they set off to strange foreign lands.

Discovering the coast of Africa

Map 6 shows the success of Portuguese sailors. In the Atlantic they reached Madeira, the Azores, the Canary and Cape Verde Islands. By the time of Prince Henry's death, Portuguese traders in forts along the coast were sending back great wealth in ivory, gold and ebony while sailors were pushing their way further south. In 1488 Bartholomew Diaz, running his ships before the winds of a gale, found he had rounded the tip of Africa and entered the Indian Ocean. Ten years later, Vasco da Gama made the first sea voyage from Europe to India. He returned with a cargo of jewels, spices and silks worth sixty times the cost of the voyage.

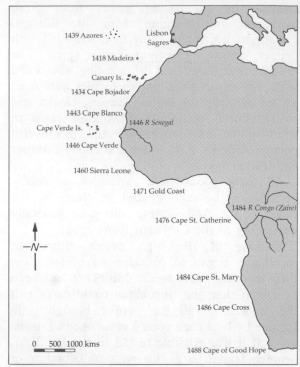

Map 6 *Portuguese exploration of the West African coast.*

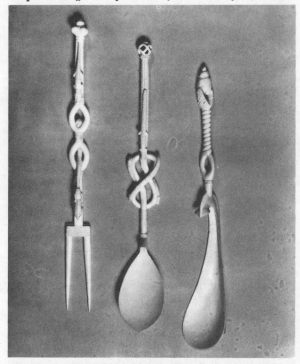

Fig. 3.1 *Ivory spoons and fork made in Benin in West Africa in the fifteenth century for sale to Portuguese sailors.*

Spain and the Canaries

In 1479 Portugal and Spain signed a treaty which shared out the results of the Portuguese explorations. Queen Isabella and King Ferdinand agreed to allow Portugal the sole right to the trading routes along the African coast. In return the Portuguese handed over the Canary Islands to the Spanish.

This arrangement pointed Spanish adventurers to the west. Soldiers went out to the Canaries to bring its people under Spanish control. They treated the conquered people in the same way as the Moors. Knights were given encomiendas over the island people and forced them to work on plantations growing sugar for Spain. When there was a shortage of local people, the Spanish bought African slaves from Portuguese traders and forced them to work in the cane fields.

Some of Isabella's advisers saw another use for the Canary Islands. Now that Spain had given up the right to explore to the south, the Canaries could be a base for voyages to explore to the west. Renaissance geographers were convinced that the world was round and not flat. That made some of them ready to listen to the theories of an unknown Italian sailor, Cristoforo Colombo who became better known as Columbus.

Columbus prepares

Columbus was born in late 1450 or 1451 in the Italian port of Genoa. Many young Genoese grew up to become sailors. Columbus gained his experience of the sea on voyages to Western Europe, Iceland, Madeira and West Africa. In

Fig. 3.2 *The cathedral of El Alcazar in Seville, Spain, where Columbus' collection of maps and books is preserved.*

1476 he moved with his brother to Lisbon where they opened a business buying and selling rare maps. Columbus kept the best documents and books for his own personal use and these have been preserved in the cathedral at Seville. The collection contains books by three authors whose writings helped Columbus to decide that Asia could be reached by sailing west across the Atlantic.

The idea

Ptolemy, a Greek geographer who lived in the second century, believed that the earth was a perfect sphere. Half of it was land stretching from Western Europe to the eastern edge of Asia. The other half was water. Columbus reasoned that if you sailed west across this ocean sea you would reach the Indies. But how wide was the ocean sea? The Arab geographer, Al-Farghani, had calculated that the distance round the earth at the equator was about 29,000 kilometres. Half of this was more than 14,500 kilometres, so Columbus would need a resting place in the middle of the ocean sea where he could take on fresh provisions. Marco Polo, an Italian merchant who travelled to Asia in the thirteenth century, wrote about the rich island of Cipango (Japan). With more guesswork than good judgement, Columbus worked out that

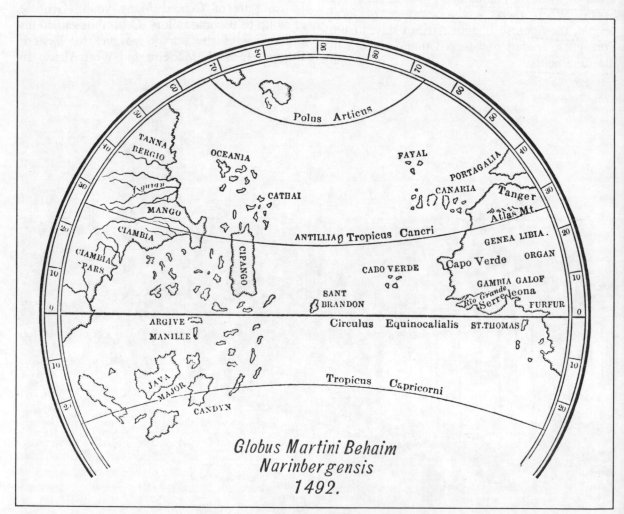

Fig. 3.3 *A modern version of a map drawn in 1492 which showed the world as Columbus expected to find it. Japan (Cipango) is to the west of Europe and Africa, and further west are the Indies.*

Japan was only 3,900 kilometres from the Canary Islands.

Search for a patron

Columbus first took his plans to the Portuguese, who turned him down because they had already decided to reach Asia by sailing round Africa.

Columbus next went to Spain where he was warmly welcomed by merchants who were willing to listen to plans for a new trade route across the Atlantic to the Far East. Isabella and Ferdinand were interested, but they were not to be rushed. Their time and money was still taken up with the end of their struggle to drive the Muslims from Spain.

Preparation

In 1492 when the war against the Moors ended, Isabella agreed to help Columbus. Wealthy Spanish followed their queen's lead. All expected to make huge profits on their investment if Columbus was successful. Columbus himself was to get one-tenth of all the profits and be made governor of any lands he discovered. The queen also promised to make him a nobleman and an admiral of the Spanish navy. She ordered that the port of Palos supply him with three ships. The *Pinta* was named after her owners, the Pinzon brothers, and the *Nina* after her owner, Juan Ninas. The *Santa Maria*, which Columbus chose as his flag ship, was the most awkward and slowest of the three. On 3 August 1492 the new Spanish admiral set sail to the Canary Islands where he took on fresh provisions. On 6 September 1492 the little fleet sailed from the Canary Islands into the uncharted Atlantic Ocean.

Columbus' first voyage

The fears of the seamen grew daily as the trade winds steadily blew their ships further and further west. By mid-September they were on the point of mutiny. Even Columbus began to doubt the wisdom of his plan. According to his earlier reckoning they should have already reached Japan. For a while he quietened his men's fears by showing them a log book in which he had underestimated the true distance they had travelled. A week later the seamen were once again talking about throwing their stubborn admiral into the sea and turning back. Columbus avoided mutiny by telling his men that they were sailing between two islands and could at any time turn towards land. On 10 October Columbus himself promised that the voyage would be abandoned if land was not sighted within forty-eight hours. As the deadline was drawing to a close, on Friday 12 October 1492, Rodrigo de Triana, keeping watch on the *Pinta*, sighted land.

Columbus went to bed convinced that the island was one of the Far Eastern spice islands. A closer look in the morning showed that the island had no exotic spices, jewels, rich clothes or gold. The natives he met had no trade goods at all, except a little inferior cotton. He could not learn where he was or what they called their island. Columbus gave it a new name, San Salvador (Holy Saviour), and pointed out to his men that the natives were willing to please and were non-believers. Their souls could be won for the Christian Church and that was sure to please Queen Isabella. Besides, the 'Indians', as Columbus mistakenly called the Arawaks, might be taught to cultivate cotton to export to Europe. In the meantime he took several Arawaks on board to guide him to the *real* spice islands.

Hispaniola

The Arawak guides led Columbus along their own trade routes between San Salvador, Cuba and Hispaniola. They continually told him – as they did all later European explorers – that there were mountains of gold further inland, or on 'just' the next island. For three months Columbus unsuccessfully looked for the fabled wealth of Asia. The search continued until one day just before Christmas when the *Santa Maria* ran aground on the north shore of Hispaniola, and sank. Thirty-nine seamen who couldn't find a place on the remaining two ships unhappily became the first European settlers in the West

Fig. 3.4 *A later European picture of Columbus landing at San Salvador. How far do you think this gives a true picture of this event?*

Indies. They used timbers from the wrecked *Santa Maria* to build themselves a fort which they called Puerto Navidad.

Columbus ordered the remaining two ships to turn back for Spain. Their strange cargo was not encouraging: a few Arawaks, some cotton samples, an alligator, several parrots, a few hammocks, a small quantity of golden nuggets and trinkets, one wooden canoe and a bundle of tobacco leaves. Columbus wrote that the tobacco was 'highly esteemed among the Indians', but had no idea what it was used for! This was all Columbus had to pay back the men who had invested money in his enterprise.

Assignments

1 *Read the following passage, then answer the questions.*
   'Columbus' voyage . . . took place at a time of great developments in ship-building, navigation and map-making. His fleet had sailed from Spain, in a part of Europe which had been eagerly seeking overseas trade and colonies throughout the fifteenth century.'

a)   What 'great developments' had taken place 'in ship-building, navigation and map-making'?
b)   How had Columbus obtained his fleet?
c)   Why had Spain 'been eagerly seeking overseas trade and colonies throughout the fifteenth century'?

2   Explain how the new knowledge of the Renaissance led to the exploration of new lands. Why was Spain the first European nation to discover the Caribbean in the fifteenth century?

3   Explain fully:
a)   Why Columbus might have been disappointed at the end of his first voyage.
b)   What reasons he might have for being pleased at the end of his first voyage.

4 THE AMERINDIANS AND THE SPANISH

The return to Hispaniola

Columbus returned to Spain in 1493 convinced that he had discovered one of the islands of the Indies. He wrote to Queen Isabella with plans for making Hispaniola the centre of a great trading empire. The first step would be to build towns from which Spaniards could trade with the Indians. The island could also be used as a base for exploring other parts of the Indies.

Isabella gave the task of collecting stores, men and ships to Juan de Fonseca, who was a priest, like most of the officials at her court. He and Columbus gathered seventeen ships and 1,200 men. Among them were builders, masons and carpenters with the materials to start work on the first towns in the 'Indies'. To organise the trade there were merchants and clerks as well as map-makers who would be useful for voyages beyond Hispaniola. To provide food for the colony there were farmers with animals and stocks of seed. An important part of the expedition was a party of priests for the work of converting the Indians to Christianity.

Columbus led his fleet back to Hispaniola through the islands of the Lesser Antilles, where he saw many Carib settlements. He wrote that the Caribs were a savage people but that they seemed healthy and intelligent and would make good slaves.

At Hispaniola the fleet landed at Navidad. Columbus found that the fort built a year before had been destroyed and the Spaniards he left behind had all been killed in fights with the Arawaks. He ordered a new trading post to be built and named after Queen Isabella, but he chose a site far away from supplies of fresh water. Plants soon wilted in the salty soil and men died from fevers carried by mosquitoes in the nearby swamps. He sent expeditions to seek gold but his men found that the Arawaks were farming people with no riches to trade. Some gold could be panned from rivers but there were no mines.

These setbacks did not stop Columbus' belief in the wealth of the Indies and he took three ships to explore further west. They sailed to Jamaica but passed quickly on to Cuba. For a month the ships explored its south coast before they returned to Hispaniola.

Destruction of the Arawaks

While Columbus was away from Hispaniola, the Spaniards had abandoned work on the buildings and farms at Isabella. Instead they forced the Arawaks to provide them with food. They had also robbed them of trinkets and assaulted their women. The Arawaks were a peaceful people who had treated the Spanish with courtesy. Now they decided to resist and came together to fight the invaders who had made themselves unwelcome. Columbus immediately organised expeditions to overcome the Arawak forces. A one-sided struggle followed.

The Arawaks had only simple bows and arrows, stone clubs and wooden spears. The Spaniards were armed with steel swords, metal-tipped pikes and cross-bows. They used fierce dogs and armour-covered horses which terrified people who had never seen animals larger than a rabbit or coney. Horses gave the Spaniards the advantage of quick attacks and retreats, while the Arawaks suffered dreadful casualties by rushing headlong at the enemy. In a very short time tens of thousands of them were killed.

The fighting marked the end of any pretence that the Spaniards would trade fairly. Instead, Columbus forced the people of the island to pay a tax. Every three months each male over fourteen had to hand over enough gold to fill a hawk's bell and every other Arawak had to supply 25 pounds (about 12 kilograms) of spun cotton. Arawaks who failed to pay were forced

Fig. 4.1 *Amerindians being forced to mine for gold, watched by Spanish soldiers.*

Fig. 4.2 *An anti-Spanish picture from the late sixteenth century showing Amerindians being burned alive by Spanish raiders.*

to give several weeks' free labour. Hundreds of Arawaks who resisted the tax were captured and sent back to Spain for sale as slaves. They were given no extra clothing and half died from cold on the voyage.

In 1496, Christopher Columbus returned to Spain, leaving his brother, Bartholomew, in charge of Hispaniola. The wars against the Arawaks continued and led to Spanish control of the whole island. In 1493 there had been between 200,000 and 300,000 Arawaks on Hispaniola. By the end of 1496 perhaps as many as two-thirds of the Arawaks were dead. They were killed not only by Spanish weapons but also by the smallpox brought to the island on Columbus' ships. The Arawaks had no immunity to the disease and it raced through the island, weakening and killing whole tribes. Within a few years great herds of European cattle, swine and goats were roaming the island destroying the Arawaks' maize and cassava crops.

In three years the Spanish plan for a trading base in Hispaniola had given way to a conquest of the whole island. Bartholomew Columbus built a line of forts from the abandoned Isabella to a new Spanish headquarters which he started at Santo Domingo. Hispaniola had become the first Caribbean colony of Spain and Santo Domingo its capital.

The third voyage

On his return to Spain Columbus found himself out of favour with Queen Isabella. She was disappointed with the way he had governed Hispaniola and annoyed that he had not found the wealth of the Indies. She had sent back the Arawak slaves and turned down Columbus' idea that Caribs might be made slaves for the same reasons. The cold would kill many of them on the voyage. Spain had no use for slave labour and as a Christian queen it was her duty to protect the Indians not enslave them. It was only in 1498 that Isabella agreed to let Columbus make a third voyage.

This time Columbus sailed far to the south through the Gulf of Paria. He saw a huge volume of fresh water pouring out of the

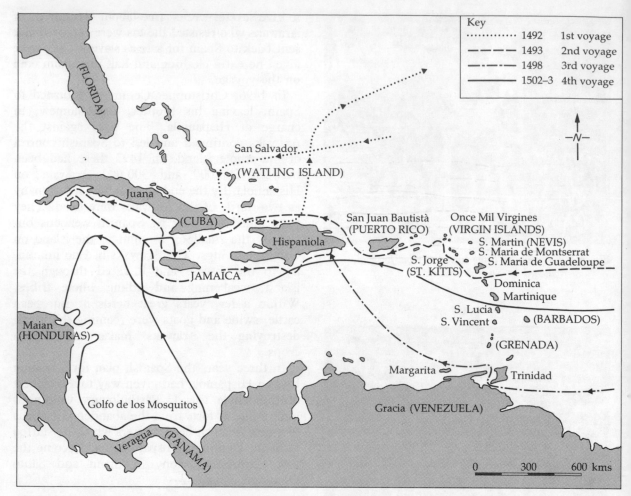

Map 7 *Columbus' four voyages to the Caribbean, showing the names he gave to places in the area.*

Orinoco River. There seemed so much that he was sure that the river must run through an entire continent and not just an island. He sailed on to Hispaniola where he found that a revolt had broken out against his brother Bartholomew. Columbus had five ringleaders hanged and tried to buy the support of the other Spanish by allowing them to take over parts of the island as private estates. This did not stop a steady stream of complaints to Spain against the Columbus brothers and, in 1499, Isabella sent Francisco de Bobadilla to Hispaniola with special powers to act on her behalf. His first act was to have the Columbus brothers arrested and sent back to Spain.

The fourth voyage

Isabella forgave Columbus and after a while allowed him to make a fourth voyage to the Caribbean to explore the coastline he had sighted across the Gulf of Paria. She warned him to stay clear of Hispaniola. Columbus did not heed the warning but sailed directly to Santo Domingo to claim his share of the taxes which had been so cruelly taken from the Arawaks. He was not allowed to enter Santo Domingo but had to take on fresh water and supplies at a nearby natural harbour.

Columbus left Hispaniola and sailed west to the coast of Honduras. Between January and May he sailed along the coast before turning his worm-eaten ships north again to Hispaniola.

Fig. 4.3 *Columbus on board one of his ships using an astrolabe to work out the angle between the sea and the sun or a star.*

The ships were not fit for the voyage and sank near St Ann's Bay, Jamaica. Columbus sent Diego Mendez by canoe to Hispaniola to beg for a rescue ship. It was almost a year before he could hire a vessel to collect Columbus and the survivors of his crew. Columbus finally arrived back in Spain in 1504 and died there in 1506, probably still believing that he had discovered part of the Indies.

Hispaniola as a Spanish colony

Ovando

What had Columbus achieved for Queen Isabella? He had promised her a way to the wealth of the Indies but all he produced was the conquest of the unfortunate Arawaks on Hispan-

iola and a Spanish colony where only 300 Spaniards were still alive in 1502. To the Queen and Juan de Fonseca, who had become her chief adviser on the Indies, the lesson was plain. The affairs of the Indies could not be left to private adventurers such as Columbus; in future they would have to be the responsibility of the government in Spain. Their first task was to choose a governor of Hispaniola who would bring order to the island and develop it as a base for further exploration.

The man chosen was a nobleman, Nicolas Ovando. He arrived in 1502 and in the next seven years governed the island in a way which became the model for the Spanish Empire which grew up in the Indies. His first aim was to produce enough food for a larger number of settlers, and to do this he experimented with different crops. It was soon found that olives and vines which flourish in Spain would not grow in the tropics, although orange and lemon trees would do very well here. European wheat and barley were unsuitable, but it was not long before the Spaniards discovered that Indian corn, or maize, could be made into bread, and rice could be planted in the wetter districts. Two crops which became very important in the history of the Caribbean, bananas and sugar cane, were brought from the Canary Islands. Sheep could not survive easily in the climate, but meat could be obtained from cattle, pigs, goats and chickens, which soon roamed freely over the island.

The new foods made it possible for Hispaniola to support ever increasing numbers of Spanish settlers. Ovando had brought 2,500 with him in 1502, to add to the 300 remaining from Columbus' day. A steady flow of emigrants from Spain raised the number of settlers to 12,000 in four years. Some of the Spaniards were drawn to Hispaniola by the news that Ovando had organised mining for gold. Others saw a chance of owning land where they could produce goods for export back to Spain. Sugar became the most important food crop once the first crushing mills were built, which was probably in 1508. Most Spaniards found cattle ranching more profitable than sugar. The cattle were not kept for their meat, but for the hides and tallow which both fetched a good price in Europe. Some ranchers also bred horses, which were sold to Spanish settlers or to explorers setting out for other islands.

Encomiendas

The Spaniards who were wealthy enough to own mines, ranches or plantations did not come to the Caribbean to work themselves. They were from hidalgo families and hoped to be granted encomiendas over the Indians, like those given to the men who had fought the Moors and the people of the Canary Islands. To set up the encomiendas Ovando carried out a distribution, or *repartimiento*, of the Indians in Hispaniola, parcelling them out into groups of thirty. A Spaniard was then granted encomiendas over one or more of these groups.

After the first repartimiento the task of sharing out the Amerindians was taken over by the *cabildo* or council of each town on the island. Each cabildo was responsible for the countryside around the town and its members came from the richest and most powerful families in the district. The Spanish in Hispaniola settled down to a life which was a copy of that in Spain, where landowners and merchants used the cabildos to protect their wealth and to control the lives of the local peasants.

A man who had been given an encomienda became the Amerindians' *encomondero*. In theory, this meant he was their protector, with the duty of seeing that they were cared for and taught to become more 'civilised' – from the Spanish point of view. Becoming more 'civilised' really meant nothing more than giving signs that they accepted the Spanish as their masters, covering their bodies as Europeans did, speaking Spanish and accepting the Christian faith. In return for Spanish 'protection' the Amerindians were to give service in the fields or mines of the encomenderos. However they were to keep their homes and farms and, by the queen's orders, were not to be made slaves.

The encomienda system was nothing more than a means of obtaining forced labour for the encomonderos. No wages were paid for the work done; churches or schools were not built

in Arawak villages. Very often the Arawaks' own farms were ruined by herds of cattle or swine belonging to their encomondero. They rarely had time to grow their own food for the forced labour left them neither time nor strength. Arawaks were not free to leave the encomienda and those who fled were hunted down by men on horseback with dogs. The results were disastrous. The death rate among Arawaks shot up as a result of hunger, weakness and despair among people whose traditional village and family life was completely destroyed. Further epidemics of smallpox helped to complete the total destruction of Amerindian life. After thirty years of Spanish settlement there were hardly any left alive.

The first slaves

The Spanish made desperate attempts to find new labour and soon turned to Amerindian slavery, although it was officially forbidden except for prisoners taken in a just war. Slaving raids were made on the Bahamas, but the Amerindians brought from these islands died just as rapidly as those from Hispaniola itself. For another source the Spanish turned to African slaves. Such labour was not new to them; for more than a hundred years small numbers of Africans had been taken to Spain itself and later to the cane fields on the Canary Islands. The few thousands brought to the Americas at this time were but the first of some twenty million transported by the end of the eighteenth century.

Conquest of the Greater Antilles

A base for explorers

The island could give a prosperous and comfortable life to only a small number of colonists. Their ill-treatment of the Amerindians meant that there was not enough labour to produce great profits from farming or mining. In any case, the mines contained only small amounts of gold. So, to most Spanish, Hispaniola became a base from which they could go on to seek great fortunes further west. In his seven years as governor, Ovando laid the foundations for a wave of exploration and conquest. He organised voyages of exploration to Cuba, which proved that it was an island, and to the Panama coast where a small Spanish settlement was set up. But, more important for the future was his success in building up Hispaniola's agriculture so that it could supply expeditions with food and horses. It was under the next governor, Diego Columbus, the son of Christopher, that all the Greater Antilles became Spanish colonies.

The spread of the Spanish Empire was carried out by private adventurers. Yet the government kept control of newly conquered lands and a share of the profits went to the royal treasury. Before he could set out, the leader of each expedition had to sign a contract known as a *capiculacion*. This gave him the title of *adelantado* and made him governor of the new territory with the right to own land there and collect customs duties on all fishing and trading. But, the capiculacion laid down that other taxes, and especially a fifth of all precious metals, were to go to the royal treasury. It was made clear that the people of conquered lands would become subjects of the Spanish king and queen. The capiculacion also stated whether the adelantado or the government would pay for work such as building towns, protecting the colony, bringing new settlers and converting the Amerindians.

Puerto Rico and Jamaica

In 1509 two adelantados set out to conquer neighbouring islands. One was Ponce de Leon who had lived in Hispaniola for some time. The year before he had made a voyage to Puerto Rico and had returned with some gold. Now he was going with a capiculacion which made him governor of the island with the right to share out its land among his party of *conquistadores*, or fighting men, some of them from Hispaniola and some from Spain itself.

In 1509 there were probably as many as 30,000 Borequino Amerindians on the island,

living in wood and thatched huts grouped in villages near the sea or rivers. Their food came from fishing or trapping birds and small animals and their only weapons were bows and arrows, hardwood swords and stone axes. Like the Arawaks of Hispaniola, these Borequinos were shared out among the conquistadores who became their encomonderos. As in Hispaniola, the result was a desperate revolt in which thousands of Borequinos were slaughtered by the Spanish. In a census taken in 1514 it was reckoned that only 4,000 remained. Yet, from the Spanish point of view, the island prospered for a few years. San Juan and other towns were built to control the countryside where mines, sugar plantations and cattle ranches replaced the villages.

The second expedition of 1509 was more disappointing for the conquistadores who went to Jamaica led by Juan d'Esquivel. They found no precious metals. D'Esquivel himself was happy to become the governor and share out the island between cattle ranchers and a few sugar planters. But Jamaica offered nothing to adventurous and greedy conquistadores who left to join in the conquest of an island that would become a more important part of Spain's American Empire – Cuba.

Cuba

The adelantado who led the Cuban expedition was Diego Velasquez, who had been deputy governor of Hispaniola. The Amerindians on Cuba did not wait to fight until the Spaniards had begun the repartimiento; they probably knew what to expect from the Amerindians who had escaped from Hispaniola and Jamaica. War broke out immediately and for three years Narvaez led his mounted soldiers against the ill-armed Amerindians, who retreated further into the mountains. Most battles were no more than simple massacres with the Spaniards slaying their enemies in thousands. At the same time, Velasquez was carrying out a repartimiento and building the island's first towns which included Santiago, the capital, and Havana, on the north coast. Two of Velasquez's followers were Bartolomé de las Casas, and Hernán Cortes.

Cuba turned out to be a richer conquest than the other islands. The shortage of Amerindian labour made cattle ranching the main form of farming, but the island had more gold than Puerto Rico or Hispaniola. Even more important, Cuba now replaced Hispaniola as the base for Spanish exploration in the New World.

Assignments

1 *Explain as fully as possible how the Arawaks' way of life was changed by the settlement of the Spaniards in the Caribbean.*

2 *Explain how and why Nicolas Ovando's work in the Caribbean was different from the work done by Christopher Columbus.*

3 *Study Fig. 4.1 on page 25 and answer the following questions:*
   a) *Suggest a territory in which this scene could have taken place. Give reasons.*
   b) *Apart from gold, what other commodities or products were obtained by Europeans from the Caribbean?*
   c) *There appear to be some seven Spanish soldiers to approximately twelve Amerindians in the illustration. Why was the smaller number of men able to force the larger number of men to mine for gold?*
   d) *Explain other ways in which the Spanish maintained control over the Amerindians.*

4 *Compare and describe why Cuba was seen by the Spanish 'to be a richer conquest than the other islands', Hispaniola, Puerto Rico, Jamaica and the islands of the Eastern Caribbean.*

5 SPAIN'S AMERICAN EMPIRE

Routes to the 'New World'

After Columbus' first voyage, Queen Isabella and King Ferdinand acted quickly to make an international claim to all the lands in the area he had discovered. Their first move was to ask for the support of the Pope, whose judgements were held to be binding by most European Christians. Pope Alexander VI was a Spaniard by birth and an ally of Isabella and Ferdinand so he was very willing to back up their claim. In a decree he divided up the world outside Europe into two zones, one each side of a line which ran 100 leagues (about 640 kilometres) west of the Azores. All lands discovered in the western zone were to belong to Spain and those in the east to Portugal.

Portugal objected that the division was unfair and refused to recognise Spanish claims to the New World unless the line was moved to 370 leagues (about 2,400 kilometres) west of the Azores. Spain agreed and the new dividing line was written into the 'Treaty of Tordesillas' which the two countries signed in 1494. This treaty gave Portugal a piece of the New World as Brazil was discovered on her side of the line.

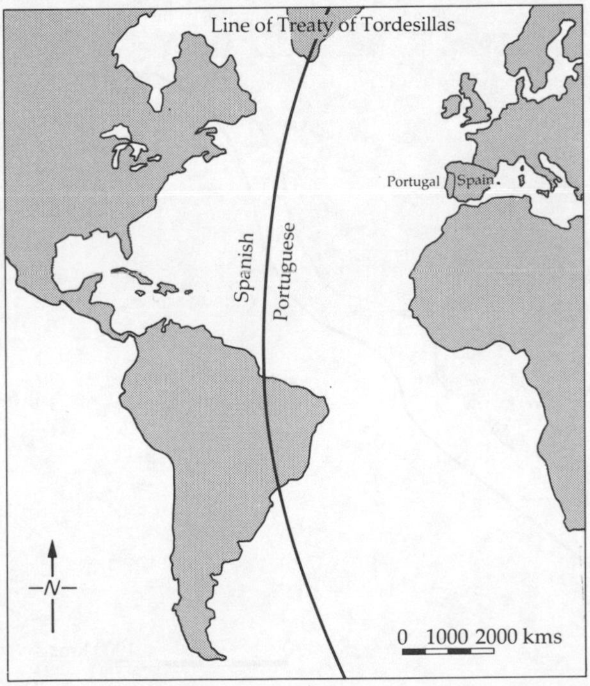

Mapping the New World

Geographers were baffled by Columbus' descriptions, which were unlike anything they had heard about Asia. Their doubts increased as more explorers crossed the Atlantic and mapped the mysterious lands. The first man to publish an account of a journey was Amerigo Vespucci, an Italian who visited the Venezuelan and Guyanese coast. Vespucci's descriptions of the American coastline led to a growing belief that Columbus had discovered a separate continent. A German geographer, Martin Waldseemuller, used Vespucci's account to produce the first map of the discoveries, calling the new land 'America' in honour of Vespucci. Waldseemuller's map showed only a small section of the

Map 8 *How the New World was divided by the Treaty of Tordesillas.*

Fig. 5.1 *A drawing of Amerindians trying to prevent Amerigo Vespucci landing.*

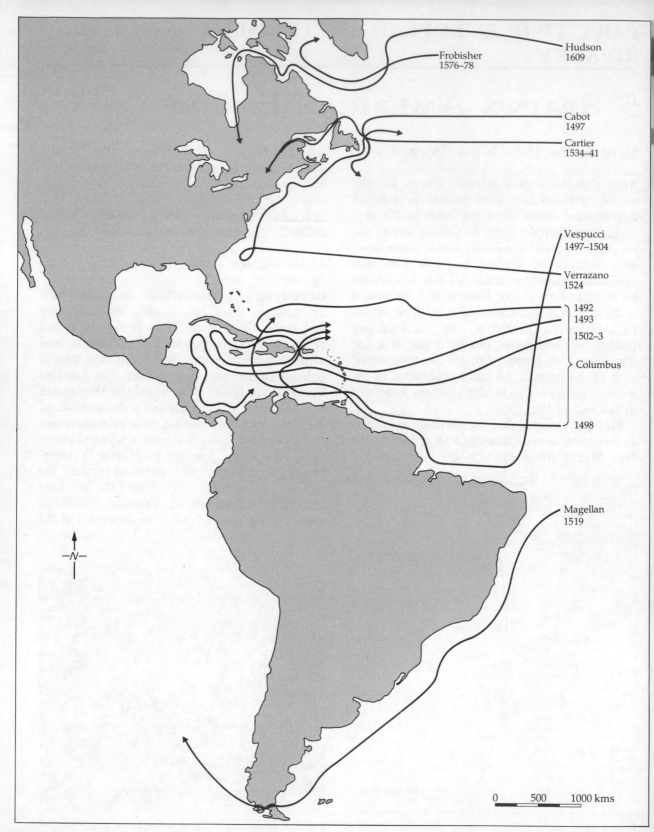

Map 9 *European explorers of the American continent.*

American coastline. There was still no proof that it was part of a new continent. Before they could be certain, the Europeans had to find out what was on both ends and on the other side.

By 1518 explorers from Spain had brought back enough information to fill in the South American coastline and the western shores of the Pacific Ocean. No one knew how wide the Pacific Ocean was or what lay beyond it. The mystery was solved in 1522 when Ferdinand Magellan, a Portuguese sailor commissioned by the Spanish king, became the first European to sail round the globe. Europeans now knew for certain that the world was round and that the new discoveries were separated from Asia by an ocean several thousand kilometres wide.

It was clear beyond all doubt that Columbus had failed to find the Indies. But he and the voyagers who followed had done more than lay claims to new lands for Spain. They had charted the winds and currents which decided the sea routes which connected the colonies with Europe.

Winds

Columbus had discovered the importance of the Trade Winds when he had started his first voyage from the Canary Islands. These winds take their strength from the masses of air which move towards the equator from the north pole. Near the equator the spinning of the earth forces the air currents to turn towards the Caribbean. They become the Trade Winds, which blow almost continuously from east to west at the latitude of the Canary Islands. After Columbus, ships from Europe sailed towards the Canaries to catch the Trades and they could then choose to stay either in the southern level, which would bring them to Trinidad and the coast of South America, or in the northern section which brought them to the Lesser Antilles. From here they entered the Caribbean through one of the many passes between the small islands. Ships sailing the southern route ran the risk of running into the Doldrums, a windless region. Here they might be stuck for weeks waiting for a breeze to blow them back into the Trades.

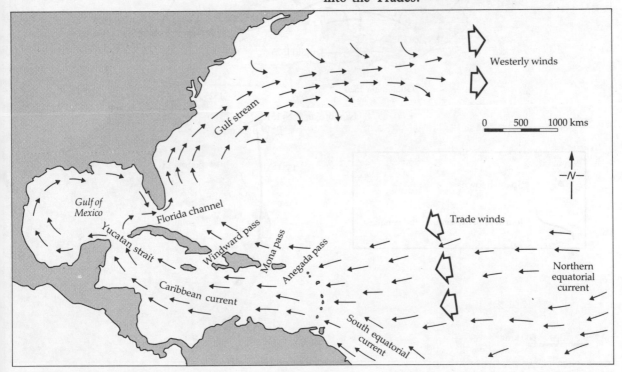

Map 10 *Winds and currents in the Caribbean.*

Once the Caribbean was reached the Trades were less welcome. It was difficult to sail against them on an easterly voyage. A voyage from Barbados to Jamaica took about a week; to go in the opposite direction needed five or six weeks!

Currents

The Spanish were also the first to chart the Caribbean currents. Like the Trade Winds, these flow from east to west. The North Equatorial Current and the South Equatorial Current flow in from the Atlantic and join north of Tobago to become the Caribbean Current. This flows to the Gulf of Mexico where it turns back through the Florida Channel as the Gulf Stream. The currents flow only at three or four knots an hour and did not influence sailing as much as the Trades, but they still forced ships in a westerly direction. On his return voyage, Columbus fought against the awkward currents and winds as he left the Caribbean through the Windward or Mona passage. Later seamen found that it was easier to follow the Trades as far west as the Yucatan Strait. Then they tacked

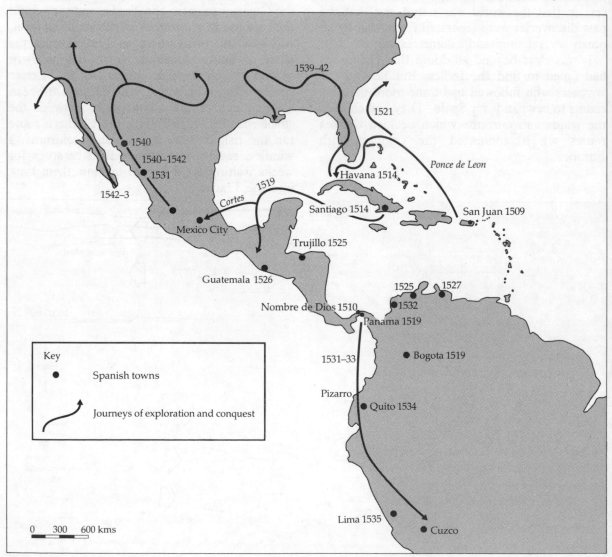

Map 11 *The Spanish conquests.*

34

north until the Gulf Stream carried them through the Florida Channel and into the Atlantic far enough north to pick up the Westerly Winds. The Spanish quickly realised the importance of controlling the Florida Channel.

The Spanish Empire

Conquest of the mainland

The Spanish would probably not have settled the mainland without their bases on the Caribbean islands. The islands had ports for refitting ships and taking food on board. They were also gathering points for conquistadores. Some of these fighting men came from Spain to join expeditions. Others had come to the islands in the hope of fortune. As the thin veins of gold ran out they were eager to move on. Such a man was Diego Velasquez who had been deputy governor of Hispaniola and conqueror of Cuba. To him, Cuba was only a stopping place in the movement west in the search of even greater wealth. Santiago, the town he founded on the island, was to be the new base for exploration in the New World.

Voyages of exploration were sent out from Santiago. They found the coast of Mexico and came back with enough loot to prove that the land held great riches. Velasquez now looked for a man to lead a force of conquistadores against the Aztecs who ruled over the peoples of Mexico. His first choice was his young secretary, Hernán Cortes. Too late, he found that Cortes had been making plans of his own. In February 1519 he slipped away taking the 600 best fighting men on Cuba, most of the island's stock of weapons and eleven ships. By September 1520 he had conquered the Aztec Empire and totally destroyed its capital, Tenochtitlan. In 1522 Cortes was made governor of Mexico which was renamed New Spain.

Mexico was not the first part of the mainland discovered by the Spanish. Earlier, Nicolas Ovando had sent a group from Hispaniola to start a small settlement on the Panama coast near Nombre de Dios. One of the settlers, Vasco Nunez de Balboa, had made a journey to be the first European to see the Pacific Ocean from a high point on the isthmus, and soon another struggling settlement had been started at Panama. But, like the islands, the Panama area gave little profit to the Spanish. They found it difficult to make a living because of hostile Amerindians and the many diseases they caught in the marshy lands. These settlements also became the base for bands of conquistadores who first gathered on the island colonies. Their goal was the great empire of the Incas in Peru.

The distant empire, whose strongholds were high in the Andes, took longer to overcome than Mexico. There were two failed expeditions and much quarrelling among the conquistadores. Then, in 1535, Francisco Pizarro captured the Inca capital at Cuzco and replaced it with a new Spanish town, Lima, on the coast. The land of the Incas became the Spanish viceroyalty of Peru, the richest part of the vast empire which Spain now had in the Americas.

Fig. 5.2 *Spaniards forcing Amerindians to carry loot taken from the Inca Empire in Peru.*

Moving on from the Caribbean

Hundreds and then thousands of Spaniards from the Caribbean moved on towards Mexico and Peru. The first were the conquistadores who went for the plunder, but close behind went men who hoped to own richer mines or cattle ranches than those on the islands. The mainland mines produced vast amounts of gold and silver, far more than those on Cuba and Hispaniola which were worn out by the 1530s. On the mainland there were thousands of square kilometres of grassland for ranching and millions of Amerindians to be forced into encomiendas.

Two towns in Cuba became well known to sailors, merchants and officials from Spain. Those travelling to Panama and Peru called in at Santo Domingo to repair their ships and take on supplies. It was still the Spanish headquarters in the Caribbean and by far the largest island town, with Spanish government officials, merchants and craftsmen who supplied the ships and their passengers. Havana was used by ships on their way to Mexico. Because it lay on this route it soon became more important than Santiago on the south coast and replaced it as the capital of Cuba. Even though its towns were important, there were only 200 Spanish land-owning families on the whole island in 1540. There had been several times that number before the riches of the mainland were discovered.

Peoples of the Spanish Caribbean

The fall in the numbers of Spanish took place throughout the Caribbean. At its time of greatest importance, Hispaniola had a population of 14,000; by 1574 there were only 500 households. Jamaica and Puerto Rico never had more than a few hundred Europeans until the mid-seventeenth century. Further south, there was a pearl-gathering settlement on Margarita, but only a few dozen Spaniards remained, because the first men on the scene had over-fished the seas. Most of the Lesser Antilles were never occupied, although the Spanish govern-ment claimed them as part of the empire. There was a settlement on Trinidad but it numbered only 70 Europeans in 1593.

The small population quickly became very mixed. To increase the numbers of European colonists the Spanish government allowed non-Spaniards to emigrate. Portuguese farmers, mostly from the Azores, were offered land in the Greater Antilles. Among the armies sent out to the New World were many Italian soldiers as well as German craftsmen who made weapons and equipment. After their army service, many settled on the islands to start a small business or farm, while the Spanish conquistadores were driving further into the mainland.

By the mid-sixteenth century the greater part of European people in the Caribbean were born here and not in Spain. Many were 'creoles', a word used by the Spanish for American-born people of European parentage. Others were of mixed parentage. So few women came among the early settlers that many men took Amerindian women. Many of the children of these unions became accepted in local society and helped to widen the differences between those born here and peninsulares – men who came from Spain to work for a time in the empire.

For creoles outside Santo Domingo and Havana, the main occupation was ranching. On all the islands there were so few landowners that it was possible to allow the cattle to roam freely without the expense of fencing. The hides and tallow fetched good prices from European leather and candle makers, and they would not suffer if they had to be stored for months waiting for a ship. Ranching did not produce as much money as sugar planting, but few creoles started plantations because of the cost of crushing mills and the shortage of labour. The government helped with loans but it was still difficult to make a profit, especially when their sugar had to compete with much larger plantations in Brazil, Mexico and the Canary Islands. After sugar and ranching a variety of products were grown on a small scale, including fruits, tobacco, cassava and maize, but none were very important, particularly when a farmer had hardly any neighbours to sell them to.

Towns and cabildos

The centre of creole life in each district was its town, or *villa*. Some, like Santo Domingo, grew into European-style cities with many stone buildings. But, throughout most of the Caribbean the towns never grew beyond a dusty main square, or *plaza major*, around which stood a few wooden buildings, a church, a town hall, a prison, and perhaps a school. The leading creole families had their homes here, too, for they did not live in great houses on the plantations as later English colonists did. The villa was more than a market town; it was the centre from which the countryside around was ruled by the cabildo, made up of the heads of the leading creole families in the district. Usually there were twenty-four councillors or *regidores* on the cabildo but small towns could have as few as four.

The cabildo was in charge of sharing out the land in the district, and arranged the repartimiento of Indians so that it controlled the supply of labour. The price of goods in the town was fixed by the cabildo whose regidores owned the land on which most of the goods were produced. The same regidores elected one of their number to be *alcades*, or magistrates, who dealt with crime and legal cases.

Governing the empire

Peninsulares

After the conquest of the mainland, the Caribbean colonies were ruled from Spain as just one part of her huge empire in the Americas. The work of running it was done by peninsulares (men from the Peninsular) sent out from Spain to serve for a time as officials. Spain's royal government intended its American lands to be ruled in the same way as the kingdoms of Castile and Aragon. Its aim was to make the crown more powerful than any group. To do this they had the aid of the Council of Castile and the Council of Aragon. Each was made up of a bishop, senior civil servants and lawyers,

and was responsible for making laws and regulations. But it was difficult to see that these were obeyed, especially where local noblemen had become wealthy and powerful enough to ignore royal officials. To keep respect for the law was the work of *audencias*, which were courts of lawyers who examined complaints of unlawful behaviour.

Only slight changes were made to this system of government in the American colonies. At first the newly conquered lands were controlled by the Council of Castile. The task became so huge that a separate Council of the Indies was set up in 1524. By 1635 this Council had made more than 400,000 laws controlling life in the colonies down to the last detail. It had set up law courts and founded new cities, schools, churches, hospitals and monasteries. But it also dealt with lesser matters, laying down what dress colonists should wear, which Spanish dialect should be taught to Amerindians, and even the order in which officials should enter church.

Audencias

To make sure that those laws were obeyed in the Americas a chain of audencias was set up. In the Americas an audencia had more power than it did in Spain for it could make its own enquiries into whether the Council's regulations were being obeyed. To back up the judges there was a staff of lawyers, officials and clerks who became the real rulers of the colonists.

When the empire had grown to its fullest size each audencia supervised an area which contained officials of many ranks. Larger districts were in the charge of presidents and each presidency was divided into several provinces each with its own governor. The more remote areas were in the charge of captain-generals. Below these senior officials were thousands of lesser government servants. All were peninsulares and could be dismissed and sent back to Spain if their work was found unsatisfactory.

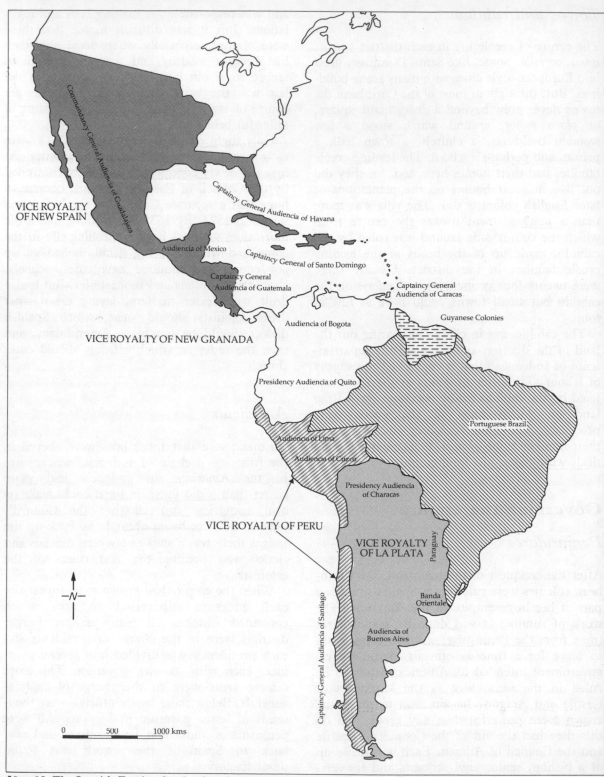

Map 12 *The Spanish Empire showing its administrative divisions. Why have the eastern Caribbean islands not been included?*

Viceroys

At the head of all the officials stood the viceroys. In the sixteenth century there were only two, governing the Viceroyalties of New Spain and Mexico. Later, the boundaries were changed and there became four: the Viceroyalties of Mexico, La Plata, Peru and New Granada. The viceroy was the representative of the king and queen; he was a great nobleman and given all the honours of royalty. But despite the magnificence of his position, his powers were carefully limited. The work of his officials was examined by the audencias and his financial records were inspected by a *visitador*, who came unannounced from Spain to check that the viceroy was not using his position for his own profit. At the end of his term of office the viceroy had to hold a *residencia* when his work could be questioned in public.

The Church in the colonies

In Spain the Church was immensely powerful. Its bishops and priests had great privileges such as being free from taxes and having the right not be accused in a royal court. Ferdinand and Isabella did not want the Church as a rival to their power in the New World. In 1508 the Pope gave the Spanish rulers complete control over who was made bishop or priest in American colonies. Tithes, or money paid to the Church by people living in its parishes, were collected by royal officials, not by priests.

The New World settlements developed into copies of Spanish society as a result of the activities of the Church. It ran all the schools from the smallest mission class up to the universities in Mexico City and Lima. Priests and nuns staffed orphanages, poorhouses and hospitals. Special Church courts dealt with matters such as marriage and the inheritance of property. The spread of new ideas was checked by the Church courts which dealt with heretics – people who spoke or wrote in a way which the Church said was false. The most famous of these courts was the Holy Office of the Inquisition, whose permission was needed for any book to be published. It is best remembered for hunting down heretics, including Protestant Dutch and English sailors who came into Spanish ports in the Americas.

The Church and the Amerindians

The leading part in the Church's work among Amerindians was taken by friars, especially the Franciscans and Dominicans. In Europe the first friars had been monks who had left their monasteries to live, without any personal belongings, among the poor. From these beginnings had sprung up the great organisations, or Orders, of friars who provided schools and hospitals across Europe. The Spanish branches of the Dominican and Franciscan Orders saw a great opportunity in the Americas. Here were millions of Amerindians, simple, ignorant people who could be cared for and cured and baptised into the Catholic Church.

Unfortunately there were two views of the purposes of the conquests. As one conquistador said, they were to: 'serve God and His Majesty and to give light to those in darkness, and also to get rich'. It was the second view which was held by the Spanish settlers who forced the Amerindians to labour for them. Queen Isabella, a very religious woman, was troubled by the ill-treatment and ordered Amerindian slaves to be set free. On the other hand, she believed the encomiendas were a way of carrying out God's work by giving the Indians protection and a chance to learn the teachings of Christianity. The truth was far different, and it was a Dominican friar, Antonio de Montesinos, who spoke it out loud in 1511.

Antonio de Montesinos

The place he chose was the main church in Santo Domingo, the capital of the empire in America. Many encomonderos sat in the congregation and heard Montesinos say: 'Are these Indians not men? Do they not have rational souls? Are you not obliged to love them as you love yourselves?' He ended his sermon by calling on the encomonderos to end the 'cruelty and tyranny you use in dealing with these innocent people'.

The congregation was outraged and so were most wealthy Spaniards on Hispaniola. They tried to silence Montesinos by sending reports to Spain that he was threatening the peace of the island. So Montesinos himself went back to Spain where his views were listened to by a Church council. This compiled the thirty-two Laws of Burgos which King Ferdinand signed in 1512. The laws attempted to make the encomienda system work without such evil effects and laid down the exact hours of labour and amount of food which each worker and his family should have. The Laws of Burgos were completely ignored in the Spanish colonies, but the campaign for fair treatment of the Amerindians was taken over by another friar.

Bartolomé de las Casas

Las Casas had first come from Spain to Hispaniola and then joined Velasquez's expedition to Cuba. There he had an encomienda but became convinced that the system was evil. He travelled to Spain to argue that the Amerindian could be converted to Christianity without being brought under encomiendas. He claimed they would work much more willingly if they were settled on their own lands. Eventually, the new ruler of Spain, Charles V, made las Casas 'Protector of the Indians' and gave him the chance to try his 'social experiments'.

The first was in Hispaniola. A few Amerindians were taken to gold mines and asked to work in return for food, clothing and shelter. They could not understand the point of such work either as free men or under force. The food was eaten but no gold mined. A few years later, las Casas tried to prove that the Amerindians could be taught to work alongside Spaniards. He took Spanish farmers and Amerindians to a remote place on the Venezuelan coast, but this experiment also ended in disaster. Spanish colonists from Hispaniola wanted to discredit las Casas and attacked the settlement, carrying off several Amerindians. Those remaining blamed their Spanish neighbours and slaughtered them.

Las Casas tried once more, in Guatemala. He had ballads written which told the Christian story in Amerindian language. These were taught to Amerindian traders who sang them on their visits around the villages. Then priests began to accompany the traders and to win the confidence of the village people. This experiment alarmed the Amerindians' own priests. In 1552 they led a rebellion in which three Christian priests were murdered, one being sacrificed before a local idol.

Las Casas failed in his efforts to protect the Amerindians from the evil consequences of the encomienda system. The creole settlers were so desperate for labour that they refused to accept laws which protected the Amerindians. Such laws were made with the encouragement of the Pope, who declared in 1537 that Amerindians were: 'not to be deprived of their liberty or the possession of their property even though they may be outside the faith of Jesus Christ . . . nor should [they] be in any case enslaved'.

This forced Charles V, king of Spain 1516–56, to issue the New Laws of 1542 which forbade new encomiendas to be granted and ordered that Amerindians should be freed on the death of their encomendero. But the Laws could not be enforced. The viceroy of Peru was murdered for trying to introduce them; the viceroy of Mexico never even published the Laws. The authorities in Spain decided to allow the encomiendas to continue rather than be faced with revolts from the colonists.

Assignments

1 *Outline the importance of wind systems and ocean currents for the activities of Europeans in the Caribbean.*

2 *Study the passage on page 36: 'At its time of greatest importance, Hispaniola had a population of 14,000.'*

a) *Explain why as many as 14,000 Spaniards were in Hispaniola.*

b) *In your own words explain, with examples, how Spain governed and controlled her empire in the New World.*

3 *Describe the role of the Catholic Church in Spain's developing empire. Why were Montesinos and las Casas critical of how the Indians were treated and what did they do about it?*

6 SIXTEENTH-CENTURY RIVALRY

Spain's monopoly system

The Spanish government believed that the wealth of its empire in the Americas existed solely to increase the power of Spain. This meant close control over buying and selling by colonists. All goods produced in the New World had to be exported to Spain and to no other country; everything the colonists bought had to be imported from Spain itself and be carried in Spanish ships. The ideas behind this economic system have been called mercantilism. Mercantilists thought that the key to a nation's wealth lay in keeping a monopoly over all its trade and keeping out foreigners. This, they said, would benefit merchants and seamen, the ship-builders and the craftsmen who made goods for the new overseas markets. It would also increase the income of the government which could tax all the goods which passed either way between Spain and the colonies. If the tax were collected in gold or silver, it would pay for the armies and navies which would make the nation more powerful than its rivals.

Fig. 6.1 *The entrance to Havana Harbour guarded by Morro Castle, which has a modern lighthouse on top. The castle was built in 1589 to protect the town from pirates.*

The Casa

To enforce Spain's monopoly of trade with her colonies the *Casa de Contratación*, or House of Trade, was set up at Seville in 1503. No other port could send ships to the colonies. All ships arriving from the Americas had to complete their journey at Seville. Here Casa officials took one-fifth of all precious metals as the king's share and charged customs duties on all other goods.

The Casa was responsible for granting licenses, or *asientos*, to foreigners who wished to ship goods to the colonies. The African slave trade first began with an asiento granted to Portuguese merchants. The Casa also maintained a school, to train map-makers, sailors and geographers, and set up special courts to deal with disputes over trade.

It was much more difficult for the Casa to control trade in the New World. Colonists were supposed to buy only goods which came through Cartagena or Nombre de Dios and, later, Portobello. It was hard to keep a check on trade between colonists and foreign merchant ships which slipped into the many Spanish settlements scattered over thousands of kilometres. To try to stop this 'smuggling', Spanish cruiser fleets patrolled the seas from bases at Santo Domingo, Havana and Cartagena.

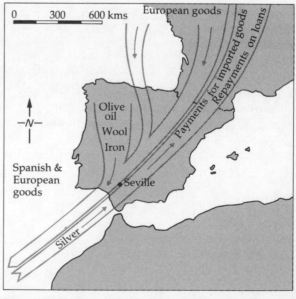

Map 13 *The flow of trade to and from the Spanish Empire.*

Challenging the monopoly

Sixteenth-century Europe

Other European nations were not prepared to accept Spain's claim to all the wealth from the New World. After the discovery of trade routes to the New World and to the Indies, European power struggles were no longer fought out just on the continent. Each country wanted to weaken its rivals by capturing their overseas bases and interrupting the flow of trading goods, silver and gold. If they succeeded they would damage the rival's power in Europe. Between 1521 and 1559 France and Spain fought for the leading position in Western Europe and the wars spilt over into the Caribbean.

The Reformation

In the later sixteenth century, Spain's main rivals were two north European peoples, the English and the Dutch. Their quarrels with the Spanish had an additional cause. Both became Protestant while Spain (like France) remained Roman Catholic. The background to this change lay in the movement we call the 'Reformation'. It began in Germany in the early sixteenth century when a priest, Martin Luther, protested at some of the practices of the Roman Catholic Church of his day. The new ideas about the Christian faith spread among people in Germany, Switzerland and the Netherlands.

The English queen, Elizabeth I, who reigned from 1558 to 1603, made herself the champion of the Protestant countries and the arch-enemy of Spain, the leading Catholic power. One of the causes she supported was the struggle of the Protestant Dutch people to free themselves from Spanish rule.

Revolt of the Netherlands

The Dutch people lived in some of the provinces of the Netherlands or low countries. Since 1519 the Netherlands had been ruled by the kings of Spain. Their people were far more experienced than the Spanish in ship-building, sailing and trading. After a few years the Dutch were managing the export to other European countries of the goods which came in to Seville from the Americas. By 1560 there were more Dutch than Spanish merchants in Seville. Bankers and traders in Antwerp and Amsterdam were leading figures in arranging trade in and out of the Spanish Empire.

The Dutch were important to the Spanish king's empire but he still ruled the Netherlands harshly. Their noblemen and city councils had little power, and leading Dutchmen who protested at this were executed. The most severe persecution was aimed at Protestants. Spain's governor in the Netherlands closed their churches and had the property of Protestant worshippers seized. Thousands fled to Germany and France, giving themselves the name of 'Beggars'.

In 1572 a revolt broke out, led by Prince William of Orange. The struggle for independence lasted until the rebel United Provinces won their freedom in 1609. Like the wars between Spain and France, and Spain and England, it had important effects on the Caribbean.

Privateers and traders

Privateers

In the sixteenth century, European countries

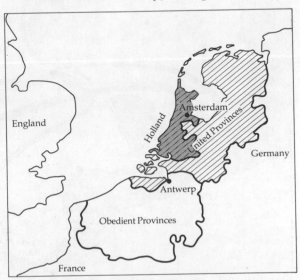

Map 14 *The Netherlands. The United Provinces revolted under the leadership of William of Orange. The Obedient Provinces remained under Spanish rule, and in 1839 became Belgium.*

apart from Spain had only small fighting navies. When war broke out, the governments would take over, or commandeer, merchant ships and fit them out with guns. They would also issue letters of *marque* to captains of merchant vessels. The letter gave authority to attack enemy ports and ships. Captains had to hand over part of any booty to their government but they could sell the rest. The advantage of the letter of marque was that it gave the sailors the right to be treated as warriors not as pirates. If their ship was captured they would be made prisoners rather than hanged as outlaws.

Fleets of French privateers, called *corsaires*, were active in the Caribbean in the war between France and Spain. In 1523 privateers led by a French merchant, Jean D'Ango, attacked a Spanish convoy and seized two galleons. Their holds were full of gold and precious objects which Cortes had stripped from Aztec palaces and temples. In 1531 D'Ango attacked Havana and Nombre de Dios with thirteen ships and 3,000 men. By 1536, French privateers were

regularly plundering Spanish ships in the Florida channel and boldly attacking settlements in Cuba, Hispaniola and Puerto Rico. In 1543 the corsaires reached the mainland, sacked New Cadiz and burned Santa Marta to the ground. Even more brutal were the raids led by François le Clerc, nicknamed 'Pie de Palo' by the Spaniards on account of his wooden leg. In 1553, his squadron captured Havana. For eighteen days the citizens were tortured to make them reveal where they had hidden their money. When the last copper coin had been extracted the French methodically destroyed the city. A French fleet which arrived two months later could not find one whole bucket to carry fresh water to the ships' barrels.

Convoys and castles

The government in Spain took strong measures to defend the treasure fleets. In 1543 ships passing to and from the Americas were ordered

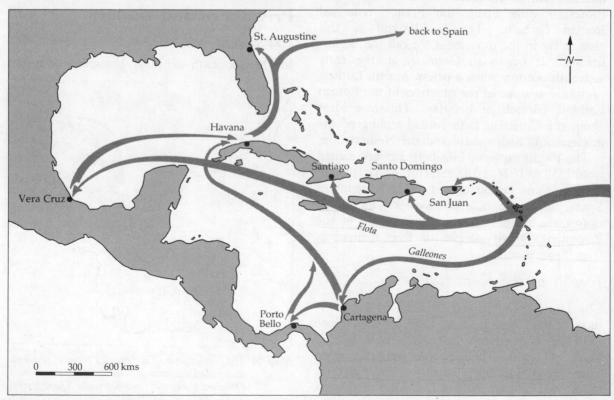

Map 15 *The convoy system.*

to sail in convoys. In 1564 and 1566, new orders laid down the convoy pattern which was followed for the next 150 years. There were to be two annual fleets. The first, the *Flota*, left Seville in April or May and sailed to the West Indies where it divided. Some ships stopped at West Indian ports and the rest continued to Vera Cruz in Mexico. In August another fleet, the *Galleones*, sailed from Seville. Part sailed to the Central American ports while the other ships turned south to Colombia and Venezuela. Both the Galleones and the Flota reassembled in Havana in April or May. After refitting and taking food on board, the combined fleet, under heavy protection from guard ships, sailed through the Florida Channel and across the Atlantic to Spain. In its long history the whole

convoy was captured only four times, although one or two ships were lost every year in storms or to pirates. In 1562 Pedro Menéndez de Aviles was sent to the colonies to strengthen their defences. He rebuilt the coastal towns the privateers had plundered, adding walls and fortifications. He had Havana rebuilt in stone, with the Morro Castle constructed at the harbour entrance to protect the fleets assembling for the homeward voyage.

De Aviles launched an attack on Florida where French corsaires had bases for their raids on the homeward-bound convoy. The French sailors were brutally slaughtered in the so-called 'Florida massacre'. It was a terrible example of Spain's determination to defend her claims. A new Spanish fort was built at St Augustine

Fig. 6.2 *Pirates raiding the Spanish settlement at Cartagena in 1555. This is a French drawing made in about 1600.*

where a permanent squadron kept guard over convoys in the Florida Channel.

English privateers

Some English sailors were given letters of marque by the French during their war with Spain. Men such as Francis Drake looted and burned Spanish settlements and stole whatever they could. Officially he was disowned by the English government for it was then still at peace with Spain. In fact officials of the court, and even Elizabeth I herself, helped to finance these raids. In 1585 war between Spain and England broke out officially. It was mainly a privateering war with English naval captains such as Drake, Anthony Shirley and Walter Raleigh raiding Spanish American strongholds. There was much senseless brutality and destruction and the raids did not lead to real gains for England or even loot for the privateers.

Fig. 6.3 *Drake's fleet outside Santo Domingo in Hispaniola. The picture shows the town's defensive walls surrounding streets laid out on a rectangular plan with a cathedral in the centre.*

Illegal traders

Europeans who wanted to carry out peaceful trade with the Spanish settlers were breaking the laws of the Spanish Empire. Yet the same regulations caused problems for the settlers who often could not get the goods or slaves they wanted from Spanish traders. The convoy system made the shortage worse as merchants could not send goods until one of the two great fleets set out from Seville. Once they had arrived in the Americas there were long delays while goods were moved on from the official ports of entry at Cartagena and Nombre de Dios.

These problems made colonists willing to break the regulations and trade with foreigners. Some were adventurers like the Englishman, John Hawkins. In 1563 he arrived on the north coast of Hispaniola with three ships carrying 400 slaves from West Africa. The colonists eagerly paid for the slaves with hides and sugar. Hawkins paid all Spanish taxes and customs duties. He insisted that local Spanish officials give him letters stating that he had traded peacefully and obeyed the laws. Two additional caravels were hired from the colonists to carry the overflowing cargoes which were sent direct to Seville. However, the Spanish government confiscated the ships and imprisoned their crews.

The following year Hawkins made another voyage, this time to the mainland settlements where the settlers were keen to pay gold for his slaves.

Back in England Hawkins gave a profit of 60 per cent to the merchants who had paid for the expedition. Money flowed in to pay for a third voyage, despite Spanish warnings that the trade was illegal.

Hawkins should have noted the warnings. In September 1569 his fleet was driven before a hurricane to seek shelter at San Juan de Ulloa. While the English were refitting their ships, the annual Flota arrived from Spain. In the battle that followed, 100 of the 300 men under Hawkins' command were killed or captured and only three ships escaped.

After that, Hawkins himself turned to priva-

teering under the French flag. But the profits he had made by trading with Spanish colonists persuaded other English merchants to take part in direct trade with them. Another group who supplied the settlers' needs was the Portuguese. Since 1530 they had held the asiento or licence to sell African slaves to settlers. This licensed trade also became the cover for shipping many other goods to the colonies, such as wine, oil, paper, tools and textiles. In addition the Portuguese sold many more slaves than their asiento permitted. The colonists paid the traders in gold, silver, tobacco, hides and sugar. In doing so they cheated the Casa in Seville of the chance to collect taxes on this produce.

By the end of the sixteenth century it was the Dutch who were the busiest illegal traders. When the revolt in the Netherlands broke out the Spanish king tried to ruin the Dutch merchants. He ordered the closing of their trading business in Spain and Portugal (which had united with Spain in 1580). To avoid ruin, merchants from Holland simply sent their ships direct to the Caribbean. They found the colonists eager to trade with them, for their goods were cheap and could be bought on easy terms. The Dutch were also forbidden to load salt for their herring industry from the salt pans in Portugal. Instead, herring fishermen crossed the Altantic to the salt pans on the coast of Venezuela and at Punta Arya. But they called first in Africa to collect slaves who were sold to Spanish colonists and Portuguese planters in Brazil.

The monopoly broken

As the sixteenth century drew to an end the monopoly system had broken down. The Caribbean sailing routes were controlled for most of each year by Dutch, English and French sailors. Spanish convoys still sailed to collect the precious metals from the mainland, but their rivals had the strongest grip on trade with agricultural settlements on the coast and islands of the Caribbean. Years passed without a single Spanish ship calling at places like Trinidad. One Spanish governor of the island pointed out that it was easier and cheaper to travel from Europe on a Dutch vessel.

Most Spanish officials were happy to grow rich themselves from taking part in illegal trade. In 1602 the Spanish king sent an agent to find out how loyal his colonial governors were. He found those in Puerto Rico, Cartagena and Havana guilty of trading with the Dutch rebels and returned with the disturbing news that Dutch ships in the Caribbean outnumbered the Spanish by five to one!

Spaniards welcomed foreigners who provided goods which could not be obtained from Spanish traders; some were even allowed to open shops in the colonies. In 1604 the new Spanish governor of Jamaica, Don Fernando Melgarejo, was dismayed to see colonists buying from Englishmen and joining them in friendly games of bowls. When he tried to drive the English traders out, the colonists threatened to hire a hundred Englishmen to kill him. The governor quickly backed down, using a phrase which all Spanish officials had to use often: 'Obedezo pero no cumplo' – I obey the law but I do not insist on it.

Effects of the monopoly system

The monopoly system had many weaknesses. The main one was that it brought little real wealth to Spain. Gold and silver poured through Seville but that simply caused inflation in the same way that a modern government printing too many banknotes does. The many restrictions on trade meant that Spain was actually discouraging her overseas people from producing far more valuable goods for export. In turn that meant that few Spanish went to settle in the empire, especially on the Caribbean islands. Each of the large islands of the Greater Antilles had only a few hundred settlers. On Trinidad and the Guyana coast there were only a few dozen and on most of the Lesser Antilles none at all. The story of Trinidad and the Guyana coast in the sixteenth century shows just how weak the Spanish were in the eastern Caribbean.

Trinidad and Guyana
El Dorado

Many Spanish adventurers believed in a mythical figure, El Dorado, the golden man, whose kingdom was said to be as rich in gold as Mexico or Peru. It was waiting to be discovered by the traveller who dared to make the journey up the Orinoco River. None tried so hard as Antonio de Berrio. His third journey was made when he was seventy and it lasted for eighteen months. After many disasters he turned back with only a handful of his men still alive, believing that he had come within four days' march of El Dorado. The survivors crossed to Trinidad by rowing boat and de Berrio decided that the island should be his base for his next attempt to reach El Dorado.

Trinidad

Columbus had sailed round the southern coast in 1498 and named the island after the Trinity. In 1520, a Spanish raid took 200 Caribs off to slavery in Puerto Rico and Santo Domingo. In 1530 a conquistador arrived to build a new colony but his small force was quickly destroyed by Caribs. It was only from de Berrio's time that Europeans managed to stay permanently on the island in tiny numbers. In 1592 de Berrio sent Domingo de Vera to conquer Trinidad. With twenty-eight soldiers, a friar and a lawyer, de Vera set out to take an island inhabited by many Amerindians. He landed at the spot which became Port of Spain and then sailed up the River Caroni to pace out the boundaries of the future city of St Joseph, the first capital of the Spanish colony on the island. The Amerindians drew back from these places. By the next year the number of soldiers had reached a hundred, and de Berrio ordered de Vera to take thirty-five of them to seek El Dorado. He returned with only some gold ornaments but falsely claimed to have discovered the golden land.

Dudley and Raleigh

Letters describing the conquest of Trinidad and the 'discovery' of the land of El Dorado were captured by an English privateer. Two English expeditions were fitted out to seize Trinidad and El Dorado. The first, led by Sir Robert Dudley,

Fig. 6.4 *Sir Walter Raleigh with a group of followers in Trinidad. This is an imaginary scene drawn in the nineteenth century.*

landed on Trinidad. From Trinidad he led a party to the Orinoco, where they got hopelessly lost and were lucky to return alive. Dudley sailed empty-handed for England, just before Sir Walter Raleigh arrived with high hopes of discovering El Dorado and setting up a rival American empire to that of Spain. The key to the scheme was the capture of the Spanish garrison on Trinidad. Raleigh easily took Port of Spain and St Joseph and made de Berrio his prisoner. Shortly afterwards, Raleigh came across a pitch lake and used some of the substance to stop leaks in his ships.

Raleigh was now ready to search for El Dorado but, after only a few days on the Orinoco, he turned back to the Caribbean. He tried to make a raid on the Spanish town of Cumana, but the Spaniards were warned and most of Raleigh's men were killed.

Raleigh's exploits brought Trinidad and Guyana to the notice of the government of Spain. In 1597 it sent de Vera to the area. His twenty-eight ships and 1,500 men recaptured the tiny settlements in Trinidad and set up a few new ones in Guyana. But within a few months most of the soldiers were dead. They had not planned to grow their own food and expected to be supplied by the Amerindians. But the Amerindians simply melted away from the Spanish camps.

With the failure of de Berrio, de Vera and Raleigh, the dream of finding El Dorado began to fade, although Sir Walter Raleigh returned to try once more in 1617. King James gave permission on condition that he did not clash with Spaniards, as the two countries were at peace. But there was fighting, and the Spanish protested to James. Seven weeks after Raleigh returned to England – still without gold – he was beheaded in the Tower of London. He was the last gold-seeking adventurer. By the time of his death men were already making fortunes from another commodity which Guyana did produce – tobacco.

Assignments

1 a) *Copy map 8 on page 31 and add France, England and the Netherlands.*
   b) *Outline the reasons that brought the French, English and Dutch to the Caribbean.*
   c) *On the map put in the route of two annual fleets, the convoys which sailed from Seville to the Caribbean and back to Spain.*
   d) *Explain briefly how the French, English and Dutch attacked Spain's monopoly in the New World.*

2 *Study the illustration on page 46 (Fig. 6.3) then answer the following questions:*
   a) *Suggest reasons for the location and layout of the town.*
   b) *What plans were made by Spain for the defence of this and similar towns in the Caribbean?*
   c) *Suggest the weaknesses of Spain's defence system in the Caribbean.*
   d) *Make an imaginary plan of how Drake would attack the town of San Domingo and outline what he would do after the attack.*

3 *Find out what you can about specific English, Dutch and French privateers and illegal traders.*

4 a) *Explain why Trinidad and Guyana were neglected by the Spanish in their earliest activities in the Caribbean.*
   b) *Why did Trinidad and Guyana gain Spain's interest at the end of the sixteenth century?*
   c) *What happened to Trinidad and Guyana after this period of interest?*

7 ENGLISH, FRENCH AND DUTCH COLONIES

Tobacco on the Guyana coast

Effective occupation

When Spain signed treaties to end her wars with France and England she refused to agree that they had any right to own land or trade in the Americas. On the other hand, England and France refused to accept that Spain had any rights in places which she did not 'effectively occupy'. The Spanish clearly had enough soldiers, officials and settlers to effectively occupy the mainland but this was less true in the western Caribbean islands. It was not at all true in the eastern islands or the Guyana coast. In the seventeenth century, Spain's rivals opened their own settlements on these lands which Spanish colonists had neglected.

Tobacco

In 1609 Robert Harcourt wrote a pamphlet to support a scheme for a tobacco plantation on the Guyana coast. He wrote:

> I dare to presume to say and hope to prove within a few years that only this commodity, tobacco, will bring as great benefit and profit as ever the Spaniards gained by their richest silver mine in all the Indies.

Tobacco had been brought back to Europe by the early explorers, but for many years it had been used mostly by sailors. In the later sixteenth century, however, pipe-smoking came into fashion in England, especially among the well-to-do. From England the pipe-smoking habit passed to Holland and then into Germany and Central Europe and on to Turkey. At the same time the Spanish were learning to like cigars and the Irish were known for taking snuff. Demand for tobacco soared, despite the

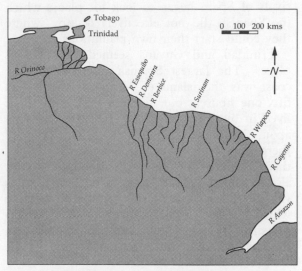

Map 16 *The Guyana coast, and Trinidad and Tobago. In the sixteenth and seventeenth centuries this region was known to Europeans as Guinea.*

efforts of some rulers to prevent the habit. For a time it was banned in Turkey and had to be smuggled there by Italian sailors. In England King James called smoking 'a custom dangerous to the eye, hateful to the nose, harmful to the brain, dangerous to the lungs'.

These efforts could not slow the demand. In 1614 an Englishman wrote:

> There has been a catalogue of all those houses that have set up that trade of selling tobacco in London, and near about London; and if a man may believe what is confidently reported, there are found to be upward of seven thousand houses that live by that trade.

There were great profits to be made from selling tobacco to shopkeepers and travelling traders in all Europe but, to do this, the merchants needed supplies. The English started their own tobacco plantations in Virginia on the American mainland. Only tiny amounts were grown there compared with in the Spanish Empire. In

51

1615–16 less than 1,360 kilograms of Virginia tobacco was landed in England against 26,300 kilograms from the Spanish Americas. All this had come from merchants who had traded illegally with Spanish settlers. Illegal Dutch traders also carried large quantities back to Amsterdam. In the early seventeenth century European rivals of Spain began to look for places which the Spanish did not effectively occupy, where they could start their own plantations.

Trinidad and Guyana seemed the obvious places. The largest Spanish colony along the coast was the island of Margarita which had fifty-one houses, but nineteen were said to be lived in by priests or widows. There were only about thirty-five other Spaniards. On Trinidad there were even fewer. No Spanish ship called there between 1597 and 1616 although, in 1611 alone, fifteen French, English or Dutch ships visited. They came mostly to take on tobacco which was grown or simply gathered by Amerindians. Trinidad tobacco was popular in England where it was known as 'Trinidada'.

Guyana

In 1604 England and Spain signed a peace treaty. Spanish and English forces would no longer attack each other, but the English king was ready to allow colonists to settle on land unoccupied by Spain. In the same year Captain Charles Leigh borrowed money from his brother and set off with forty-six men to build the first colony in Guyana. He selected a site for the first crops of tobacco, sugar, cotton and flax on the banks of the Wiapoco River. The colony began well but tropical heat and fever took their toll; nine men died before the provision grounds were prepared. Within two months the ship's supplies had run out and Leigh was forced to exchange his farming tools and even some of his men's clothes for food from the Amerindians. By January 1605 Leigh was dead. In March a Dutch ship carrying slaves to the Spanish colonies stopped at the little settlement and fourteen of the settlers agreed to load salt at Punta Arya in return for a passage back to England. A month later, ten more colonists left on a French ship. The remaining men stayed on to harvest a pitifully small crop of tobacco and flax. This they hoarded until 1606 when five survivors traded it for a passage to England on a Dutch merchant ship.

After Leigh, other small bands of French, English and Dutch arrived with high hopes of hacking plantations out of the tangled jungle. The first French efforts were organised by René de Montbarrot who sent his deputy, Daniel de la Ravardière, to select a suitable spot. He chose one on the Cayenne River and in 1607 three ships and 400 Frenchmen arrived to plant tobacco. The month after their arrival most were killed in a fierce Carib raid. The survivors moved south to the Amazon but this time were forced to flee by the Portuguese. Of all the attempts only one was successful, when the Dutch managed to start a small colony on the Berbice River.

Joint stock companies

Would-be settlers learned many lessons from these early failures to set up colonies on the Guyana coast. There had to be some way of supporting a colony over the first few difficult years. Money was needed for a good store of provisions, for building materials so that strongholds could be made, and, above all, to bring out more stores, food, ammunition, farming equipment and new colonists to replace those who had died. The English solution to this need for money was the joint stock company.

Before the joint stock company, most trading ventures were paid for by one merchant or a group of merchants. Even when the costs were shared, the risks were very great. A sudden raid by Amerindians, a storm or an outbreak of fever meant danger to the sailors and settlers and financial ruin to those who had sent them. The risks, however, could be spread much more widely by setting up a joint stock company and selling shares in the planned colony. In the early days a share usually cost 12 pounds, 10 shillings which was the estimated cost of 'planting a settler', that is getting one man established in the colony as a grower of tobacco or cotton. The settlers were looked on as the tenant-farmers of the company, which would take his produce back to England and sell it to make a profit from which the shareholders would be paid a dividend.

One of the earliest joint stock companies was the Amazon Company, started by Roger North in 1620 to plant settlers on the Guyana coast. North led the expedition himself and the scheme began well, but disaster then overtook him, for reasons which later companies did well to remember. A joint stock company needed a licence from the king. This gave it the sole right to colonise in a stated area, but what the king gave he could just as easily take away. In 1620, James I was trying to make an alliance with Spain by marrying his son to a Spanish princess. So, when the Spanish pointed out that North's settlement was a threat to Spaniards in nearby Venezuela, James I withdrew the licence. He had North recalled from Guyana and imprisoned in the Tower of London for three months.

Map 17 *The Lesser Antilles.*

The English in the Leewards

St Kitts

The harsh treatment of Roger North led Englishmen to shift their attention towards the islands of the Lesser Antilles. The Leewards were a favourite stopping place of an English pirate, Captain Painton. After North had been recalled to London, Painton had called in on the Guyana settlement where he became a close friend of Captain Thomas Warner, one of the men left in charge. Warner listened intently as Painton spoke of the healthy climate in the Leewards where the air was always fresh and cool because of the continual easterly Trade Winds. There were no swamps and the soils were fertile. The only drawback, Warner learned, might be the local Caribs, who had already massacred a shipload of colonists who had called in to St Lucia on their way to Guyana.

On his way back to England in 1622 Warner stopped at St Christopher. He studied the soil and planted a few tobacco seeds which soon sprouted into healthy plants. Before leaving he

gave gifts to the local Carib chieftain, Tegramond, and promised more, provided he was welcome to return with men to plant on the island. Back in England Warner kept his plans to himself and made a secret arrangement with a merchant, Ralph Merrifield, who agreed to supply money and stores in return for any tobacco that was grown on St Kitts, as the island became known.

In November 1622 Warner set out from England with one small ship, his wife, thirteen-year-old son and fourteen companions. They chose a site on the north coast near the middle of the island. Their first shelter was made by sticking a few branches in the ground and covering them with brush and leaves. All shared this hut while they cleared the ground for the first tobacco crop. The work was slow and hard for so few people. They ringed tree trunks with an axe and planted the tobacco between the dead stumps. One of the colonists, Captain John Smith, kept a diary in which he wrote on 20 September 1624: 'By September we made a crop of tobacco; but upon the 19 September came a hurricane and blew it away.'

The colonists planted a second crop, which was ready for shipment to England in 1625 when the *Hopewell* arrived with more supplies and colonists sent by Merrifield. Warner himself returned to England to ask for a royal licence for the company he and Merrifield had started in secret. Much to his surprise the plan to colonise St Kitts was warmly welcomed. While he had been away England's friendship with Spain had broken down and she was again preparing for war. The king's military advisers were looking for men to settle islands in the West Indies to serve as naval bases. Many merchants were also pressing for colonies to supply England direct with tobacco and other goods without having to buy them from Dutch, Portuguese or Spanish traders.

Lord proprietors

The merchants had learned not to trust the king and looked for someone with power and influence at court to act as a lord proprietor of the colonies. They would pay him to protect their interests and prevent the king from granting the charter to someone else. The lord proprietor chosen by Merrifield and Warner was the Earl of Carlisle. In 1625 the king granted him a charter to colonise St Kitts, Nevis, Montserrat and Barbados. Carlisle could appoint governors, raise taxes and make laws for the colonies. He was responsible for making arrangements for the defence of the islands and for recruiting new colonists. Each year Carlisle was to pay the king £100 to have the charter renewed.

Carlisle left the management of the colonies to Merrifield and his fellow merchants who ran the joint stock company. In the Caribbean the real master of St Kitts was Warner, who was made governor by the Earl of Carlisle.

Barbados

Carlisle's charter did not remain unchallenged for long. In 1624, on his way to England from Guyana with a cargo of tobacco, John Powell called at Barbados. On reaching England he suggested a scheme for growing tobacco on Barbados to his employer, Sir William Courteen. Courteen knew of Merrifield's schemes and hurried to set up a rival company for tobacco planting on Barbados. In February 1627 John Powell led a party of eighty men to the island. He left some there to build shelters and sailed to Guyana where he 'furnished himself with roots, plants, fowls, tobacco seeds, sugar canes and other materials together with thirty-two Indians which he carried to the said island'.

The little colony was growing quickly, but Courteen could make no profits because the king had already granted the licence to colonise Barbados to the Earl of Carlisle. In 1628 Courteen arranged for the Earl of Pembroke to be made lord proprietor of Barbados as well as Trinidad. Carlisle immediately protested and used his influence with the king to have Pembroke's claim set aside and himself granted a new charter making him lord proprietor of all the Lesser Antilles.

Carlisle's company then made great efforts to establish colonies on all the islands named in the new charter. Anthony Hilton left St Kitts and began planting tobacco on Nevis. In 1632 settlers began planting tobacco on Montserrat and Antigua.

Fig. 7.1 *Thomas Warner's gravestone. It refers to him as Lieutenant-General of the Caribee Company and Governor of St Christophers.*

Problems for English settlers

Carlisle and the merchants in England did not understand the difficulties which the settlers had to face before they could begin a profitable export trade. In addition to clearing the land and facing hurricanes, drought and disease they had to cope with raids from Caribs. In a Carib raid on Antigua in 1640 fifty colonists were killed and the governor's wife, his two children and three other women were carried off as hostages. It was difficult to force the Caribs away from settlements on the windward side of the island. In their war canoes they could push out to sea against the wind and so move freely up and down the coast. Sailing ships found this difficult to do without being forced back to the shore. So most European settlements were on the leeward of islands.

Occasionally there were raids by Spaniards. In 1629, the Spanish fleet on its way to Mexico turned aside to call at St Kitts. The Spaniards destroyed the few buildings and burnt the crops. Most of the English colonists were forced to sail back to England. Within a year they were back and planting in the ashes of the last year's crop.

As the number of settlements grew so did the difficulty of finding men willing to emigrate from England. Usually the companies looked for someone to 'plant' as a tenant farmer. Often these settlers were small farmers looking for more land than they had in England, but others were craftsmen with no knowledge of agriculture. Many were members of non-conformist religions seeking new homes where they could practise their beliefs freely.

Such men were often independent-minded and reluctant to grow export crops for the companies. They could often make a much better living as craftsmen, traders or builders. This meant that the shareholders' chances of making a profit lay in the large plantations owned by the company and not let out to tenants. As the Spanish colonists had discovered, the greatest problem on the plantation was finding a large enough supply of labour. The first English solution was the indenture or bondservant system.

Bondservants

Under the indenture system the companies gave a special contract to poor emigrants who were usually agricultural labourers. In return for a free passage to the Caribbean they signed an indenture bond agreeing to work for five years on one of the plantations. When their five-year bond ran out they were to be given a few simple farming tools and allowed to take up 5 acres (about 2 hectares) of land to begin their own small plantation. Bondservants suffered terribly for this chance to escape from a hard life in England. The journey to the Lesser Antilles took between four and six weeks, with each emigrant sleeping in a space 60 by 180 centimetres and living on cold and raw food. Yet a steady stream of men took up indentures, and the flow of bondservants raised the European population on Barbados from 6,000 to 36,000 between 1636 and 1645, and on St Kitts from 3,000 to over 20,000 between 1629 and 1643.

Even as more bondservants arrived, a new difficulty arose: growing tobacco on the English islands was becoming less profitable. Tobacco planters faced competition from the Spanish and French colonies but especially from the English plantations in Virginia which had now gained the largest part of the European market. In 1638, the port of London received 1.1 million tonnes of Caribbean tobacco and 3.4 million tonnes of Virginian. With larger areas of land, Virginia was able to produce tobacco at a much lower cost and its flavour was greatly preferred by European smokers. Even the French bought Virginian tobacco in preference to that produced on French plantations in the Caribbean.

At the height of the tobacco crisis, Henry Winthrop borrowed money from his father, sailed to Barbados and bought a small tobacco farm. After receiving the first shipment his father wrote back to say that no profit could be made from a tobacco 'so very ill-conditioned, foul, full of stalks and evil coloured'. He advised his son to find another cash crop. Some planters tried growing cotton, but the European markets were well supplied with cloth from the Far East. In 1640 one planter reported: 'This year has been so base [poor] a cotton year that the inhabitants have not made so much cotton as will buy necessaries for their servants.'

Quarrels with England

Because of poor profits, merchants in England became less willing to risk their money by lending it to Carlisle's company. Fewer ships arrived with supplies and the colonists found themselves almost abandoned and increasingly poor. This was especially true on the smaller islands. 'If you go to St Christophers', said one visitor in 1645, 'you will see the ruins of a flourishing place'. Ten years later the island was described as 'almost worn out'.

The white settlers began to object to making payments to the lord proprietor. When Carlisle sent an agent to collect overdue rents and taxes on St Kitts the planters simply refused to pay and 'took it ill and mutinied'. The colonists in Barbados drove out the man appointed as governor by Carlisle. They tore up his letter of appointment under a gallows and elected their own governor in his place.

In 1642 ties between the colonies and England became even weaker. In that year civil war broke out in England between supporters of King Charles I and the armies of Parliament under the leadership of Oliver Cromwell. During the six years of fighting the English neglected the Caribbean colonies, and settlers there were able to ignore the lord proprietor. In 1643 settlers on Barbados stopped paying the rents they owed him. The chance for an even more complete break came in 1649 when Charles I was executed and England became a 'Commonwealth' ruled by Oliver Cromwell. The colonists then declared themselves supporters of the dead king's son, hoping that this would mean they need not accept the laws made by the new government in London. In Barbados two royalist soldiers, Colonel Humphrey Walround and his brother Edward, persuaded the settlers to support a new governor, Lord Willoughby, appointed by the dead king's son. Other colonies took similar action. In Bermuda the col-onists condemned 'that horrid act of slaying His Majesty' and drove out all those they suspected of supporting the Commonwealth government. The refugees fled to Eleutheria in the Bahamas and helped to give England a strong claim to these islands. The governor and most of the colonists in Antigua declared support for the king's son. By 1651 most of the English territories in the Caribbean were free from London's rule.

The French in the Leewards

St Kitts

When Warner had returned as governor to St Kitts in 1626 he had been greeted by a number of Frenchmen, led by Pierre Belain, who had landed to refit their ship after a fight with a Spanish man-of-war. The English colonists had welcomed the French as they needed help against the Caribs, who became more hostile as Europeans spread over the island. Warner and Belain led a joint expedition in which Chief Tegramond and many of his men were killed and the remaining Caribs driven off the island. In return for their help Warner agreed to divide the island, giving the French the ends and keeping the middle for his company. The arrangement was followed by many quarrels as each side accused the other of taking the best lands.

In 1629, Belain was given support for his new colony by Cardinal Richelieu who governed France as regent on behalf of the young king, Louis XIII. Richelieu was determined that France should have a share in the New World. He had already claimed parts of Canada and followed this by founding a number of com-panies to settle Caribbean islands which were not 'effectively occupied' by other European powers. The French companies, like the English, were financed by private merchants, but the government kept much closer control because it saw the colonies as possible naval bases. The Company of St Christophers was the first to be formed and Belain returned as governor of the French colony to St Kitts.

Company of the Isles of America

In 1635 the Company of the Isles of America was founded and given a twenty-year monopoly of all trade between the West Indies and France. It had to pay a large rent to the French government in the form of tobacco and cotton. All company ships had to carry a number of *engagés* to the islands. Engagés were French bondservants who had engaged to work for three years on the plantations; they were commonly known as *les trente-six mois*, the thirty-six-month men.

The Company of the Isles of America soon settled colonists on St Lucia, Grenada, Martinique and Guadeloupe. All were occupied by Caribs, so the first years were ones of frequent fighting. In the end the Caribs were driven away from the land most wanted by the French. The warfare meant that the colonists were slow to establish plantations and send produce to France. As a result many French merchants lost interest in the Caribbean. The French government, too, found little use for them after it made peace with Spain in 1648.

The French colonies abandoned

Without support from merchants or the government, the Company of the Isles of America went bankrupt. For several months it looked as if the colonies would be abandoned altogether. Eventually it was decided that each colony could be purchased privately from the bankrupt company. The king of France appointed the French governor of St Kitts as his lieutenant-governor, but otherwise the French colonies remained neglected for nearly twenty years.

The Dutch

The West India Company

Between 1609 and 1621 there was a truce in the long war between the Dutch and the Spanish. At the end of the truce the Dutch set up the West India Company to fight all-out war in the Americas against Spain and Portugal, which were a united kingdom between 1580 and 1640. The Company had its own army and navy. All Dutch seamen and merchant companies wishing to trade in the Americas or the west coast of Africa had to belong to the Company, accept its rules and use its factories as trading bases.

The war at sea

In a few years the West India Company's admirals cleared the west Atlantic and Caribbean of all Spanish shipping apart from the annual convoys. In 1628 even this life-line was cut when Piet Hein ambushed the homeward-bound convoy off the north coast of Cuba. The first nine galleons were captured without a shot. Their cargoes of hides, cochineal, ginger, cocoa and other valuable goods would have satisfied Hein, but behind them came four treasure galleons carrying the year's output from the gold and silver mines in Peru. Hein returned to Holland with nearly 90,600 kilograms of silver, 61 kilograms of gold, a large quantity of pearls and several bags of precious stones.

For Spain the loss was a disaster; her soldiers went without pay and ammunition for a year. The Italian bankers who made loans each year to the Spanish government flatly refused to do so any longer. For shareholders in the West India Company there was a 50 per cent dividend and still enough money to pay for an expedition to capture the Portuguese sugar plantations in Brazil.

Fig. 7.2 *A Dutch warship of the seventeenth century.*

AFBEELDINGE IN WAT MANIER DE **SILUER VLOOT VANDEN GENERAEL**
PIETER PIETERSEN HEYN VEROOUERT IS Anno 1628.

Fig. 7.3 *Piet Hein's fleet comes out of its hiding place in Matanzas Bay to ambush the Spanish treasure convoy in 1628.*

The Dutch in Brazil 1630–54

The north-east of Brazil was the largest supplier of sugar to Europe. Most of the planters came from wealthy Portuguese families. These families could pay the heavy costs of starting a sugar plantation, especially the price of a mill to crush the cane. There were two kinds of mill: the *trapiche* powered by horses, oxen or sometimes slaves, and the *ingenio* powered by water. The trapiche could handle twenty-five to thirty-five cartloads of cane every day and the ingenio forty to fifty, so that the owners needed a large plantation to supply them. Large plantations meant a large labour force and the Portuguese, like the

Spanish, had turned to the use of African slaves. At the time of the Dutch conquest, there were 350 plantations with mills in Brazil, most of them worked by between thirty and forty slaves, although some were much larger.

Between 1630 and 1635 the West India Company conquered 1,600 kilometres of the north-east coastline of Brazil, and took a very large share of the profits from sugar. Portuguese planters had no choice but to ship their sugar to Europe in Dutch ships and to buy their copper boiling kettles from the Dutch. Most important, they bought their slaves from them, as the West India Company's forces had captured the Portuguese slaving posts on the

Fig. 7.4 *A Portuguese settlement in Brazil, drawn in 1628.*

West African coast. Dutch merchant ships called there to load with a human cargo before crossing the Atlantic.

The Dutch Empire in Brazil did not last long. In 1640 the Portuguese broke away from Spanish rule and began a war to drive the Dutch from Brazil. By 1654 they had recaptured the whole country. But this short period of Dutch control over Brazil was important for the history of the Caribbean. The Dutch had learned from the Portuguese planters about the use of African slaves to work large sugar plantations. They had also found that huge profits could be made by carrying slaves and plantation supplies across the Atlantic and returning with sugar.

The Dutch in the Caribbean

As well as supplying Brazil, the Dutch also brought slaves and goods to the Caribbean. They showed hardly any interest in planting here, apart from small settlements on the Berbice and Essequibo rivers. Instead they seized two groups of tiny islands as bases for trading with the Spanish colonies. The islands in the southern group of Aruba, Curaçao and Bonaire lay close to the ports of the Spanish mainland. The northern islands of Saba, St Eustatius and St Martin were near to the Spanish colonies in the Greater Antilles.

In 1648 Spain recognised these islands as Dutch colonies in the Treaty of Munster, which ended the war which had been restarted in 1621. The Treaty was the first in which the Spanish agreed that another nation could own colonies here. However, they still refused to allow their colonists to trade with other Europeans. But Spain did not have the sea-power to prevent the Dutch being their main suppliers of Spanish colonists. At the same time Dutch ships kept open Europe's links with the French and English settlements in the Caribbean.

The foster-fathers

The Dutch have been called the foster-fathers of the French and English settlements in the Caribbean for the way they kept them supplied when they were abandoned by France or rebelling against England. Dutch merchants carried tobacco and other produce back to Europe and, as one colonist said, brought to the Caribbean 'all things that were in any way necessary for their comfortable subsistence'. Dutch warehouses lined the harbours of the Lesser Antilles colonies. When fire broke out at Basseterre on the French part of St Kitts it destroyed sixty Dutch warehouses and their contents.

It was from the Dutch that English and French settlers learned of the profits which could be made from large-scale sugar planting. A small amount was already grown on Barbados and turned into a strong wine, but no sugar was exported until two Barbadian planters, James Holdip and John Drax, visited the Dutch plantations in Brazil. There, they saw cane fields and factories worked by African slaves. Back in Barbados they planted canes and cropped their first harvest, probably in 1643. Very soon sugar was the main export crop on the island.

The Dutch had many reasons for encouraging sugar planting. It brought more work for their ships and seamen; their merchants could lend money to planters to set up mills and buy the copper kettles needed for boiling. Refineries in Holland needed supplies of raw sugar. But, sadly, the greatest profits were to be made from carrying slaves across the Atlantic to work on the plantations.

Despite the profits, other English islands were slow to turn from tobacco to the new crop, and Barbados was the only prosperous English

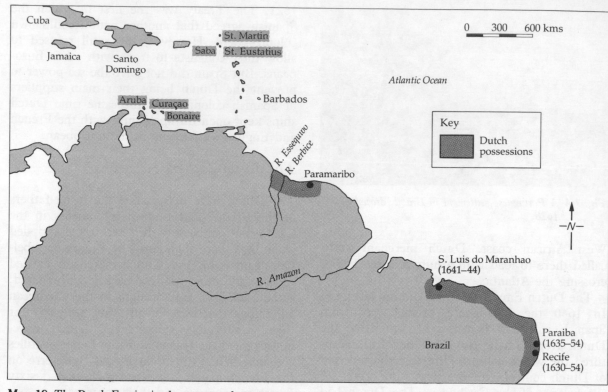

Map 18 *The Dutch Empire in the seventeenth century.*

island for twenty years. However, the Dutch also encouraged sugar planting by the French in Guadeloupe and Martinique in the 1640s. Dutchmen fled to these islands when they were driven out of Brazil in the years between 1640 and 1650. A thousand came to Martinique and 300 to Guadeloupe, bringing their knowledge of sugar and slavery with them.

For a few years in the 1640s and early 1650s the Dutch were the only Europeans carrying regular trade to and from the Caribbean. But they were too successful not to attract the attention of rivals. Soon the merchants of England and France were pressing their governments to take a new interest in the Caribbean. The first to move was the English government, as the following chapter shows.

Assignments

1 *Which sites in your country were first settled by Europeans? Can you account for their choice?*

2 *Make a copy of map 17 on page 53:*
   a) *Indicate where the English, French and Dutch had settlements in the early seventeeth century.*
   b) *Give examples of co-operation between the English, French and Dutch at this time.*

3 *What were the main problems faced by the English, French and Dutch in the Caribbean in the first half of the seventeenth century? How did they try to overcome these problems?*

4 *'For a few years in the 1640s and early 1650s the Dutch were the only Europeans carrying regular trade to and from the Caribbean,'* page 60:

a) *Explain why the above statement was the case.*

b) *Why and how do you think the English and French were going to turn against the Dutch in the Caribbean?*

8 THE FRENCH AND BRITISH EMPIRES

England and the Dutch

In the 1640s the Dutch were the only Europeans who traded regularly with the Caribbean. With Dutch help the rebel English colonies in the Lesser Antilles were able to survive without links with Oliver Cromwell's England. On Barbados, planters were making profits on sugar sold to the merchants of the Dutch West India Company.

British merchants saw no reason why Dutch traders and refiners should have all the trade. They persuaded the English Parliament to pass the Navigation Act of 1650 which forbade the other nations to trade with Antigua, Bermuda and Barbados. Willoughby, the rebel 'governor' in Barbados, ignored the law and the island went on trading with the Dutch. A soldier such as Cromwell saw only one way of dealing with rebellion. He ordered Sir George Ayescue to lead an expedition to recapture the islands.

Barbados retaken

When Ayescue's fleet reached Barbados it immediately seized twelve Dutch ships and blockaded the ports to stop any others coming in or going out. The blockade meant that the rebel colonists would soon starve. Lord Willoughby slipped away with some followers to start a colony in Surinam. The rest of the islanders surrendered to Ayescue. Soon afterwards planters on the Leewards also gave up their rebellion and accepted Cromwell's government.

The Navigation Act, 1651

The English Parliament set about making their position in the Caribbean even stronger by passing a second Navigation Act in 1651. This ordered that no produce from a colony could be carried to England or another English colony except in English owned ships. At least three-quarters of the crew had to be English, too. Goods going to the colony could be carried in ships from the country where they were made or in English vessels. They could not be carried by ships from any other country acting purely as a carrier.

The Act was aimed at stopping the Dutch. It meant that they could not ship tobacco and sugar back to England through their warehouses in Amsterdam. The only food and estate supplies they could take to the English colonies were those made in Holland. But the Dutch mainly lived by trade and the Navigation Act was proof that England was going to fight to make London, not Amsterdam, the greatest warehousing and shipping centre for trade with the colonies. One sign that the English were determined was that 200 ships were added to the British navy between 1651 and 1660.

The First Dutch War 1652–4

The Dutch refused to accept the Navigation Act and in 1652 they declared war on England. This First Dutch War was fought almost entirely in European waters where armed English ships blockaded Dutch ports to stop their ships sailing to the colonies. The blockade was never complete but it did make regular Dutch sailings impossible. Ships which did get through to the colonies found Cromwell's governors in control and ready to prevent English settlers from trading with them. The colonists had no choice but to use English ships, borrow money from London merchants and accept English manufactures, however expensive. They were particular annoyed by being forced to buy English woollen cloth. Even the most finely woven caused terrible itching in the tropical climate.

From the London point of view the war was

Fig. 8.1 *Casks of sugar being unloaded at Bristol.*

a huge success. Colonial sugar, cotton and dyewoods poured into English warehouses and a busy trade in re-exporting them to the rest of Europe grew up. Cromwell and his supporters were not ready to listen to the colonists' complaints or to give way to the Dutch. In 1654, the Dutch put their desire for peace first and agreed in the Treaty of Westminster to accept the Navigation Act.

England and Spain

The Western Design

For the moment the Dutch were no threat to the English in the Caribbean. Cromwell then turned his attention to the 'Western Design', a scheme for forcing Spain to recognise Britain's right to own colonies in the Caribbean and trade with Spanish settlers here. The Western Design was to begin with a surprise attack on Hispaniola. Once captured, it would be settled with Englishmen already living in the eastern Caribbean and become a supply base for raids on Spanish settlements in Central America.

An army of 2,500 men, commanded by General Robert Venables, set off from Plymouth in December 1654. Its first call was Barbados where Venables offered freedom to any bondsmen who wished to join the expedition. This roused the anger of planters who had paid for the bondservants' passage, and who were seriously short of labourers. The bondservants, of course, were eager to take the chance of freedom and land of their own. When the Barbados assembly refused to grant funds to buy arms for the new recruits, Venables issued the recruits with sharpened sticks.

His next call was to the Leewards, which were already overcrowded with European small farmers living on the edge of poverty. Four thousand of them were attracted by the chance of a larger plantation on one of the western islands. They, too, were not a serious addition to the fighting strength of Venables' force, for they came on board with their wives, children and slaves and even herds of animals and flocks of geese and chickens.

The attack on Hispaniola was a disaster. Admiral Penn put the men ashore in the middle of an unhealthy swamp, about 50 kilometres from Santo Domingo. The untrained troops lacked the food and water for a 50-kilometre march and were easily scattered by a force of Spanish lancers. They fled in confusion to the ships, where they refused to listen to Venables' pleas to face the Spaniards again. General Venables and Admiral Penn were faced with mutiny in the Caribbean and the certain anger of Cromwell at their failure. To repair the damage as much as possible they decided on the capture of Jamaica, the least wealthy and worst defended of the Spanish islands.

The capture of Jamaica

The total Spanish population of Jamaica was no more than 1,400 and only 500 were men of fighting age. Thirty-eight English ships sailed into Kingston harbour and were able to take the fort without a fight. The Spanish governor was old and sick and he left Cristoval de Ysasi to handle the problem of the English invasion. De Ysasi organised two forms of local resistance. First, the Spanish ranchers turned their cattle loose, freed their slaves, and set off with their valuables to the north coast where they sailed to Cuba. So, when the English marched into Spanish Town they found it empty with nothing

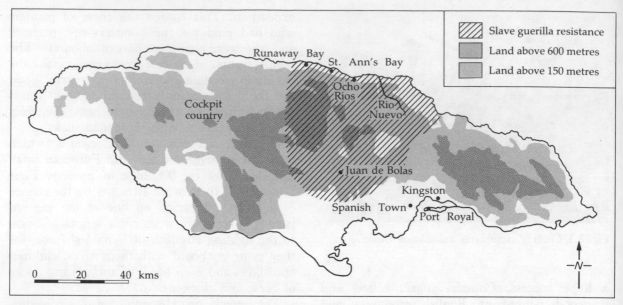

Map 19 *Jamaica in the mid-seventeenth century.*

to loot. Worse, the farms around were bare of food. They had to hunt down wild cattle and swine and supplies of these soon gave out.

De Ysasi's second form of resistance was to organise the freed slaves into guerilla bands. Their main base was at Juan de Bolas, called after the Spanish name for the slave chief, Lubolo. From here they attacked and killed any English who strayed too far in their search for food. Soon the English forces were dying from starvation, lack of medicines and disease.

Cromwell was determined to make the most of Jamaica, despite these setbacks. He ordered the military governor, Edward D'Oyley, to press ahead with building forts at Port Royal and around the coast. Troops were sent out from England and ordered to grow their own food, open new roads and build towns. To build up the population, Cromwell ordered a thousand Irishmen and as many women, mostly prisoners taken in his wars against the Irish, to be deported to Jamaica. From Nevis, Luke Stokes brought 1,600 farmers hoping for grants of land in Jamaica. D'Oyley ordered all new male settlers to serve in local militia bands which could be called on to help the regular soldiers fight de Ysasi's bands.

The English strengthened their position just

in time to deal with another Spanish threat. An invasion force of fighting men mostly from Mexico set out from Cuba to retake Jamaica. It landed in 1658 on the north coast at Rio Nuevo and built a strong fort where they were joined by de Ysasi and some of his guerillas. D'Oyley brought an English force by sea to attack the fort. More than 300 Spanish were killed and most of their supplies captured. De Ysasi escaped and fought on for two more years. But his resistance was weakened because Juan de Bolas went over to the English. He was the first Maroon, or independently living African (see Chapter 16), to come to terms with Europeans. He was allowed to take his fellow Maroons to a settlement in the Cockpit country. Without de Bolas's knowledge of the mountains, it was impossible for de Ysasi to carry on. In 1660 with his few remaining Spanish followers he escaped to Cuba in canoes from Runaway Bay.

Buccaneers

D'Oyley was not only military governor of Jamaica. He was in charge of trying to carry through Cromwell's grand design against the Spanish. He built up Port Royal into a naval base for raids on nearby Spanish colonies. In 1655 a raiding party destroyed the small

Spanish settlement at Santa Marta but the plunder did not 'pay for the powder and shot spent'. In 1656 an attack on Rio de la Hacha in Cuba led to the capture of only 'four great brass pieces of ordnance of near 4,000 pound [about 1,800 kilograms] weight each'. There were similar failures in 1657 and D'Oyley hit on the idea of inviting the buccaneers to join the British campaign against the Spaniards.

The first buccaneers were runaway bond-servants and men fleeing from the law. They had found safety on the north-west coast of Hispaniola which the Spanish had abandoned because of Dutch raids in the 1630s. The living they made was a poor one, hunting wild cattle and swine for their hides, which were then bargained for powder and shot from passing ships. The hard life and raids by Spaniards from Santo Domingo led the buccaneers to move to Tortuga, a few kilometres away, and join bands of pirates already there. With these pirates the buccaneers formed bands to raid shipping and defenceless settlements.

Most of the bands were made up of men from the same nation, England, France or the Netherlands. From time to time an Englishman or Frenchman would try to unite all the bands but they never succeeded in bringing foreigners under their rule. When Governor D'Oyley called on the English buccaneers to move to Jamaica they left behind the French, who were usually known as *flibustiers* (pirates).

The English fleet working from Jamaica was immediately helped by the buccaneers' skill in navigating the Caribbean currents and shoals, and by their knowledge of Spanish shipping movements. In 1659 the fleet returned from an expedition which had destroyed Campeche, Coro, Cumana and Puerto Cabello and captured loot valued at over £300,000. The regular fleet was then recalled to England. But D'Oyley increased the number of buccaneering ships under his command and their raiding of Spanish villages increased. Loot from these raids poured into Port Royal which, for a time, became the fastest growing town in the British Empire. The wild spending of the buccaneers also made it the most lawless port in the Americas.

Fig. 8.2 *A seventeenth-century artist's impression of the burning of Panama City by Morgan's pirates.*

The most famous buccaneer was Henry Morgan, an escaped indentured servant who had won a name for cruel and murderous treatment of captives. He continued with his cruel career until 1670 with a round of attacks on Cuba, Hispaniola and Central America. His last expedition was to seize and pillage Panama before withdrawing with £10,000 worth of loot. But, even before he set out, Spain had signed a treaty which recognised the British right to own territories in the Caribbean. In return, Britain agreed to bring pillaging by the buccaneers to an end.

Morgan had known about the Treaty before he sailed from Port Royal for Panama. He had probably gone with the good wishes of the governor, but on his return he was arrested and sent back to England to stand trial for piracy. However, anti-Spanish feeling was high in England, and Morgan was welcomed as a hero. He was acquitted in court and soon after knighted and sent back to Jamaica as lieutenant-governor.

For a few years Morgan played a double game; officially his task was to suppress the buccaneers, but secretly he helped finance more raids against the Spanish. Yet buccaneering no longer received support from the most powerful merchants in Jamaica or England. The raiding made the Spaniards reluctant to grant them legal trading arrangements. Planters, too, objected that privateering took away the labourers they needed. In 1685 the British government sent naval forces to suppress buccaneering. Within four years most of the English buccaneers had fled from the Caribbean to the mainland around Carolina or Virginia. Other gave up sea-roving altogether and settled as planters or sailed to Campeche to cut logwood. A last blow was the destruction of their main base, Port Royal, in an earthquake in 1692.

The Second Dutch War

The Navigation Act, 1660

With Jamaica safely in her hands, England turned again to her campaign to drive the Dutch from her growing trading empire in the Caribbean. Cromwell was now dead and the new government of Charles II gave itself further powers over trade in another Navigation Act.

The Navigation Act of 1660 said that valuable colonial goods were to be 'enumerated' or placed on a list of items which could be exported only to England or another English colony. The most important enumerated goods were sugar, tobacco, cotton, indigo, ginger and dyewoods. None of these could now be carried direct to a trading rival's ports. They had to be taken first to England then re-exported. This increased the profits of English merchant companies and industries such as tobacco curing and sugar refining. The king's treasury also collected increased customs duties. Another section of the Act closed all colonial ports to foreign vessels, apart from certain free ports such as those in Jamaica where Spanish ships were allowed to buy English manufactured goods and slaves.

More pressure on the Dutch

The 1660 Navigation Act, like those in 1650 and 1651, was aimed at the Dutch. But the

Fig. 8.3 *A drawing from a seventeenth-century French book illustrating the life of a buccaneer. What evidence can you find for their way of life?*

pressure did not stop there. In 1662 Parliament passed the Staples Act which laid down that all non-British goods had to be landed in England before they were sent on to the colonies. In this way Charles II's government collected both import and export duties. The extra duties made the foreign goods more expensive in the colonies than those which were manufactured in England.

The only items to escape the Staples Act were those which England did not produce herself such as wine and slaves. To gain control of the Dutch business of supplying slaves to the colonies, the Company of Royal Adventurers Trading into Africa was set up in 1660. In 1663, Captain Robert Holmes was sent to Africa with a fleet to arrange for slaves to be supplied to the Company's ships from the Portuguese trading factories on the coast. The Dutch tried to prevent Holmes's activities. In 1664, acting without orders, he seized several Dutch trading factories and used them as bases for supplying slaves to the Company of Royal Adventurers. In the same year the British captured the town of New Amsterdam, which later became New York. These British captures signalled the start of the Second Dutch War.

The Second Dutch War 1665–7

The Dutch struck the first blow in 1665 with a surprise attack on Barbados. Although unable to land, they destroyed several English merchant ships before sailing on to plunder Montserrat and Antigua. In reply the new governor of Jamaica, Thomas Modyford, called on the buccaneers to attack the Dutch islands. The buccaneers attacked St Eustatius and Saba.

In 1666, the English faced new dangers when France joined the war on the side of Holland. The quarrelling English buccaneers were no match for the French fleet which soon arrived on the scene. St Kitts, Montserrat, Anguilla and Antigua fell to the French and their English settlers were deported to Nevis. Governor Modyford reported that they had been plundered 'to their very shirt tails'. In 1667 only Nevis, Barbados and Jamaica were in English hands. The British government realised that

buccaneers could not be relied on and sent a fleet with trained soldiers and sailors in the spring of 1667. Within a few months Montserrat, Antigua and Anguilla were retaken. The war was then brought to an end by the Peace Treaty signed at Breda.

Treaty of Breda

All colonies were returned to their owners, except that the British allowed the Dutch to keep Tobago, and the colony founded by Lord Willoughby in Surinam, in exchange for New York. The treaty's greatest importance, however, was that it marked the end of the Netherlands' position as chief supplier to the Caribbean settlements. They had been driven from trading with the English islands. The way was now open for the British to replace them as the main carriers of slaves and manufactured goods to the Spanish colonies. By 1700 English traders were selling £1.5 million worth of goods to Spanish America each year.

The French Empire

French settlements in the 1650s

While the British government was building an empire out of the Caribbean colonies, the French islands had remained in private hands. Under their proprietors, the French settlements had increased in number and in wealth. There were three distinct types. In the eastern Caribbean lay the colonies on Martinique, Guadeloupe, Marie Galante, Desirade, the Saintes, Grenada and part of St Kitts. As in the English colonies, the first tobacco farms had given way to sugar plantations; African slaves had been imported and profits were increasing yearly. For their slaves and for shipping produce back to Europe, the French settlers relied on the Dutch.

The second group of French settlers had moved on from the Lesser Antilles to the deserted parts of the western Caribbean. In western Hispaniola, or St Domingue, which had been abandoned by the Spaniards, flourishing sugar plantations had grown up. Nearby, the flibustiers still had their base on Tortuga. The third group were plantations in the Cayenne region of the Guyana coast.

For years there was no official communication between France and her colonies, even though the governor of the French colony on St Kitts had the title of lieutenant-governor to the king. But the growing wealth of the colonies attracted the notice of French finance officials who began to argue that France should take advantage of them as her European rivals were doing. In 1658 the Finance Minister, Nicholas Fouquet, wrote to the Council of State:

> The great number of vessels which Dutch merchants send to the French islands is proof that trade with these islands is very profitable, for otherwise they would not send 100 or 120 large ships there every year. In order that the French may profit from this commerce, it is necessary to exclude all foreigners from privileges of trade there, as the Dutch, Spaniards and English have done in their colonies.

Colbert

Jean-Baptiste Colbert, the French Minister for Trade, agreed with Fouquet. In 1664 he bought the colonies back from the proprietors and set about strengthening French trade with them. To increase the supply of slaves he ordered the small French fort of St Louis on the Senegal River to be enlarged and had new ones built in Gambia and Sierra Leone. In the West Indies he planned a trading base on Grenada to hold slaves and manufactured goods for sale to the Spanish colonies.

Colbert set up a French West India Company to manage trading depots and collect customs duties. The goods which passed through the Company's hands were to be carried to and from the Caribbean in the ships of private French merchants. He sent a new lieutenant-governor to force the colonists to trade through the French and not the Dutch West India Company.

The French colonists continued to deal with the Dutch. So, in 1670, Colbert sent a naval fleet, commanded by the Sieur de Gabaret, to

Fig. 8.4 *Jean-Baptiste Colbert.*

drive the Dutch from the French islands. Within a year de Gabaret had cleared the Dutch from the eastern Caribbean, but he was faced by revolts of French colonists and Dutch merchants in western Hispaniola. One by one, its towns refused to obey the French government. De Gabaret succeeded in gaining control but the lesson was not lost on Colbert. The Dutch, he said, had to be crushed once and for all.

Collapse of the Dutch West India Company

The First and Second Dutch Wars had arisen from the English determination to drive the Dutch from their empire. The Third was started by Colbert's intention to do the same thing. During the first two years France had the support of England, but from 1673 she fought on alone against the Dutch who had some help from the Spanish. The combined Dutch and Spanish forces were no match for the well-armed French fleets and armies. In 1674, the Netherlands withdrew all her ships from the

Caribbean to fight on for a while in European waters. In 1678 she admitted defeat and agreed to withdraw all Dutch agents from French West Indian colonies. The Dutch also recognised France as owner of Tobago and the Cayenne settlements.

The war finished the effort begun by the English to break the Dutch hold on American trade. The great Dutch West India Company, which had opened the Spanish Indies to English and French settlers, collapsed into bankruptcy.

Colbert and Spain

France, like England before her, still had a quarrel with Spain who refused to accept her claims to western Hispaniola or to an open door for her trade with the Spanish settlements. In 1679, Colbert sent Le Comte d'Estrées with eleven ships and orders to enlist the aid of the flibustiers in a round of attacks to persuade the Spaniards to allow French ships into their American ports. The first raid was on Santo Domingo in 1680; in the following year Cartegena, Santa Marta and the coast of Venezuela were plundered. In 1683 the flibustier bands combined for their greatest success, the capture of San Juan de Ulloa. The town was taken without the Spaniards firing a single shot, and for two weeks a fleet of fourteen Spanish ships lay outside the harbour not daring to interfere while the flibustiers plundered and burned the churches and public buildings.

The raid on San Juan, the chief port of the Viceroyalty of Mexico, was proof of how helpless the Spaniards had become at defending their possessions. But, instead of following up this military success, Colbert made a truce with Spain. Buccaneering would bring far less profit to France than building up St Domingue into a vast sugar-producing colony.

St Domingue

Immediately after the truce, Colbert sent the Sieur Tarin de Tracy to St Domingue to suppress the buccaneers. De Tracy encouraged the flibustiers to use the loot from raids on the Spanish to set up sugar mills and purchase slaves. He continued the schemes of the previous governor of bringing women from France and auctioning them as wives. The wives, he said, had done more than the king's fleet to stop the flibustiers. Flibustiers' leaders were given pensions or made officers in the French navy. One, de Grammant, was appointed a lieutenant-governor of St Dominigue.

Both the Spanish and English were opposed to the French settlement on St Domingue. Jamaican planters complained loudly about the competition from such a near neighbour. In 1689 France and England went to war and the Spaniards made an alliance with the English to get their help in driving the French from St Domingue. The French, however, were determined to remain. In 1690 the governor of St Domingue led a raid on the Spanish part of the island and burned St Jago de Los Caballeros. In 1695 a new governor led the French in a last great privateering raid against Jamaica. For more than three weeks they pillaged the south shore, carrying off slaves, mills, livestock and even trees to their new plantations in St Domingue.

The war, known to the English colonists as 'King William's War', ended with the Treaty of Ryswick in 1697. The Spanish and English finally recognised St Domingue as French. Already it was on its way to becoming the largest and most prosperous sugar colony in the Caribbean.

Brandenburgers and Danes

After the Third Dutch War, merchants from Holland faced ruin unless they could find some way of continuing their trade in the Caribbean. Many of them hit on the plan of sending goods to the West Indies on ships registered in Denmark or Brandenburg, the small German state which had Berlin as its capital. Denmark and Brandenburg were neutral nations and there was a chance that their ships would be ignored by English and French customs officials. Several Dutch merchants moved their businesses to Denmark or Brandenburg.

These men put money into the Danish Guinea Company so that it would open two new slaving stations at Anamabo and Christiansborg near Accra. They financed a Danish West India Company which opened a trading base on St Thomas in the Virgin Islands. St Thomas had a fine harbour and was close to the slave markets in Puerto Rico and the Leewards. In 1682 Dutch merchants were behind similar Brandenburg schemes. A Brandenburg-Guinea company was set up and a fort, Gross Frederichsburg, was built on the Gold Coast. In 1685 the Dutch got the Danes to agree to allow Brandenburgers to build a warehouse and slave compound on St Thomas.

The combined Dutch, Danish and Brandenburg enterprise was short-lived because of the opposition of the English and French. After only thirty years the new companies had dwindled into bankruptcy. The Brandenburgers completely disappeared from the scene although the Danish settlement at St Thomas survived. It was too small to be a threat to the other colonies, and it was a useful shelter for merchant ships in times of war or for men escaping the laws in their own colonies. In 1685 its numbers were swollen by Protestant French who were driven from their own colonies. As the number of refugees increased, the little colony spilled over to include the neighbouring St John and, after 1733, St Croix.

Economic control of the empires

The last war of the seventeenth century ended, as we have seen, with the Treaty of Ryswick in 1697. By that time Britain and France had both created large Caribbean empires. Away from the American mainland they had no serious rivals. The Spanish island colonies held few settlers and the Dutch had ceased to be a major power in the area. There were only four unclaimed or neutral islands left in the Caribbean.

The European empires remained very little changed from 1697 until recent times. The most important changes were to the advantage of Britain who took over some French, Spanish and Dutch colonies as a result of the wars of the eighteenth and early nineteenth centuries. The chart opposite shows the European empires in 1697 and the later changes in ownership.

Mercantilism

By building empires in the Caribbean, England and France had broken the trading monopoly of the Spanish. They then set up their own monopolies. Like the Spanish system, the French and British trading rules were based on the ideas which were later called 'mercantilism'. Each country wanted to keep the trade with its empires for its own people and out of the hands of foreigners. A large colonial trade meant a large navy and ship-building industry. It meant profits for merchants and for people making goods which went out to the colonies or refining the sugar and tobacco that came back. It meant high earnings from customs duties which gave the government the money to pay the soldiers and sailors needed to defend the empire.

If a country was forced to share any of the profits with another nation then it lost some of its wealth – which in those days was thought of as the same as losing some of its power. Those were the reasons why England passed Navigation Acts to keep the foreigners out of trade with her colonies. At first they were aimed at the Dutch but later they were used against Britain's new rivals, the French.

There was another side to the mercantilist system. Mother countries such as England and France believed they would lose profits and employment if their colonies were anything more than suppliers. Suppose settlers in the Caribbean began refining their own sugar, making their own cotton cloth and building their own ships. This would harm sugar refining, textiles and shipbuilding in Britain.

Suppose the colonies started trading with each other so that planters in Jamaica sold their sugar to colonists in New England in return for iron goods made there. That would take business away from merchants, seamen, refinery workers and iron workers in Britain. To stop this threat to the mother country's wealth, the English Parliament passed the Plantations Duties Act in 1673.

European empires in the Caribbean 1697–1815

		1697	1713	1748	1763	1783	1815
British Empire	Antigua						
	Barbados						
	Jamaica						
	Montserrat						
	Nevis						
	St Kitts (part)						
	Virgin Islands						
French Empire	Cayenne						
	Desirade						
	Grenada				To Britain		
	Guadeloupe						
	Marie Galante						
	Martinique						
	St Bartholomew					To Sweden	
	St Domingue						Independent
	St Kitts		To Britain				
Spanish Empire	Cuba						
	St Domingo						Independent
	Puerto Rico						
	Trinidad						To Britain
Dutch Empire	Aruba						
	Berbice						To Britain
	Bonaire						
	Curaçao						
	Demerara						To Britain
	Essequibo						To Britain
	St Eustatius						
	Saba						
Danish bases	St John						
	St Thomas						
Neutral islands	Dominica				To Britain		
	St Lucia				To France		To Britain
	St Vincent				To Britain		
	Tobago				To Britain	To France	To Britain

Plantations Duties Act, 1673

The Act had two main parts. One gave a list of 'enumerated' goods. If any goods on the list were shipped from one colony to another then a high customs duty would have to be paid. This made it very expensive for West Indian planters to send their sugar to British colonies in North America in return for food or plantation supplies because all these items were on the list. The second part put heavy duties on all West Indian sugars except for wet unrefined muscovado. That meant the colonists could not refine their own sugar and sell it to Britain. Instead, the refining industry grew rapidly in British port towns, especially Glasgow and Bristol.

The French 'exclusive'

The French had a similar system of economic control over their colonies. It was generally known as the 'exclusive', which describes its main aim of excluding foreigners from the trading wealth of the French Empire. It was the work of Colbert and continued long after his death in 1683. The exclusive was made up of a series of laws, such as the Ordinance of Marine in 1671 and the Ordinance of Commerce in 1673, which forbade foreigners to trade with the French colonies. Colbert was firm in allowing no breaks from this rule. He refused to allow Guadeloupe and Martinique to send molasses and rum to the British colonies in North America even though there was no market for them in France. This was because the rum and molasses would have been exchanged for salt meat from the British colonies and not from France.

The exclusive also prevented French colonists competing with industry in France. Sugar refining gave work to many colonists but it was banned in 1684. When the colonists continued to refine their own sugar, a duty was placed of 22 livres a hundredweight (about 50 kilograms), while unrefined sugar was allowed into France at only 1 livre a hundredweight. This completely strangled the colonial industry.

In 1698 a general decree brought together all the regulations and laid down harsh penalties for those who broke them. Foreign smugglers would have ships and cargo confiscated while French colonists who traded illegally could be fined, imprisoned or sent to work in the galleys.

English political controls

To make the mercantile system work, England and France needed close political control over the colonies. In England this became the task of the Council of Trade and Plantations whose President was an important member of the government. The Council later became the Board of Trade and Plantations and underwent many changes in the eighteenth century as the British Empire grew. In the nineteenth century it became two government departments, the Board of Trade and the Colonial Office.

Barbados

The Council of Trade and Plantations soon put an end to the proprietory system. This had already been abolished in Barbados when Sir George Ayescue had retaken the rebel colony in 1651. From then on, the colony was ruled by a governor appointed by the government in London. Yet, Ayescue agreed that the Barbados settlers should keep their own elected assembly which had started under the proprietors. The assembly would make local laws, although they had to be approved by the English Parliament. It also had the power to object to any local taxes or customs duties.

The Lesser Antilles

After the government of Barbados was settled there were still quarrels over who owned the other Lesser Antilles islands which Charles I had granted at different times to two lord proprietors, the Earls of Pembroke and Carlisle. The heir of each earl tried to get the English law courts to rule that he alone should have the profits from the colonies. The government stopped the quarrel by taking over the colonies on the same terms as it had taken over Barbados. The colonies were to have elected

Fig. 8.5 *A view of Bridgetown, Barbados, in 1695. What does it suggest about the development of the colonies from the first settlers in the sixteenth century?*

assemblies and in return they would have to accept British governors.

To save money the Leewards were placed under the same governor as Barbados. This first attempt to build a small federation of West Indian colonies did not last long because of the rivalry between them for biggest share of the English sugar market. After they had suffered from raiding in the Second Dutch War, the Leeward planters complained in a petition to the king that the Barbadians were pleased that their people had been driven away and their export trade damaged:

> It is in the interest of the Council and Assembly of Barbados that these islands be no more settled, for one pound of their sugar will be worth as much as two before these islands were lost, and petitioners can prove that several Barbadians have wished these islands sunk.

In 1671 the Council of Trade gave in to the demands for a separate administration in the Leewards. A governor-in-chief was appointed for St Kitts, Nevis, Montserrat, Antigua, Barbuda, Anguilla and 'all the other of the Leeward islands which His Majesty has thought fit to separate from the Government in Barbados'.

Jamaica

From 1656, Edward D'Oyley was military governor of Jamaica. But in 1660 the new plantation owners complained that the time for military rule was over. The last Spaniards had been driven away and the island was well protected by the forts at Port Royal and around the coast. They wanted a system of local government similar to that in the Lesser Antilles. In 1662 the Council of Trade gave in and sent a new governor, Lord Windsor, with instructions to set up a council and call elections for an assembly. The island was divided into twelve parishes. The leading figure in the parish government was the *custos*, a title which came from the old English official, the Custos Rotulorum or Keeper of the Records. Each custos had a seat on the council and the landowners in each parish also elected two members of the Jamaica assembly.

Governing English colonies

The governors

The first responsibility of colonial governors was to act as representative of the king. They had to enforce all laws and regulations, such as the Navigation Acts, take charge of the defence of the colony and collect taxes and customs owing to the king. In the name of the king they could summon and dismiss assemblies and call for elections to new ones. They were responsible for enforcing the local laws made by the assembly and for overseeing the work of the many officials who were appointed in England to serve in the colonies: chief justices, lieutenant-governors, customs inspectors, tax collectors, clerks of the court and so on.

Fig. 8.6 *The Court House in St Johns, Antigua, drawn in 1823. What contrast can you see between the lives of the blacks and the whites?*

The councils

In each colony, the governor chose leading merchants and planters to sit on his council. Councils had the duty of advising the governor and supporting him in enforcing regulations which came from the imperial government in England. A councillor who did not do this would be almost certainly dismissed. The council was also the upper law-making body in the colony. Laws suggested by the elected assemblies had to be agreed by them as well. Laws which the governor wished to see brought into force would be first agreed by the council and then passed down to the assembly to seek its approval. Finally, in most colonies the council acted as a court of appeal against decisions made by magistrates and judges.

The assemblies

The right to vote in elections to the assemblies was held only by the wealthier freeholders – men who owned property and were not tenants. In most of the Leewards, to claim the right to vote a colonist needed to own 10 acres (4 hectares) of land or property which could be rented for £10 a year. If he actually wished to stand for election to the assembly he needed 40 acres (16 hectares) of property worth £40 a year. These property qualifications meant that assemblies represented the interests of the wealthier colonists, who made up the group sometimes called the 'plantocracy'.

The assemblies' greatest power was their control of the local taxes. They alone, without the council, had the right to vote taxes to raise money for governing the colony. Sometimes an assembly used this power to force the governor and the English government to accept laws they disagreed with. In 1677 the English government tried to challenge this power of the Jamaican assembly. In London, it prepared thirty-seven Acts dealing with Jamaican affairs. They sent these to Jamaica with a new governor under orders to see that the assembly passed the Acts. If the assembly had done this, the English government would have claimed that it had been established that assemblies must always accept laws passed in England. Not only the Jamaican assembly but also the council flatly refused. Indeed, they emphasised their independence by leaving the king's name off all future local laws which were always passed in the name of 'the Assembly, the Council and the Governor'.

Such quarrels between the English government and the local assemblies were common. Often, too, locally-born planters and businessmen considered they could run their colony far better than the governor and the officials,

judges and bishops appointed in England. But the balance of power was clearly tipped in favour of the imperial government in London. It frequently refused to give its agreement to laws made by the local assemblies; it controlled the appointment of officials and, from afar, it could decide on the prosperity of the colonies by the taxes and duties it placed on their goods.

The roots of underdevelopment

Later it was seen that the greatest weakness of this system was that neither the imperial nor local governments gave attention to the need to develop the colonial territories. The English government was interested chiefly in supplies of raw materials and food, as well as ports of call for the Royal Navy. Beyond that it was not prepared to spend money on colonial development. The assemblies, because they represented the interests of rich colonials, were reluctant to vote taxes to be spent on roads and bridges, hospitals and schools. The roots of the underdevelopment of the colonies at independence lay in the mercantile and political systems of the seventeenth century.

Parishes

English colonies in the Caribbean were divided into parishes. They were based on the English system of the time where the whole kingdom was divided into parishes which were run by committees or vestries, elected by all freeholders. The vestries supervised tasks such as road-building and appointed constables to keep law and order. This method of managing local government in the countryside was brought to the colonies, where many of the seventeenth-century parish names have lasted to the present day.

In England the most powerful men on the vestries were usually the wealthiest landowners. Some of them became magistrates or justices of the peace, who held courts to try all people accused of small or 'petty' crimes. This system, too, developed in the colonies. The wealthiest planters became magistrates, responsible for law

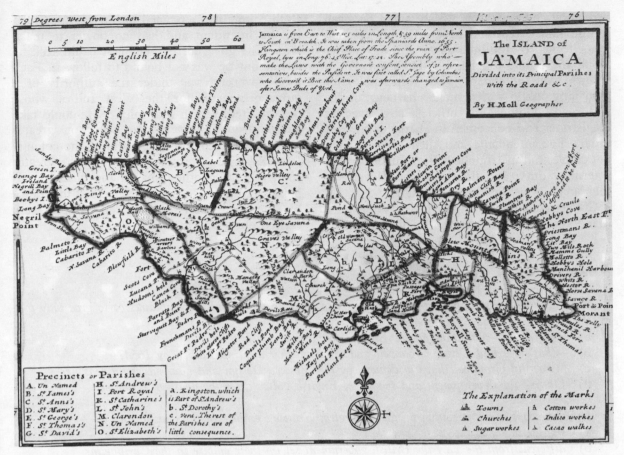

Fig. 8.7 *An eighteenth-century map of Jamaica showing that it then had fourteen parishes. Twelve parishes were initially created on the island in the 1660s.*

and order in their district. But, whereas magistrates in England controlled the lives of labourers and tenant farmers, in the colonies they dealt mainly with the enforcement of the slave laws made in the assemblies.

One of the duties of a parish magistrate was to see that the militia was always in readiness. The militia was a force of volunteer soldiers who could be called out to deal with any riot or disturbance or to hunt down runaway slaves. Occasionally coloureds served in the militias but they were usually made up of whites – planters and their sons, overseers and book-keepers and any others likely to be willing to defend the planters' property.

French colonial government

Power in seventeenth-century England was shared by king and Parliament. France was governed by an absolute monarchy with all decisions taken by the king's personal ministers. Instead of allowing local affairs to be managed by magistrates and parish committees, the districts of France were ruled by royal officials known as *intendants*.

Colbert placed a centralised and absolute system of government in the colonies. It was headed by the Conseil d'Etat (Council of State) in France which appointed all officials and wrote all laws for the colonies. Each colony had a governor who was a nobleman and soldier. The governor was responsible for the colony's defence and acted as a figure-head with all the ceremony and privileges which would be given to the king's representative. But his position was checked by the intendant, who was master to all the public officials on the island. As in France, the intendant was responsible for managing public works, such as harbour, bridge and road-building. His officials also acted as magistrates and policemen in charge of law and order. The intendants and their officials were not creoles but metropolitan Frenchmen serving a term of duty, and they gave their loyalty to their masters in the Conseil d'Etat.

Creole colonists had far less say in their island's government than the English colonials.

Each colony had a council but it was appointed by the intendant and had no power to make laws. The governor or intendant could seek its advice but he was not bound to follow it. Each local governor was under the authority of a governor-general for the West Indies whose headquarters was in Martinique. He could take advice from a *conseil supérieur*, or greater council, selected from members of the colonial councils. The governor-general and the greater council were another link in the chain of officials set up to see that laws decided in France by the king and his Conseil d'Etat were carried out.

Assignments

1 'Cromwell and his supporters were not ready to listen to the colonists' complaints or to give way to the Dutch', page 62:
   a) Describe the complaints of the English colonists in the 1650s.
   b) What steps had Oliver Cromwell and the English Parliament taken by 1654?
   c) What did Cromwell hope to achieve by the Western Design and how successful was he?
   d) Outline the development and success of English policy after the death of Cromwell.

2 In what ways was the setting up and control of France's empire in the Caribbean:
   a) similar to
   b) different from the way the British government set up their empire in the Caribbean?

3 How was mercantilism meant to work? How did it favour the metropolitan countries rather than the colonies?

4 Why did the British set up governors, councils and assemblies in their colonies in the Caribbean?
   a) How did this compare with the way in which England was governed?
   b) Which people in the English colonies did not have a say in the way in which they were governed?
   c) What quarrels were likely to develop between the English government and the local assemblies?

9 THE RISE OF KING SUGAR

Profits and land prices

There was an immense demand for sugar in Europe. Most fruits which grow there are cropped between July and September and for the rest of the year are eaten preserved in sugar or made into jam. Sugar was also needed for distilling and brewing as well as making cakes and biscuits. In the sixteenth century Europe's only native source of sugar came from bees, and its needs could not be met by the sugar grown on the Mediterranean coast, the islands of Cyprus and Sicily and in the Spanish colonies of Madeira and the Azores. The sugar which came from the early Spanish and Portuguese plantations in the New World sold for good prices and the demand grew as new uses were found, especially as a sweetener for coffee, tea and cocoa.

The idea of planting sugar on a large scale had been brought to the Caribbean from Brazil by the Dutch. Barbados had been the first English island to take up the new crop in the 1640s. Guadeloupe and Martinique became the first French sugar islands in the 1650s. Sugar went hand in hand with the growth of large plantations. It was generally reckoned that at least eighty to a hundred hectares had to be planted before a farmer could make a reasonable profit on the money he spent on mills, boiling houses, haulage animals and a large labour force. The successful sugar planters bought tobacco lands from their neighbours and amalgamated them into large sugar estates. According to John Scott, who visited Barbados in 1668, the number of landowners there had fallen from 11,200 in 1645 to 745 in 1667. The amalgamations led to a steep rise in the value of land. In the 1640s land prices in Barbados rose by more than fifteen times and in Nevis by more than ten.

Displaced settlers

There were always a few farmers who made a living from tobacco, indigo and cotton. Often they managed to do this by selling their most fertile land to sugar planters and keeping hilly and rocky sections for their own crops. But when an island changed to sugar, most of the poor settlers and the freed bondservants looked for any chance to move on. Many of the early settlers in Jamaica came from Barbados, Nevis and Antigua. Some joined the buccaneering bands before they settled as farmers. Poor French settlers from Guadeloupe and Martinique moved to St Domingue. Other migrants from sugar islands started colonies on the smaller territories such as the Bahamas, the Virgin Islands and Surinam. Many English left the Caribbean altogether and moved to the British colonies in North America.

Not all migrating settlers were farmers. Many were craftsmen who lost their livelihood when large estates began to keep their own slave carpenters and builders. Small pedlars suffered when planters bought all their estate supplies in bulk from overseas merchant firms.

European labour

Bondservants and convicts

The profits of the sugar planters depended on having enough labour for the yearly cycle of planting, hoeing, cutting, hauling, crushing, boiling and packing. Yet the spread of large plantations meant that it became more difficult to recruit European labourers. The first English bondservants or French engagés had found the chance of a small farm after three or five years' labour worth the terrible conditions of the Atlantic crossing. But these men had been brought to the Caribbean to work on small farms, whose owners may have treated them no worse than their masters in Europe. On the sugar plantations there was nothing but the most grinding toil. In 1659, bondservants in Barbados were described as:

Grinding at the mills and attending the furnaces or digging in this scorching island; having nothing to feed on (nothwithstanding their hard labour) but potato roots, nor to drink but water with such roots washed in it. . . . being bought and sold still from one planter to another . . . being whipped at the whipping post (as rogues) for their masters' pleasure, and sleeping in sties worse than hogs in England.

No wonder that there were outbursts of rebellion. When Richard Ligon visited Barbados in 1647 an island-wide revolt of bondservants had just been put down. Eighteen ringleaders had been executed but the planters feared more trouble. Ligon noted that they were frantically rebuilding houses 'in all manner of fortifications', adding bulwarks from which they could pour boiling water on mutinous workers.

Only the most desperate Europeans would leave home for such plantation work, and so the planters came to rely for their labour on dishonest recruiters who travelled through the country districts of Europe. They signed up simple youths who had no idea where the 'sugar islands' were and what future to expect. Ships' captains found it a profitable business. In Jamaica they were paid £6 or £7 for every bondservant they brought to the island. Catholic priests complained about the methods of French captains:

> Some have been mean and knavish enough to entice children aboard their vessels under various pretexts and force them to go to the islands where they were sold to masters who fed them poorly and made them go to work so excessively and treated them so inhumanely that many of them died in a short time.

Some European suppliers used kidnapping raids in seaside towns where sailors and fishermen were 'barbodised'; that is seized, often when drunk, and hustled on board ship. Labourers recruited by these methods never received proper indenture papers. Many did not live to the end of bondservice. For those who did, there was usually no grant of land. In Jamaica they were given 136 kilograms of sugar. This was worth just £2, which was the same as the cash paid to freed bondservants in Barbados.

Prisoners

After about 1650 many European labourers were convicts or prisoners of war. European courts sentenced men to be transported to the colonies for the time of their prison sentence. Perhaps the saddest groups of all were the Scots and Irish sent to the Caribbean by Oliver Cromwell. Some were prisoners taken in the wars he fought to spread his rule in Scotland and Ireland. Nearly 8,000 men were sent from a Scottish army he defeated in 1651. Others were simply rounded up after his army had won a victory, like the 2,000 Irish men and women ordered to be sent to Jamaica in 1656.

Convicts and prisoners did not meet the growing demand of the English and French planters for more labour. Increasingly, they turned to the use of Africans. For more than a century and a half the prosperity of the planters and the comfort of sugar-using Europeans depended on a particularly inhuman form of the age-old evil of slavery.

African slave labour

Slavery in the Caribbean had begun in the earliest days of colonisation. The Spanish had enslaved Amerindians before Queen Isabella had ordered them to be placed in encomiendas which were different from slavery only in name. But, as early as 1501, slaves were brought across the Atlantic, mostly from Spain itself. Some were Moors, taken prisoner in the reconquista, some were black Africans captured earlier and taken to Spain or Portugal as slaves; others were European prisoners.

In 1518, the first ship-load of slaves was brought direct from the African coast and soon the Spanish government placed the evil trade on a regular footing. Slaves were not usually brought in Spanish ships; instead the government gave the asiento, or licence, to merchants usually from Portugal. The Portuguese were well placed to carry on the slave trade because they had forts and trading posts down the coast of West Africa. By the end of the sixteenth century, the Portuguese had built up a regular

Fig. 9.1 *A shop for the sale of slaves in Brazil.*

trade to the Spanish colonies and to Brazil, where large sugar plantations had been opened. Most of the trade then fell into the hands of the Dutch, who captured several Portuguese trading posts in Africa and were masters of Brazil between 1630 and 1654.

Up to the 1640s, African slavery had not been introduced on a large scale to the new English and French settlements. Tobacco was mostly grown by smallholders with the help of a few bondservants. Then, in a few years, the Dutch showed them the profits to be made from sugar planting and the use of African labour. Very few men of the time considered the morality of slavery. What mattered to most Europeans in the sixteenth and seventeenth centuries was the fact that slavery seemed to answer *their* labour problems and brought profits to the slavers.

Dutch slavers pointed out to likely buyers that the cost of an African slave compared favourably with that of a European labourer. In 1650 an African sold for between £15 and £20, and the price of a European convict was between £10 and £15, but the buyer had to pay transport and take the risk that the condemned man could escape or die on route. The planter also expected his labour supply to increase from the birth of slave children, whereas the sons and daughters of bondservants were not bound by their parents' indentures. Owners of both slaves and bondservants could raise money by mortgaging them to a lender, but the servant with a five-year indenture was poorer security for a long-term loan than an African enslaved for life. Finally, the Dutch could guarantee a steady supply of African slaves, whereas the flow of bondservants was uncertain.

But it was more than costs which made the planters favour African slaves. In 1640, the Barbadian planters who visited the Dutch plantations in Brazil were impressed by the ease with which a few Dutch overseers managed large gangs of African slaves. The Africans were just as hostile to their masters as bondservants were, but their resistance had less chance of success now they were torn from their homeland. Bondservants knew their master's culture, language and weaknesses too well to be easily subdued. They could escape by mixing with the thousands of other Europeans who came to and left the islands each year; because of his colour the African could not disappear into the crowd.

The Dutch pointed out that the Africans' death rate in the tropics was about one third less than that of Europeans, although death rates in their first few months in the Caribbean were terribly high. This gave rise later to racist theories that blacks were physically better suited to work in the tropics. Such theories are not true. Both Africans and Europeans could survive the work and heat as the Europeans who cleared the first farms and plantations did. But the Africans did come to the West Indies with immunities to several diseases common to both West Africa and the Caribbean and it took Europeans several generations to build up the same resistance. The visitors noted one other important value of African slaves; they were usually more skilful at agriculture than bondservants. Nearly all Africans came from agricultural societies used to hoe cultivation, whereas most bondservants and convicts were brought from cities and port towns.

Fig. 9.2 *A late seventeenth-century French illustration of a sugar factory in the Caribbean. The cane is crushed by the large roller in the background and the juice boiled in the copper at the front left. What evidence is there for a change from European to African labour at this time?*

African and European labourers

	1678		1700		1774	
	Black	White	Black	White	Black	White
Nevis	3,849	3,521	3,676	1,104	10,000	1,000
Antigua	2,172	2,308	12,960	2,892	37,808	2,590
St Kitts	1,436	1,897	3,294	1,670	23,462	1,900
Montserrat	992	2,882	3,570	1,545	10,000	1,300
	8,449	10,608	23,500	7,211	81,270	6,790

The switch from European bondservants to African slaves took many years. The chart shows the gradualness of the change in the Leeward Islands. In 1678 whites outnumbered blacks everywhere except Nevis, and by 1700 there was still almost one white for every three blacks. The greatest change took place between 1700 and 1775 when the ratio became one white to every twelve blacks. On all the sugar islands white bondservants and black slaves at first worked side by side, but by the 1770s the only whites were owners or overseers.

The evil of slavery was present throughout the Caribbean, but the number of Africans was smaller on the Spanish islands where sugar was not the main crop. Cuba in the 1770s still depended mostly on tobacco and cattle ranching, and there were more whites than blacks on the island. In Trinidad, cotton, coffee and cocoa were grown but not sugar and, in 1783, although there were 310 slaves to 126 Europeans, there were also 295 free non-white people, probably *mestizos*. Because the island was then still not fully developed by European farmers, there were 2,032 Amerindians, more than the Europeans and Africans together. The chart above shows the rise in black populations in four areas, and compares the fall in the white populations.

Assignments

1 *How was the population of the Caribbean made up by 1650?*
   or
   Who were the various people living in the Caribbean by 1650?
   What work did each group do?

2 *Using the information in this chapter, make a chart to show the increase in African slaves in the Caribbean between 1501 and the 1770s.*
   Outline the reasons given for bringing African slaves to the Caribbean.

3 *What alternatives to African slave labour do you think could have taken place in the Caribbean?*

4 *Study Fig 9.2. Use it to describe the main stages of sugar production at the time of the illustration.*

10 WEST AFRICA

Birth place of the human race

Planters had no real knowledge of the background and culture of their slaves. They were interested only in their usefulness as labour. They advised each other to avoid Igbos because they often became depressed and committed suicide and not to buy Angolans because they were lazy. They would do better to buy Popos or Ibibios for they were cheerful and hardworking. Slave-owners of the fifteenth to eighteenth centuries would have been surprised to read that twentieth-century scholars believe that the first true human people appeared in Africa.

Remains of such early people and their pebble tools have been found by archaeologists

Fig. 10.1 *A hand-axe, used by early man, found in Tanzania.*

digging in Tanzania and Ethiopia. In the hundreds of thousands of years which followed, these early Africans developed the skills to make improved stone weapons and tools. They discovered the art of hunting and how to use a wide variety of wild plants for food. By about 12,000 years ago there were small numbers of hunters and gatherers in most parts of Africa. The largest number were the ancestors of the different groups of black Africans. A smaller number were a light-coloured folk who never reached more than about a metre and a half high. They are the ancestors of the Bushmen and Pygmies of south-west Africa. Along the north of the continent were another light-skinned group who had some ancestors who came from Asia.

Mastering the continent

The next great step forward was the art of growing food and raising cattle. Few people in Africa remained as hunters and gatherers. By 4000 B.C. people along the Nile valley were ploughing fields to grow wheat and barley. They kept cattle as did people on huge stretches of the modern Sahara desert which were then covered with grass and trees. Farming skills spread over the rest of the continent especially after Africans mastered the use of iron. Outside Egypt this skill first developed in central Nigeria about 300 B.C. Iron axes and hoes, spears and arrow-heads meant that many groups of African people were able to settle an area and grow a surplus of food.

As with the Amerindians, a food surplus led to a more complex society with specialist craftsmen, warriors, priests and rulers. Again, in the same way as the Amerindians, these societies can be divided into those where great empires arose and those where people of the same culture lived in separate communities. In Africa the reason for these differences often began with climate and vegetation.

Savannah and forest

Most of the slaves who were shipped to the Caribbean came from a section of West Africa between the Senegal and Congo Rivers. The northern part of this area is covered with savannah, open grassland which stretches for hundreds of kilometres. As you move south through the savannah, the rainfall increases and the grass is mixed with woodland. You also enter the region infested by the tsetse fly which means that cattle will not survive. Further south still you come to the tropical forests of the Guinea coast, and the Congo River.

When the slave trade began in the fifteenth century (as for many years before), the savannah and tropical forests were each home for Africans with different skills, technologies, and political organisation. They will be studied separately before we consider the ideas and beliefs and forms of social organisation which West Africans shared.

Societies of the savannah

Technology and skill

The farmers of these fertile grasslands grew peanuts, millet, yams and many green vegetables. North of the tsetse line they also reared goats, cattle and sheep. The foods, leather and wool were plentiful enough to support the many people who were not farmers. Across the savannah there were families where the knowledge of iron-working, leather-working or weaving passed from father to son. Farmers traded with these craft communities but even more of their products went to towns on the northern fringe of the savannah: Timbuctu, Kumbi Saleh, Walata and Jenne. There were

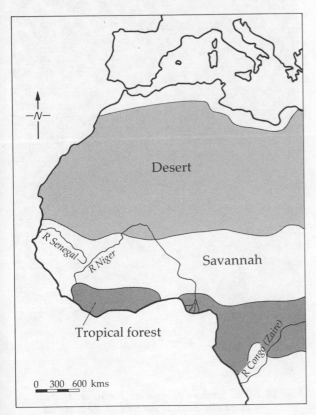

Map 20 *Vegetation zones in West Africa.*

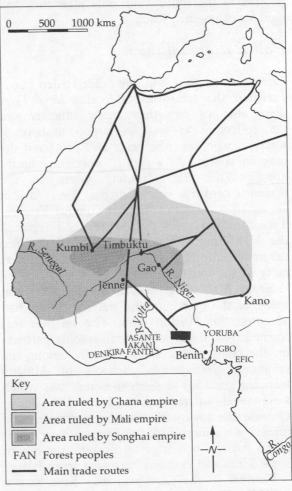

Map 21 *Important empires and peoples in West Africa.*

potters, weavers, metal- and leather-workers in these towns and there were also the merchants, known as *dyula*. Dyula usually worked in small companies which moved about with their own escorts of mounted guards.

The towns had grown up at the end of trading routes which crossed the Sahara to the coast of north Africa. The dyula's caravans of camels set off along these routes loaded with the finely worked cloth and leather articles made by savannah craftsmen but they had even more valuable trades. They collected gold from the skilled miners of the Senegal and Niger valleys, brought it to their towns, paid taxes on it, and then took it on to the north. On their return journeys they brought salt which they could sell at very high prices to the forest peoples of the south – but only after they had paid taxes on each load.

Political organisation

The taxes on gold, salt and other traded goods enriched the treasuries of local rulers. They were able to pay their many officials and tax collectors as well as large numbers of warriors who kept the peace and protected the caravan routes. As a result, powerful empires arose. When slave trading began in the fifteenth century, nearly all the West African savannah was part of the vast Songhai Empire. Two hundred years earlier they had replaced the Mali Empire which had enlarged the first savannah empire, Ghana, which had begun as early as the fourth century.

From Mali times the savannah rulers and many of the merchant and warrior classes had accepted the Muslim faith. The religion was learned from their Berber Arab trading partners on the coast and it spread rapidly among the savannah townspeople. Schools of Muslim learning grew up to teach the civil laws which were used to regulate trade and business. Outside the towns, the farming craftsmen and miners were more likely to keep to their traditional African beliefs or to combine these with some ideas and customs borrowed from Islam.

Planters in the Caribbean may have known little about the wealth of the savannah people, their political organisation or their learning. But these were well known to Arab travellers and to some Europeans. In the fourteenth century the Arab Ibn Battuta praised the Mali people and their government. He wrote that they:

> possess some admirable qualities. They are seldom unjust and have a greater abhorrence of injustice than any other people. Their Sultan shows no mercy to anyone guilty of the least act of it. There is complete security in the country. Neither travellers nor inhabitants in it have anything to fear from robbers or men of violence.

In 1550 a European from Granada, whose Latin name was Leo Africanus, wrote about Timbuktu under the Songhai:

> There you may find many judges, professors and devout men, all handsomely maintained by the king, who holds scholars in much honour. There, too, they sell many handwritten North African books and more profit is made there from the sale of books than from any other branch of trade.

Fig. 10.2 *The Sankoré Mosque at Timbuctu. It was originally built at the time of the Songhai Empire.*

Probably few of the scholars, merchants and officials of the savannah cities ended up as slaves. But many other people of the savannah did. Some would have learned the skills involved in trade from their dealings with the dyula. Even more would have come from advanced farming communities who were used to exchanging their surplus food for goods made by other people. Many slaves would have belonged to families with long traditions of skill in iron and copperwork, in fishing or in mining. Most would probably have been far more finely dressed than they were in the coarse Osnaburg pants, made from a cloth first manufactured in Germany, and the simple petticoats doled out to plantation slaves.

Peoples of the forest

Technology and skill

In the dense tropical forests the only links between settlements were footpaths. The cascading rivers were too dangerous for canoes, and work animals could not be kept because of the tsetse. Poor communications kept the peoples of the West African forests separated. Yet, in most of them experienced village farmers could produce a food surplus. An important skill in forest farming was to know how to use land properly. Many forest communities kept part of their land unplanted to allow it to recover its fertility. Others shifted their village every few years to a new site cleared in the forest. Another skill was to know how to combine crops. Root crops such as yams and cassava could be protected by banana fronds while the banana could be shaded by tall forest trees. With these skills and a careful use of wood-ash and animal manure a rich variety of crops was grown, along with small animals such as chickens, pigs, goats and guinea fowl.

The food surplus supported the craftsmen of the forest regions. There were many centres for pottery, carpentry and cloth weaving. Sixteenth-century Europeans were impressed by the African skill in dyeing cloth with brilliant colours which they were not able to match for two hundred years. In some places salt was dried and prepared for sale. However, metal-working was probably the most important and widely spread skill in the forest areas.

It involved large numbers of men working in different specialisms. Right across the forest region there were miners digging for iron ore. In the centre of the Ashanti lands, miners also brought out enough gold ore to produce many hundreds of tons of gold between 1350 and 1500. After the miners there were the workers who crushed and smelted the ores in charcoal furnaces. Blacksmiths then turned the iron into tools and weapons, and other items such as hinges and bolts. Goldsmiths had more delicate work beating gold into thin leaf or turning it into fine ornaments. Some forest centres specialised in yet another branch of metalwork. They made brass and bronze from copper and tin. Sculptors in forest towns such as Ife and Benin turned these into fine figures and models using the complicated 'lost-wax' method.

Because there was so much exchange of food for other goods, many people of the forest region took part in trade. For some it was mostly a matter of knowing how to find their way along jungle paths with the aid only of the sun and stars. But many goods went north to the savannah empires. After the Portuguese found the sea routes to West Africa there were new trading partners to deal with. Merchants dealing in these export trades had to understand a great deal of the world outside West Africa, to have knowledge of the value of many goods and to be able to keep records and accounts. Few Africans could write because their own languages had no written forms. But just as Africans of the savannah learned the Arabic scripts of the Muslim scholars, some officials and traders in forest towns could write in the language of the Portuguese who became their trading partners in the fifteenth century.

Political organisation

At the time when slavery began, the pattern of farming, industry and trade in the forest zone had not produced vast empires like those of the savannah. For some people the village was still the most important organisation. This was so for the Igbo. Young Igbo grew up believing that they were all direct descendants of one common ancestor and were distinct from the people of other Igbo villages. Each village managed its own affairs through a council of elders headed by a chief or headman. However, Igbo political life was very democratic. Every adult man had a right to voice his opinions in the village assembly. Elders had to accept the will of these assemblies.

Although Igbos clung to their village groups, they understood that they belonged to a wider society. All Igbos shared a common language and Igbo men chose their wives from another village. Above all there was constant movement of food, iron goods, pottery and cloth from one Igbo group to another. When difficult disputes arose over trade the villagers would send elders to consult the priest at one of the shrines where oracles were kept. The greatest of these oracles was at Orachuku. After listening to the dispute, the priest would give a judgement which all Igbo communities would respect. This obedience to the oracle's judgement made up for the fact that the Igbo had no one ruler to control the complex patterns of trade between villages.

The political organisation of the Akan people on the Gulf of Guinea started with groups of villages in a small area whose people believed they had the same ancestor. In the fifteenth century most of the Akan people still lived in these independent village groups or clans. Among them there were a few strong states ruled by people who had conquered their neighbours such as the Fante and Denkirya. In future centuries many of the Akan clans and small states were brought into one state by another Akan people, the Ashanti. But in the fifteenth century many of the Akan peoples had a political organisation which was only one stage different from the independent villages of the Igbo.

Yoruba political life was similar to the Igbos except that it was centred on forest towns rather than villages. Yoruba farmers preferred to live in towns and walk out to their fields each day and the towns became the centres of small kingdoms which ruled over the nearby forest land.

The town made up a community equal to a collection of Igbo villages for it held farmers, priests, traders and craftsmen. The greatest of these Yoruba town kingdoms was Ife, which became famous for its fine bronze and terracotta sculptures.

Because each small town kingdom was ruled by a king or *oba*, the Yoruba had a less democratic form of government than the Igbo. In other ways they were similar. In the fifteenth century there was no king or emperor ruling all Yoruba. It was enough for them that they shared a common culture, a language and their trade. Another powerful bond was the belief that all Yoruba shared a common ancestor, Oduduwa, the first king of Ife.

The political organisation of the Yoruba was copied and then developed by the Edo people.

Fig. 10.3 *A Benin bronze statue of the oba's horn-blower.*

They built a state based on the town of Benin which had begun, like Ife, as the centre of a small kingdom. Like the Yoruba kings, the rulers of Benin called themselves obas. However, unlike the Yoruba obas, those in Benin brought the chiefs of neighbouring families under their control and forced them to live in Benin.

The reason for the greater power of the oba of Benin was the wealth of his government. Benin stood at the southern edge of the routes leading to the savannah towns. In the early days the Edo merchants sent ivory, pepper and ebony to the north. In the fifteenth century a new trading opportunity arose when the Portuguese ships arrived on the coast. Benin became famed in Europe for the work of its craftsmen who produced beautifully carved ivory and wooden sculptures, finely woven cloth and exquisite jewellery in gold, ivory and copper. Bronze sculptures from fifteenth-century Benin are often said to be among the world's finest works of art.

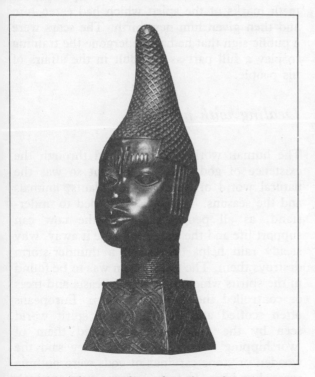

Fig. 10.4 *A bronze sculpture from sixteenth-century Benin. It shows the Queen Mother and is one of Benin's finest works of art.*

Forest people on the plantations

As with the slaves of the savannah, the Africans of the forest region brought skills with them that were quite unrecognised by most planters. Men who were put to work hoeing and cutting a single crop may have been skilled in the management of a village's mixed farming. African villagers generally knew far more about growing tropical crops than the European on the Caribbean estates. Among the slaves there must have been tens of thousands of metal-workers, as well as other skilled craftsmen. There were men who had taken part in governing an Igbo village, an Akan clan or a Yoruba town. These chiefs, elders and officials shared one thing with warriors, priests, doctors and merchants. On the plantation all were forced to do simple labouring tasks with no chance to use their experience in making decisions, their bravery or their wisdom.

Culture and beliefs

The world of the West African

Slavery tore each group of West African slaves away from its homeland and threw them together haphazardly on the Caribbean plantations. Here the different African peoples found that they shared many beliefs and explanations for the experiences which are common to all men: birth and death, the sense of belonging to a family, a clan and a wider group, the benefits of rain and the disaster of flood or drought. An explanation of these mysteries was found in the belief of the existence of gods. Many West Africans believed that their ancestors had been brought into being by a creator god. He was far removed from their daily lives and could not be worshipped as a being who controlled people's behaviour and expected them to be good rather than evil. Sharing a belief in the god was a powerful way of helping people to understand what it meant to say 'I am one of the Edo people' or 'I live in the land which was given to the Yorubas at the beginning of time'. Tales of the gods often described how they had taught ancestors to farm, fish, use iron, discover the best season for sowing and planting and so on. These stories were acted out in dances and the drummers at the god's shrine would beat out the rhythms which reminded people of their common ancestry.

Social bonds

In many African societies it was accepted that there were three groups of people in a village: the living, the ancestors whom the living joined at death, and those waiting to be born. These bonds between the living and dead, between temporary humans and spirits, helped explain the sense of belonging to a family, clan or village group. The shrines of ancestral spirits in village compounds were a practical way of reminding the living of the importance of rules and customs which had helped them survive in the past. The same rules and customs must be kept if those about to be born were to have a secure home. The dead were not thought of as separate from the community and were often called on to give advice, especially in times of trouble. For many African peoples, burial ceremonies were a way of handing down these traditions. When an Edo elder died it was his eldest son's duty to see that he was buried with the equipment he would need to join the other spirits of the clan and become a spirit-elder. At the same time a shrine was set up so that the living could show respect to the leadership and guidance he had given when alive. The ceremony also showed that, while the father was being accepted by his dead spirit-relatives, the son was being recognised as the new family elder.

Like most African peoples, the society of living Edos was grouped into grades according to age. In this case there were headmen and elders and below them the younger men who were warriors and organised the villages' farming and trade; finally there were the youths who were the village workers. Some African people had even more age-sets; there were seven among the Tiriki people of north-west Kenya. Sometimes entry into the different ranks and

age-sets was controlled by societies whose elders had kept alive the traditions and rules of an African people for many centuries. The societies organised the times of initiation for men ready to move from one age-set to the next. The lives of the people of several African societies in the area which is now Sierra Leone and Liberia were regulated by the Poro society. Elders of the society took boys of about fourteen to a sacred area of bush away from their village. The boy was now said to have been eaten by the spirit *namu*, whose priests wore wooden masks fringed with strands of raffia straw. Inside the sacred bush, he was taught the history of his people and the skills he would need in the future: farming, crafts, house-building, fighting and the use of medicines. He had to undergo tests of physical strength and was given harsh punishments to train him to accept the authority of the society's elders. After this initiation, the boy was said to have been reborn and returned to his village with a 'bush name' and with scars on his back and chest to represent the teeth marks of the spirit which had eaten him and then given him new birth. The scars were a public sign that he had undergone the training to play a full part as an adult in the affairs of his people.

Dealing with nature

The human world was explained through the existence of gods and spirits, but so was the natural world of water, earth, plants, animals and the seasons. The African needed to understand, as all people do, why the cow can support life and the snake can take it away, why steady rain helps crops and a thunder-storm destroys them. The explanation was to be found in the spirits which lived in the beasts and trees or controlled the forces of nature. Europeans often scoffed at the complicated spirit world seen by the Africans and accused them of 'worshipping' stones and trees. They said the wooden or stone carvings of gods were nothing more than idols. In fact, Africans were not idol-worshippers. The many dances and ceremonies and the sacrifices at gods' shrines were much more a way of showing that mere men have no real control over the forces of nature. They were part of the education of the young who learned to fear the dangers of certain forest paths or streams and to understand the anxiety of their elders that they could do nothing to stop a god, such as Shango – the Yoruba god of lightning – striking at their homes or their livestock.

The gods and spirits had to be served by priests, men who understood them and could explain their power over humans. Priests were thus important in African societies, and respected for the years of study which brought them the wisdom to keep alive traditions or give help in times of trouble. Many priests were also medicine men. The best of these had great skill in curing illness with medicines made from herbs and plants, a skill which could only be learned after a long apprenticeship. The African's belief in a spirit world also meant that medicine men had to be able to drive out spirits. A young person with a snake bite would not believe it had happened accidentally but that he had offended a mischievous spirit. So the cure would not be complete if the medicine man did not drive away the spirit.

A rich heritage

In African societies the individual was regarded first and foremost as a member of a community. From earliest childhood the African learned to know the sounds and rhythms of the many drums beating out from the shrines or playing for the village dances. He learned to take part in the dances, or to play the drums and other musical instruments, and through them to learn the history of his people, their rules of good citizenship, their techniques of farming and the way they counted time – whether by the seasons or the phases of the moon. He was surrounded by carvings which told him the same stories in a different way.

The Africans who came to the Caribbean were richer than the planters realised, in more than skill and technology. Each group also had a culture which had kept their society secure and stable over many centuries. A slave came with a strong sense of his people's history, a rich store of stories and songs which were far more significant than simple work chants. They also had dignity and pride. In Chapter 13 you will read how African culture was maintained on the plantation and in Chapter 16 how the dignity and pride led so often to resistance and rebellion.

Assignments

1 *Explain why Europeans knew so little about the people of West Africa.*

2 *Outline, with examples, what you think were the main achievements of:*
   a) *the African societies of the savannah.*
   b) *the African peoples of the forests.*

3 *What do you think were the main problems faced by the people of West Africa?*

4 *Although there were many differences, what were the main similarities of belief and heritage shared by the people of West Africa?*

11 THE SLAVE TRADE

Origins of African slavery

The story of the connection between sugar and African slavery began in the twelfth century when Italians planted cane fields on the island of Cyprus. Arab suppliers sold them African slaves who were skilled in cane cultivation. By the fourteenth century, sugar cultivation had spread westward to southern Spain and Portugal. More black African slaves were bought from Arab traders, but they were put to work as unskilled labourers rather than skilled artisans. In the fifteenth century many of these captives were shipped from Spain and Portugal to work the cane fields in their colonies in Madeira, the Azores and the Canary Islands. By the close of the century, Portuguese traders shipped slaves there direct from their new forts along the West African coast. In the sixteenth century they brought them still further west to the new colonies in the Americas.

In the Americas sugar planters remained the greatest users of slaves. By 1700, sugar and slavery had moved across the Caribbean from Barbados and the Leewards to Jamaica and St Domingue. A century later the cattle ranches in Puerto Rico and Cuba were changed by African slave gangs into cane fields. In the United States the close link between sugar and plantation slavery centred in Louisiana. Most of the millions of Africans in the rest of the southern United States were put to labour in the tobacco, cotton and rice fields.

The table gives the destination and estimated total of African slaves brought to each part of the Americas. It lists only the live arrivals. For every African who arrived alive at least one other perished in the slaving raids, on the trek to the coast or during the trans-Atlantic crossing. So, it has been calculated that, over a period of 400 years, about twenty million Africans fell victim to the Atlantic slave trade.

European companies and the slave trade

In the first stage of the Atlantic slave trade costs were low as only small numbers of Africans were carried to Spanish and Portuguese colonies. A new stage began in the seventeenth century when there was a rapid growth of sugar plantations in Brazil and the Lesser Antilles. There was now a bigger demand for slaves. Traders had to hire or buy more ships. They needed cash to pay for warehouses and slave pens on the African coast and to buy the slaves. To find the money, Europeans began to spread the costs over many investors.

Numbers of live slaves taken from West Africa 1451–1870

British Caribbean	
Jamaica	747,500
Barbados	387,000
Leeward Islands	346,000
St Vincent, St Lucia, Tobago & Dominica	70,000
Trinidad	22,000
Grenada	67,000
Other places	25,000
French Caribbean	
St Domingue	864,300
Martinique	365,800
Guadeloupe	290,800
Louisiana	28,000
French Guyana	51,000
Dutch Caribbean	500,000
Danish Caribbean	28,000
Brazil	3,646,800
North America	399,000
Spanish America	1,552,100
Europe	175,000
São Thomé	100,000
Atlantic islands (Madeira and Canaries)	25,000
	9,566,100

Averages per year	
1451–1600	1,800 each year
1601–1700	13,400
1701–1810	55,000
1810–1870	31,600

(Adapted from P. D. Curtin, *The Atlantic Slave Trade: A Census*, University of Wisconsin Press, 1972.)

The Dutch were the first to do this when they set up their West India Company in 1621. The British government followed their example in 1660 and gave the sole right of selling slaves in English colonies to the Company of Royal Adventurers Trading into Africa. In 1672 this was turned into the Royal Africa Company. Money was put into it by rich merchants, noble landowners and members of the royal family. In 1664 France's government encouraged its country's merchants to found the French West India Company. Later Denmark and Brandenburg had their own smaller trading companies.

By the beginning of the eighteenth century each nation's company controlled separate sections of the West African coast. The French were the leading traders in Senegal, the Ivory Coast, the Cameroons and part of the Congo, while the English were strongest in Gambia, the Windward Coast and the Niger Delta. The Portuguese still had a large trade in Angola and parts of the Congo. Scattered in between were the Dutch, Brandenburgers and Danes.

The government-sponsored companies never made large profits. One reason was the cost of the trading stations on the African coast. Each was protected by a fort with a garrison of soldiers paid by the company. Another reason was the large number of company agents in Africa and the Americas. They often cheated by selling slaves who they reported as having died on the crossing or declaring a lower price than they actually received. Some simply disappeared with company funds.

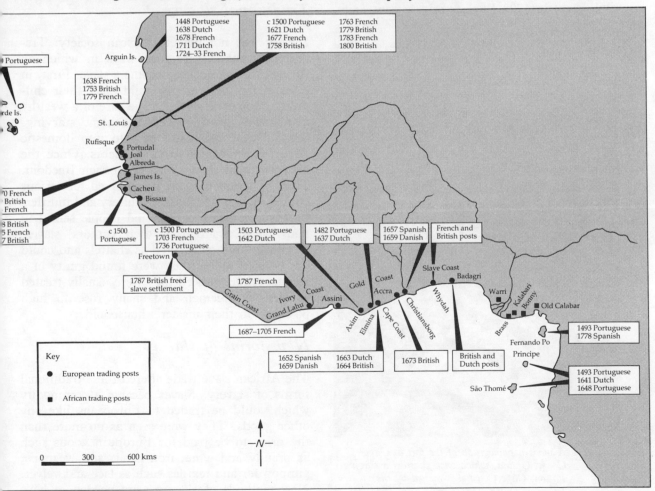

Map 22 *The main trading posts in West Africa.*

Private trade

These difficulties led to changes in the British slave trade. The Royal Africa Company gave way to large numbers of private traders. They bought slaves direct from African slavers instead of from the company trading posts. This made the slaves cheaper so planters preferred to buy from the private traders. The British government accepted their place in the trade and granted them licences to deal in slaves, provided they made a small payment towards keeping the British forts on the African coast in good order. The new traders greatly increased the number of slaves brought to the Americas. Between 1680 and 1688 the Royal Africa Company delivered an average of 5,155 each year; in 1708 English private companies,

Fig. 11.1 *A modern photograph of the fort at Cape Coast, Ghana, which once guarded a slaving station. Cape Coast was owned by the Spanish, Dutch, Danes and, after 1664, by the British.*

using over 100 ships, carried 25,000. Most of the trade was in the hands of well-organised merchants who directed their ships from offices in Liverpool, Bristol and London. After 1720 merchants from Boston and Charleston also took part.

The French and Dutch governments continued to support government companies and their share of the trade fell as that of the British private traders rose. In 1768 approximately 96,100 Africans were shipped to the Americas. British vessels brought 53,100 and British American ships a further 6,200, while the French carried only 23,000, the Dutch 11,300, the Portuguese 1,700 and the Danes 1,200.

Traditional slavery

Slavery was not new to African society. Traditionally there were four ways in which an African freeman could become a slave. First, in cases of famine, parents could place their children as domestic slaves in the care of a wealthy man who would prevent them starving. Secondly, people could be sold into domestic slavery as payment for their debts. Once the debt was paid they could regain their freedom. Thirdly, freemen could be enslaved for serious crimes such as witchcraft, adultery and murder. Finally, prisoners of war and people seized in raids were regarded as their captors' slaves. They were not considered as chattels and could not be sold unless they were found guilty of a serious crime. Indeed they were usually treated as well as freemen and many rose to high positions in their master's household.

New forms of slavery

The African slave trade altered these traditional forms of slavery. Slaves became a commodity which could be traded to Europeans like any other goods. They were seen as no more than the price to be paid for European goods such as brandy and wine, iron goods and weapons, gunpowder and textiles such as lace and velvet. New methods of slaving were needed to have enough slaves to exchange. One group would invent a cause for war against a neighbour, solely to collect slaves. Frequently European traders encouraged such slaving wars by supplying one people with guns in return for the slaves. Often they would arm the other side if they also agreed to deliver slaves.

African rulers usually needed no encouragement to raid their neighbours. John Atkins visited Whydah in 1721 and reported how one of the petty African kings there first bargained with his neighbours for slaves but, if he 'can not obtain a sufficient number of slaves that way, he marches an Army inland and depopulates'. This sort of thing happened all along the coast. C. B. Waldstrom gave evidence against the slave trade in 1789 and stated that, for African kings, 'Public pillage [raiding] is of all the others, the most plentiful source, from which the slave trade derives its continuance and support.'

For some African rulers the profits came in another way. Slaves captured in the interior were brought to the coast through inland market towns. Here the local ruler collected taxes on them just as he would on any other trading item that passed through. These taxes were often the biggest part of a chief or king's income.

Effects of slaving in Africa

At the time, few Africans saw the damage that was being done to their stable societies. Traditional crafts such as iron-working and weaving died when African merchants imported cheap cooking pots and hoes or cloth made in European factories. Many African industries suffered when skilled craftsmen were seized as slaves. Villages and kingdoms lost their natural leaders, and the men and women skilled in healing.

The barbarous trade

Slaving raids

No West African was altogether free from the risk of enslavement, but generally the raiders

Fig. 11.2 *A seventeenth-century picture of a slave coffle. The European soldiers carry pikes. Slave coffles in later years were much longer and often had women and children as well as men.*

came from the well-organised kingdoms and the victims from inland villages and tiny separated communities. For the majority of our West African ancestors the first step to slavery began with a surprise night attack. The raiders quickly fired the houses and, in the panic, collected the villagers, yoking them two by two with forked sticks around their necks into a slave coffle. Speed was important; the coffles had to be on their way before the fires died down and the villagers regrouped and overpowered the raiders. Quickly they were prodded towards the coast. The strongest and fittest survived; the very young, the old, the weak and sick were cut from the coffles to die along the wayside or make their way back to their ruined village as best they could. After a march, often lasting several weeks and covering three or four hundred kilometres, the coffles reached the slaving markets of the inland capitals at Salago, Oke-Odan, Kumasi, Abomey or Oyo. Here the coffles were broken for the first time and the slaves sold to the dealers who traded with the Europeans on the coast. They formed their purchases into new coffles, paid the taxes due on them and marched them down the well-worn routes to the coast.

At the coast

At the coast the slaves were finally sold to Europeans. The chief factor (the agent of a European trading company) at Elmina castle in 1701 was a Dutchman, William Bosman. In a letter Bosman described this final stage.

> When these slaves come to Fida they are put in prison all together, and when we treat concerning buying them, they are throughly examined by our surgeons, even to the smallest member . . . .
> Those which are approved as good are set on one side; and the lame or faulty are set by as invalids, which are here called Mackrons. These are such as are above five and thirty years old, or are maimed in arms, legs, hands or feet, have lost a tooth, are grey-haired or have films over eyes; as well as those which are affected with any venereal distemper, or with several other diseases. The invalids and maimed being thrown out . . . the remainder are numbered and in the meanwhile a

burning iron with the arms or name of the Company lies in the fire; with which ours are marked on the breast.

Here Bosman paused to offer some excuses for the inhumanity he has described.

> I doubt not this trade seems very barbarous to you, but since it is followed by mere necessity, it must go on; but we yet take all possible care that they are not burned too hard, especially the women, who are more tender than the men.

The middle passage

Captains of slaving ships acquired their human cargoes in one of two ways. Either they cruised along the coast dealing with several small African dealers, or they sailed directly to a trading station and bought their slaves from a European factor. The first method was used mainly by private shipowners who could not afford the overhead charges at the trading stations. As a result they could often sell their slaves slightly cheaper in America. However, they could seldom load a complete cargo at one point and had to ply up and down the coast for a few slaves here and there. These delays could be costly as additional provisions had to be taken on board and wages paid to seamen for little work. The risk of losing both cargo and crew from disease in the unhealthy coastal swamps increased each day.

The ships of merchant companies who called at the trading stations often took on a full load straight away. The captain, along with his 'surgeon', went ashore to select the slaves and bargain for them with the goods on board. John Atkins describes the procedure at Whydah in 1721:

> The commanders with their surgeons (as skilled in the choice of slaves) attend the whole time on shore, where they purchase in what they call a fair open market. The mates reside on board, receiving from time to time their masters' directions as to the goods wanted, and to prepare the ship for the reception and security of the slaves sent him; where this is a rule always observed, to keep males apart from the women and children, to handcuff the former . . .

The middle passage began with a short trip in open boats to the waiting ship. For the slaves it provided a last glimpse of a homeland few would see again.

Slave ships

The waiting ships were fully prepared for their human cargoes. Along the whole length, under deck, ran tier upon tier of open-ended, box-like trays 150 centimetres long and 50 centimetres wide and high. The men were placed in these with iron shackles around their ankles, joined by chains looped to the shackles of their neighbours. Women and children were crowded below decks in the fore section. The slavers' equipment included feeding bowls, food containers, guns and special chisels to knock out front teeth so that slaves who were determined to starve to death could be forcibly fed. Provisions were simple: rice, yams, oil, a few fresh fruits and water. The ships were horribly crowded as it was reckoned that one-fifth of the slaves would die during the crossing. To offset these losses, the captain crammed in one-fifth more slaves than the number he had insured his voyage for.

When all was ready the hatches were bolted, the sails raised and course charted west from Africa to America. For the first days, until the ship was well out to sea, the slaves were kept below deck. Then a steady routine set in. The ship's doctor made morning rounds attending to the sick and disposing of the dead. Relays of slaves were allowed on deck where they were closely watched while being allowed to exercise and take their meal. In fair weather, women and children were generally allowed to remain on deck and sometimes captains forced groups of men to join in songs and dances.

But such times were rare. Heavy seas often kept the hatches bolted for days on end and few captains considered more than the most basic needs of their cargo. The gloom, stench and sweltering heat below deck brought unbelievable misery. Slaves and crew alike suffered from

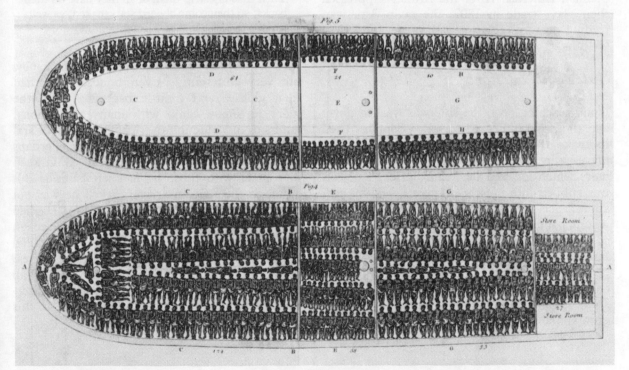

Fig. 11.3 *Plan of a slave ship showing the inhuman packing to make use of every centimetre. The bottom diagram shows the lower deck and the top one shows a platform fixed round the sides of the ship's walls between the lower and upper decks.*

inflammations, fevers and smallpox. Their limbs swelled and bodies rotted from yaws and dropsy. Despair made the possibility of infection and death all the greater. The captain of the slave ship *Hannibal* had taken on 700 slaves. Before reaching American waters 320 had died and he lamented:

> After all our pains and care to give them their messes in due order and season, keeping their lodges clean and sweet as possible, and enduring so much misery and stench among a parcel of creatures nastier than swine . . . to be defeated by their mortality!

The middle passage lasted from six to ten weeks, depending on the weather and destination. The shortest route was to Brazil and the longest to the continental United States. The main slave markets in the Caribbean during the eighteenth century were at Barbados, Martinique, Jamaica and Hispaniola. The Dutch island, Curacao, also served as a trans-shipment port for slaves for the mainland colonies of Spanish America. After the British suppressed their slave trade in 1807, the main American trading centres became Havana and New Orleans.

Sales and auctions

Upon reaching port, the ship was washed down and the slaves prepared for sale. Captains tried to make their cargo as attractive as possible. Slaves were stripped and shaved to remove grey hairs which lowered the selling price. Palm oil was rubbed into muscles to give a healthy firm appearance. Some captains tried to conceal wounds and scars by rubbing them with cosmetic mixtures which included gunpowder, lime juice and even iron rust.

The final sale to the planter was conducted either by a 'slave scramble' or an auction. In a slave scramble the Africans were divided into groups for which set prices were fixed. At a signal, the planters rushed on board to assess which group offered the best quality for the least money. The practice was extremely cruel; at the on-rush of the planters many of the terrified Africans flung themselves desperately into the sea. The scramble was eventually outlawed in most colonies and replaced by the auction when planters were allowed to inspect the slaves before the bidding began. After the scramble or auction the slaves were branded again, this time with their new master's mark. They were issued with a set of Osnaburg clothes – pants and a hat for men, a petticoat and scarf for women – and taken to the plantation where the long process of converting an African into a seasoned American slave began.

The African heritage

The beginning of the African's journey to America was described in 1700 by William Bosman in a few plain words:

> Their masters strip them of all they have on their backs; so they come aboard stark-naked, as well women as men: in which condition they are obliged to continue.

Most European immigrants started their new life very differently. Even bondservants had their clothes and a little baggage; while the more fortunate came with many possessions, letters of introduction to friends or relatives and perhaps even a farm waiting for them. Perhaps most important of all the European could keep in contact with those he had left behind. But although the African arrived naked he was not completely cut off from his homeland. He had his language, beliefs, skills and a place in society as perhaps a warrior, priest or skilled craftsman. He had a rich store of memories, stories and dances. In time he would use all these to piece together a life in his new American surroundings which owed much to his African heritage.

Assignments

1 *Examine the table given on page 90, 'Numbers of live slaves taken from West Africa 1451–1870' and answer the following questions:*
   a) *Which two Caribbean islands received the largest number of slaves?*
   b) *Which country received the largest number of slaves?*
   c) *Give reasons why the above three territories received such vast numbers of slaves.*
   d) *What effect do you think that this loss of manpower to Africa would have on West Africa?*

2 *'For every African who arrived alive at least one other perished in the slaving raids, on the trek to the coast or during the trans-Atlantic crossing', page 90.*
   Explain how so many Africans died on 'the trek to the coast and during the trans-Atlantic crossing'.

3 *Make a table or diagram to show how Europe organised the slave trade. Include the private individuals and the highly organised national companies.*

12 THE EIGHTEENTH-CENTURY PLANTATION

The plantation in British colonies

It has been reckoned that in 1774 the typical plantation in Jamaica was 240 hectares and worth £19,324. At that time an Englishman could live very comfortably on a few hundred pounds a year and a farm labourer in England earned only a few shillings a week. The value of such a plantation can be broken down like this:

105 hectares sugar cane	£4,273
135 hectares other land	£1,728
Sugar works	£3,962
Slaves	£7,641
Livestock	£1,380
Other equipment	£340
	£19,324

Of course, not all plantations on the sugar islands were of 240 hectares. Many were much larger, especially in Jamaica where land was used more wastefully, and where it was also usual to give slaves plots to grow provisions. On Barbados and Antigua estates were rarely more than 120 hectares. But there was less waste or mountain ground and each hectare was used with more care so that plantations on the smaller islands were roughly the same value as those on Jamaica. The table shows two features which were true for most estates. First, the most valuable property was the slaves, generally worth about two-fifths of all the planter owned. Second, a sugar plantation was a combination of industry and agriculture; the sugar works were worth nearly as much as the cane fields.

Sugar production in the ten leading Caribbean islands

	Area in sq. km.	Yearly average in tonnes 1741–5	1766–70
St Domingue (Fr)	27,856	43,078	62,227
Jamaica (Br)	11,424	15,827	36,597
Antigua (Br)	280	6,329	10,861
St Christopher (Br)	176	7,345	9,856
Martinique (Fr)	1,105	14,389	8,918
St Croix (Danish)	218	742	8,361
Guadeloupe (Fr)	1,702	8,241	8,024
Barbados (Br)	430	6,746	7,944
Grenada (Br)	345	–	6,657
Cuba (Sp)	110,922	2,032	5,283
Total	154,458	104,729	164,728

Comparison of plantation sizes in St Kitts and Jamaica in the eighteenth century

St Kitts		Jamaica	
Size in acres (1 acre = 0.4 hectares)	Number of owners	Size in acres (1 acre = 0.4 hectares)	Number of owners
1–9	19	0–99	263
10–24	21	100–499	566
25–49	23	500–999	303
50–99	26	1,000–1,999	253
100–149	18	2,000–4,999	153
150–199	12	5,000–9,999	52
200–523	15	10,000–22,999	9
Total 134		Total 1,599	

Location and layout

Close by a river was ideal as water could be carried by an aqueduct to turn the mill; it was also useful for irrigating the fields. If possible, a place near the coast was chosen so that a small dock could be built to send sugar to the main ports of the island for shipping overseas. It would also be the means of bringing in the plantation's supplies.

A plantation was described by one Jamaican as being like a little town which bought goods from all over the world. One estate's account books for the 1780s show that in one shipment from Europe it received 15 barrels of beef, 70 barrels of herring for feeding slaves, 200 lb (90 kilograms) of butter and four kegs of tallow for making candles and soap. To clothe its slaves it also bought quantities of Osnaburg cloth, made in Germany, and supplies of 'negro hats'.

Most plantations on Barbados ran in narrow strips from the coast, and planters fed their slaves chiefly on imported foods. In Jamaica this was not always possible as many plantations were opened in inland valleys. Some Jamaican planters built roads to the coast and charged tolls for other people to use them. But they also found ways of cutting down on the need for transport. Inland plantations were usually larger, in some cases more than 2,000 hectares. More of the land was used for provision crops and often slaves were allowed one and half days per week to grow their own food. The large

estate could provide its own timber for building. Owners of these plantations did not need to be such careful farmers. Edward Long wrote in 1750 that they often wore out their plantations by 'incessant cultivation and after throwing it up, pass on to a new piece which is destined to be worked to the bone in the same manner'. The planters with less land to waste, like those on Barbados, were noted for careful manuring which kept their fields fertile.

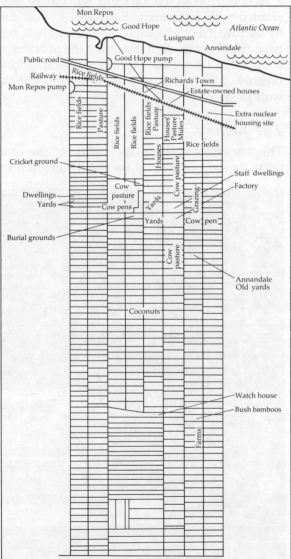

Map 24 *Plantations in Guyana ran from the sea inland in long narrow strips. The layout of eighteenth-century plantations near Georgetown can be seen in this diagram of a modern estate.*

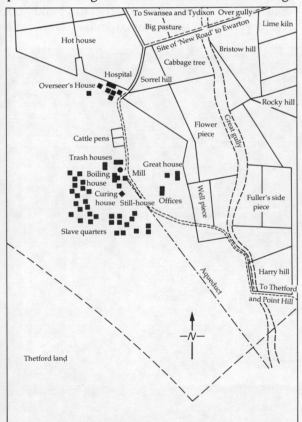

Map 23 *A plan of Worthy Park, Jamaica, in 1794. The estate, situated in St John's parish in the central region of the island, covered an area of 614 hectares.*

Fields

Plantation lands were divided into several sections: cane fields, pastures, woodlands, provision grounds, workyards and living quarters for managers and labourers. Most plantations had from three to five cane fields, each surrounded by a closely trimmed hedge or stone wall to keep out cattle. Each year one field was generally left fallow, another grew a second crop of ratoons and the others were planted with new canes. Each field was divided by narrow roads into smaller square plots of 6–9 hectares. This made it easier for the overseer to control the rate of the slave gangs' work and to organise the movement of cut cane to the workyard.

The factory

The workyard stood in the middle of the cane fields. It was made up of the mill boiling house,

curing house and the blacksmith's and carpenter's sheds. Close by stood the cattle pens, poultry houses and a small 'hospital' which was also used as a jail for runaway slaves. There was sometimes a trash house in which the crushed cane stalks were dried to burn in the furnace.

The mill and boiling house were often built from elaborately cut stone but their mechanisms were not very efficient by modern standards. Juice was taken from the cane by crushing it between three upright rollers made of iron (or wood covered with iron). The power to run the rollers came from animals, wind or water. Animal mills were the simplest and cheapest. Cattle or mules were yoked on to a pole which turned the rollers as the animals walked in a wide circle. Windmills were possible only in certain places, such as the windward side of small islands where the Trade Winds blew constantly. They were costly to build but cheaper to run than animal mills. Watermills

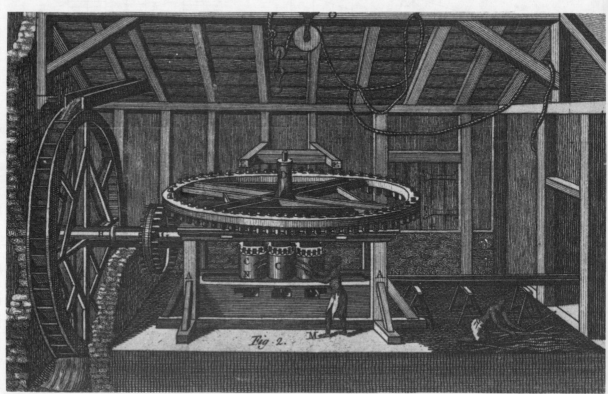

Fig. 12.1 *A water-driven mill from an eighteenth-century book. The slave in the centre is pushing cane between the rollers so that the juice will fall into the trough below and will be carried to the boiling house along the gutter leading to the right.*

were the most powerful and efficient. They cost little to run but needed expensive aqueducts to carry the water which drove the huge wheel. Only a few planters could afford aqueducts.

Lead-covered wooden troughs carried the fresh cane juice from the mill to storage cisterns at the head of each furnace in the boiling house. The furnaces were rectangular boxes of brick or stone, with openings near the bottom of one side to stoke the fires and pull out the ashes. Set in the top of each furnace were up to seven copper kettles. Cane juice was taken from the cistern, strained and ladled into the first and largest copper. It was heated and a little lime was added to remove impurities. The juice was then skimmed and ladled down the line of coppers, each smaller and hotter than the one before, until it reached the smallest and hottest, the teache. In the teache the sugar bubbled to a sticky syrup which was ladled into cooling troughs where the sugar crystals hardened around a sticky core of molasses. The raw sugar was shovelled from the cooling troughs into hogsheads which were wheeled away to the curing house. Here, the molasses drained off through holes in the bottom of the hogsheads leaving the muscovado sugar stuck to the sides. After four weeks the holes were plugged and the hogsheads were ready for export to Europe.

The raw muscovado still had to be turned into many grades of fine white powdered sugar, but the Navigation Laws forbade refining in the Caribbean. Refining became an important industry in the chief western ports of Britain: Bristol, Liverpool and Glasgow – as it did in towns in western France supplied by French Caribbean islands.

Europeans on the plantation

Planters and attorneys

It was only on the very small islands such as Antigua that nearly all planters owned and lived on one plantation. On Jamaica and Barbados it became common for the wealthiest planters to own several plantations, but often they had no home on any. At different times up to a third of the planters were absentees living in England. Absentee planters employed attorneys to be their agents and take care of the plantations. Attorneys inspected the plantation books, purchased supplies and appointed overseers and managers. For this they often received a commission of 6 per cent of the yearly profits and could share in the privileges of the planter class. Some attorneys lived in the owners' great house and became members of the parish vestry.

Great houses

The richest plantation owners usually lived in England and stayed in towns when they visited the Caribbean. Rich planters who spent their lives in the Caribbean often lived in towns rather than on one of their estates. This meant that eighteenth-century great houses were not so magnificent as those of the seventeenth

Fig. 12.2 *A modern photograph of a great house. The lower storey and the verandah can be seen clearly.*

century. Some planters even chose not to waste money on a house which would stay empty for most of the year. They would stay in the bookkeeper's house if they visited their property. But most planters built great houses to a fairly simple design. The bottom storey was made of stone and used as a storage shed, storm cellar and a stronghold in case of a slave revolt. The living quarters were on the second floor, built of wood with a verandah around. One large central hall served as the dining room, sitting room, office and occasionally banqueting hall. Around this were the bedrooms. The kitchens and servants' quarters were in a separate building.

The position of the great house showed the planter's desire for comfort but also his fear and suspicion of the slaves. It usually stood on a mound about a kilometre away from the heat and noise of the workyard and slave quarters. On the verandah the planter's family and guests could catch the cooling breezes; at the same time they could keep a watchful eye on the slaves at work in fields and factory. For extra safety some planters made their house the centre of a compound which also held the homes of the more loyal workers: the overseers and book-keepers, white craftsmen, occasionally a doctor, and the domestic slaves.

Other whites

The overseer managed the daily work on the plantation. It was his job to keep the plantation books for the planter or his attorney, order the daily work to be done and distribute food, clothing, equipment and stores. He was helped by the book-keepers who, despite their titles, did very little book-keeping. Each day they checked the stock of implements and animals and saw that the slaves got to the fields on time and carried out the day's work set by the overseer. When there were white mechanics and craftsmen to repair the buildings and machinery they worked under the orders of the book-keepers, although they generally earned a higher wage than him because of their skills. Even if they were bondservants, as Europeans they had a superior position and many were given charge over artisan and domestic slaves.

Slaves on the plantation

Beyond the compound were the slave quarters. These were simple huts made from wattle, daub and thatch, often with a small garden patch at the back and a living yard at the front. Some island assemblies passed regulations that slave quarters could have only one room, one window and one door. Planters preferred to have their slaves do all their domestic work in the front yard where they were in full view. The huts were sleeping, not living, quarters.

Plantation owners kept stock books which listed their slaves in almost the same way as cattle. In the book for Worthy Park Estate in Jamaica you can find entries like this:

Name	Qualifications	Condition
Quashie	Head carpenter	Able
Nero	Field labourer	Able
Waller	Head boiler	Sickly
Grace	Driver	Elderly
Little Dido	Field labourer	Weakly and runaway

These books remind us that the first thing an African lost when he arrived on the plantation was the name he came with. It was replaced with one which the planter could pronounce and which pleased him in some way. Africans were named after Roman emperors, like Nero on this list. In the same stock book there are slaves with the names of European poets such as Pope and Homer, European countries such as Russia and Germany. Scottish planters often gave their slaves the names of clans in Scotland, such as Mackenzie and Macdonald.

Field slaves

Slaves on a plantation were classified according to the work that they did. Most slaves spent some of their lives as field labourers working in one of the two or three field gangs. The great gang contained the strongest, and especially newly arrived slaves whom the planter wanted to 'season' before deciding whether they had the skill for other work. The stock books show that

Fig. 12.3 *A painting of slave huts near St Johns, Antigua. The great house stands on the rising ground on the left.*

Fig. 12.4 *An early nineteenth-century drawing of slaves cutting and carting cane.*

some of them rose out of the field gangs to specialised positions such as boilers and carpenters. But as they became weak and elderly they often became field labourers again, this time working at the lighter tasks given to the second or third gangs.

In the fields the gangs were commanded by a slave who had risen to the position of driver. His task was to see that the day's work ordered by the overseer was completed. As fields were divided into squares it was easy to see which men or women moved more slowly than the others along the lines to be dug, weeded or manured. The driver had permission to use the whip and some could call on another slave, known as the 'jumper' or 'Johnny Jumper', to carry out the whippings.

Artisans

The most valuable group of slaves were the artisans in the workyard. The head man of each section had the help of journeymen slaves and younger apprentices. The head boiler was the most important of all the artisans. He had to decide how long the sugar should boil in each copper to produce the best quality. Whether the plantation made a good profit or not depended on his skill and judgement. Planters recognised the value of their artisan slaves by giving them special privileges such as extra allowances of clothing, food, drink and more comfortable quarters. When they were not needed on the plantation they were given the chance to 'job away' for another planter or perhaps to work in a nearby town. They paid their owner a percentage of their earnings.

There was also a group of less skilled specialised slaves which included cattlemen, mulemen, midwives and watchmen. Slave children were not free from plantation work. Between the ages of 4 and 10 they had to work in the 'pickney' gang, under the care of an old slave lady who was usually greatly respected by the others. Under her supervision the children moved around the plantation picking up sticks, stones and trash. They carried water and food to the field gangs and fed the poultry. The oldest children were sometimes divided into a separate 'grass gang' to go out and collect feed for the animals.

Domestic slaves

Each planter had domestic slaves to serve his family as maids, cooks, butlers, gardeners, coachmen, valets and nursemaids. Sometimes the domestic slaves were looked on as more fortunate than their fellow Africans in the fields and workyards but it was rarely so. Living close to the master and his family, they were more often the victims of the white man's anger. In the worst households they were punished very frequently. Many of the tasks they had to do were humiliating, especially when they were serving one of the planter's children. One young mistress was described as having three slaves attending her when she took her afternoon nap; two to fan her face and one to lightly scratch her feet. They usually had to live in a compound near the great house and away from the other slaves who often treated them as outcasts. Unfairly, they became thought of as 'Uncle Toms', that is slaves who took the master's side against their own people.

Like the artisans, the domestic slaves would be returned to the plantation as field labourers if they displeased their master or if he no longer had a use for them. Some slave women kept by overseers and managers succeeded in avoiding this fate, but not always. The Worthy Park stock book tells the story of the slave, Dolly. In 1787 she was described as 'in the overseer's house' with a baby, Mulatto Patty. A few years later there are two more coloured babies against her name but Dolly had become a field labourer, presumably because she was too old to be attractive. Whether the father freed the children is not known.

Hired slaves

Between 15 and 20 per cent of the slaves were not attached to a plantation. They belonged to a master who rented them out. The most fortunate were artisans who paid their master for a ticket of leave which allowed them to travel about on work such as carpentry, tailoring, fishing, piloting, higgling and catching rats. Many could earn a fairly comfortable living. A skilled rat-catcher, for instance, could catch sixty to a hundred each week at a $\frac{1}{2}$-cent per rat.

Perhaps the least fortunate of all slaves were those in the unskilled jobbing gangs, which belonged to slave contractors, small landowners or occasionally to a group of planters who shared the use of their labour. They were hired out to do extra work which could not be handled by regular plantation slaves. Sometimes this involved hard and dangerous tasks which the planter feared might cause injury or death to his own slaves. The jobbing slaves had no permanent homes, or regular rations. At night they slept chained together wherever they happened to be working. It was reckoned that a jobbing slave lived on average about seven years.

The weekly round

The slave's sixteen-and-a-half-hour working day began at 4 a.m. when the driver rang a bell or blew on a conch shell. Work like feeding the poultry and cleaning the cattle pens had to be done before daylight. At sunrise all assembled for the roll-call by the overseer. The day's tasks were given and work began again until 10 a.m., when there was a half-hour for breakfast. The slaves were given a two-hour break at 12.30 p.m. to attend to their personal chores. Some went to their food plots and others to clean out and feed their pigs and poultry. Work began again at 2 p.m. and continued until sunset. Only after another roll-call were the slaves allowed to go back to their quarters until 4 a.m. the next morning. This routine was broken on Sunday mornings when slaves were allowed to go to market to sell the small animals and provisions they had raised. Holidays were given during Christmas week and for a few days after crop time.

The yearly cycle

The yearly cycle of cultivation began in spring with the planting of new canes. The great gang had to open up the soil to a depth of 15 centimetres. The task was doubly difficult if old ratoons had to be pried out by the roots. Dr Tullideph in Antigua estimated that his field slaves wore out 'near half a ton' of hoes each planting season. Once the field was planted the great gang was kept busy weeding, thinning, hoeing and replanting. They were helped by the second and third gangs who also manured the cane holes.

When the crop was growing well the gangs were put to work at other tasks. Provisions had to be planted, fences repaired and roads built. Towards the end of March there was a rush to complete work which could not be done during crop time. The provisions were reaped and stored, staves were cut and piled ready for the coopers to make hogsheads, and cane trash was collected for the boiling house.

During the five months of crop time the working day lengthened to eighteen-and-a-half hours. Most plantations worked a shift-system which allowed each shift only four hours sleep every twenty-four. The shifts alternated between cutting canes and working in the factory. Both were monotonous and back-breaking. The last field shift of the day had to cut enough canes to keep the mill running all night. Artisans had to be on duty night and day to fix breakdowns. The slaves dreaded work in the mills more than cane cutting. The factory work was hot and dangerous as canes had to be fed into the rollers by hand. There was an axe hanging by to cut off tired fingers which became caught up in the rollers. In the boiling house slaves suffered terribly from burns while stoking the furnaces and ladling the boiling sugar from copper to copper. Working such incredibly long hours in dangerous conditions with little food helped make plantation slavery a terrible experience and meant that most slaves' lives were short.

Assignments

1 *The slaves were the most valuable property of a sugar plantation:*
   a) *Why was this so?*
   b) *If this was so why were the slaves treated so harshly by the planters?*

2 *Compare the size and layout of sugar plantations throughout the Caribbean. What dictated whether a plantation would be large or small and where it would be located?*

3 *There were different categories of slaves on each sugar estate. Which slaves do you think had the most difficult time – explain why. In what ways were all slaves similar?*

4 *Describe the way of life of eighteenth-century sugar planters, their attorneys and other whites in the Caribbean.*

13 AFRICAN CULTURAL FORMS

A surviving society

Newly arrived Africans went through long periods of training called 'seasoning'. Arriving at the plantation, they were put in the charge of slave families who helped them to build houses, prepare provision grounds and taught them the ways of the plantation. If they rebelled or ran away they were severely punished; if they worked hard they were rewarded with extra rations or better jobs.

What happened when slaves were given a newly arrived African-born person to 'season'? They did learn to use some of the European language and to live and work in the way enforced by European planters. But at the same time links with the traditions of Africa were strengthened. In some cases they could even make slaves better informed about their homeland, for men and women from different African groups were able to discover how much heritage they shared in common.

As in Africa much of the culture of the West Indian slaves survived in dance and song. Many planters believed that when the slaves danced it was a sign of the contentment of a simple people. In fact, they were keeping alive their history and cultural life. Sometimes they were enlarging their heritage as people from different West African groups mingled together and developed new dances and stories. The dance for which there are most records in eighteenth-century Jamaica was the John Canoe. The descriptions of the dance leaders' masks remind us of the head-dress worn by secret society elders in African village ceremonies and processions.

Time has made changes, but all the forms of Caribbean song and dance still carry signs of African origins. They appear in the rhythms of jazz, the satire of calypsoes, the vigour of reggae and 'jump ups' and the feeling of soul. Drum-ming has survived as an important part of religious and social festivals too. Planters feared it and made it illegal, perhaps knowing that it was the main way of drawing African people together. But it was one of the things which no laws could suppress even if it had sometimes to be disguised. A planter, Bryan Edwards, described the Leewards slaves as very fond of beating on a wooden board with a stick. The musical instruments used by slaves in their dances were all of African origin. Many, such as the marimbas and maracas, have changed little in three hundred years.

Families and social life

Planters usually cared little for family relationships among the slaves. The position of fathers was often under the greatest threat. Marriages were not encouraged and most men did not live in the huts of their children's mothers. Sometimes male slaves were rotated around different plantations to break up family stability. In a society where men and women, children and the old all toiled under orders there was no special place for the man as the family protector. On islands where slaves grew their own food, the man might still have a place as the provider of food but on most plantations even this position was taken away from him. Yet Africans continued to teach respect for the authority of fathers. On large estates with a settled slave community children did grow up to have a relationship with their fathers.

The tradition of age-sets was continued. Bryan Edwards commented that 'old age was held in great veneration' and noted that older slaves had considerable authority over the younger ones. Slave children grew up to address the men and women of their mother's generation as 'Daddy' or 'Uncle', 'Mammy' or

Fig. 13.1 *A picture of slaves dancing in Dominica, painted by an Englishman in 1779. How accurate a picture of plantation life is it likely to be?*

'Aunty'. Among newly arrived slaves strong bonds were often created among peoples wrenched from different villages and different societies in Africa. Those who came over on the same boat would know each other as 'ship-mates', an important relationship which lasted a lifetime.

To keep up the relationship with ship-mates or a loved one some slaves risked leaving the plantation at night without permission and going 'night walking'. But the most common place for such meetings was the Sunday market, described by David McKinnen, in 1802, as the 'day of market and also the day of mirth and recreation when the whole negro population seemed to be in motion'. The market was of course the place where slaves sold or exchanged provision crops and articles they had made such as bedmats or baskets. But it also gave opportunity to consult a herbal doctor or *Obeah-man*,

listen to stories or music and take part in dances. Some descriptions of markets show how the slaves would divide up and spend the day in the company of their own age-set.

Beliefs and customs

Slave funerals were carried out with much of the ceremony of Africa, and slavery did not destroy the belief that the dead person remained part of the community. Corpses were carried in processions which 'stepped up' to the places that the dead person had known in life. Sometimes a bowl of soup was placed at the head and a bottle of rum at the feet to help the dead man to join his spirit relatives.

At first it was common for slaves to believe that they would return over the seas to join spirit relatives. As the years passed and more ancestors were Caribbean born the direct links were broken, but slaves continued to draw many of their ideas and beliefs from the African past. This was true of the beliefs held by followers of Vodun and Shango.

Vodun was chiefly found in French St Domingue, modern Haiti. Most of the slaves came from the Dahomey region where Africans recognised a creator male-female god, Maur-Lisa, and a host of lesser gods, or voduns, each caring for some aspect of life. Many slaves were compulsorily baptised into the Roman Catholic Church and it may have been at these services that priests of the Vodun gods noted that a Catholic Church has an altar to a high God and shrines for saints. Out of this arose the mixture of Catholic and African beliefs which has usually been called Voodoo.

Shangoism became particularly strong in Trinidad. It stemmed from Yoruba beliefs about Shango, the god of thunder or lightning. Shangoism like other West African religions encouraged a belief in life after death and in the idea of creator-gods. Planters usually refused to allow Christian missionaries on the plantations for fear that Christianity might give them a common bond and unite them against their masters. Yet black slaves did not need Christianity to give them a deep spiritual life. This was their heritage from West African culture. Traditional African ideas about birth and death, God and man, spirits and the spirit world, as well as respect for the natural world all survived in the Caribbean. Later they came to merge with Christian beliefs.

Some Africans kept a strong belief in the power of Obeahism and Myalism, which was kept alive by Obeah-men and Myal-men who came on the slave ships. Obeahism, at its crudest, was a belief in sorcery. Obeah-men used charms and shadow-catching to harm a person who was thought to be the cause of things which went wrong. Some Obeah-men, however, set out to use their powers for healing. To many Africans, Myalism was a more certain way of dealing with disaster. Myal-men led ritual dances in which people became united with ancestral spirits and got strength and guidance from them. Myal-men were also skilled in herbal medicine and some planters allowed

them to practise in plantation hospitals. It is interesting to note that many Europeans during the slavery period also believed firmly in witchcraft or sorcery. As late as the 1700s old Scottish women were executed as witches!

The lesser spirits of things like rocks, trees and streams, which were so important in the African explanation of the natural world, often found a place in the Caribbean. Tales of duppies and other spirits were widespread. So were the fables and stories from the oral traditions of Africa, which were handed down by word of mouth from one generation to the next. Anancy stories were told to plantation children. Originally based on the spider hero Ananse of the Akan people, they became known to Africans of other groups as well, and were gradually given a West Indian setting. In the plantations of the southern American states the tortoise tales of the Yoruba and the hare tales of the Igbo were retold.

Surviving skills and language

African crafts survived in the West Indies. The most common were basket-work and straw-plaiting used to make bed-mats, wicker-chairs, baskets and occasionally plaited shoes. Traditional pottery skills continued in the making of earthern pots and jars. Some groups kept alive some of the highly decorative fashions of Africa, such as those found in the combs, paddles, stools and doorposts of the free Maroons in Surinam. Women's fashions lasted through the years of slavery to the present day. The practice of wrapping women's heads with distinctive ties can be traced to West Africa. Today, among the Ashanti, there are at least fifty recognised styles of tying headkerchiefs. The braiding and plaiting of hair into delicate cane rows and pieces is a fashion still shared by women in the Caribbean and West Africa.

One of the great tragedies of the slave societies was that so few records have been left of the cultural and social lives of the African people. Even when Europeans bothered to describe slave life they rarely understood it and, of course, they knew very little indeed about the African society from which they had taken their plantation labour. So their attitudes to African culture in the West Indies show not only fear but also ignorance. Sometimes, therefore, we can best work out how much African tradition survived on the slave plantation by looking at what has lasted to the present day.

For instance, it is only recently that careful studies of language have shown that the syntax (or grammar) and idiom (or forms of speech) of the many West Indian creoles are based on elements found in the speech of peoples such as the Yoruba, the Ewe, the Twi and many others. In most cases the African word had been replaced by an English, Spanish or French equivalent. Sometimes, too, slaves took Amerindian words. But African terms survived too. Many West Indian dialects still retain the word *Tata* for a beloved relative or grandmother. *Nyam*, to eat, is probably the same as the Twi word for meat.

European attempts at control

The plantocracy

At the centre of the history of the eighteenth-century colonies is the life of the plantation slaves. What they endured has been the most important influence on the development of the free Caribbean societies of today. But, at the time, it was not the slaves who controlled colonies even though they outnumbered whites everywhere by about twelve to one. Undoubtedly, power in the eighteenth century rested in the hands of a small section of whites, the plantocracy. In turn, it was only a small number of these, usually the wealthiest, who sat in the island assemblies and wrote the laws. Others, however, held positions of local power through the parish vestries. A planter could serve as a custos, magistrate, justice of the peace, collecting constable and an officer of the militia.

The greatest fear of the planters in the assemblies and vestries was that their numbers and strength would fall to dangerously low levels. The plantocracy on the larger colonies already lived with the threat from Maroons in the interior (see pp. 135–9). On all colonies there was an ever-present anxiety about black rebellion.

Deficiency Acts

As we saw in Chapter 9 the ratio of whites to blacks began to fall rapidly in the early eighteenth century. To try to stop this most island assemblies passed a Deficiency Act. This usually stated that a planter must hire one white servant for every ten slaves on his plantation. In fact the Deficiency Acts actually led to a fall in the number of white settlers. The reason was that planters kept their own doctors, store-keepers, carpenters and masons, and so men with private businesses had to close their shops and leave the islands. In time, too, the planters found that it was cheaper to train a slave than to pay a white craftsman. The fine for breaking the Deficiency Acts was not more than £10 whereas it would cost considerably more a year to employ a European.

The failure of the Deficiency Acts meant that whites on the sugar islands were everywhere in a tiny minority. In Jamaica in 1774 there were only 18,420 compared to 205,261 slaves, a proportion of about 1 to 11. But the whites were not evenly spread. Most of them lived in Kingston and other island towns, or were soldiers in the garrison. In the countryside there were only a few to each plantation and most of these were men. Lady Nugent, the governor's wife, travelled from Kingston to Port Antonio in 1802 and met only one white woman. The result was fear of the Africans and strong measures to keep them under control.

Police laws

Each colony passed a series of police laws controlling the movement and behaviour of slaves. Some dealt with the capture and punishment of runaways. Slaves were forbidden to travel away from the plantation without a ticket from their master giving the destination and time of return. Other laws made it illegal for slaves to carry weapons, to blow horns, beat drums or assemble together in large numbers. They were not allowed to inherit land or to own private property without their master's permission. A master could punish slaves for minor offences. More serious cases were tried by a

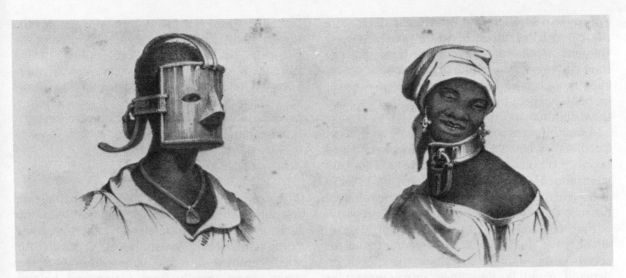

Fig. 13.2 *Two ways of punishing slaves, taken from an old British guidebook to the West Indies.*

justice of the peace and three freeholders, who would all be white property owners. At these trials slaves could not speak in their defence. No slave was allowed to give evidence in a trial for a freeman, which meant that there was no evidence to convict a white who had ill-treated a slave. In Nevis a planter, Edward Huggins, was brought to court for cruelty in whipping slaves after he had given 365 lashes to a man and 292 to a woman. The jury found him not guilty. The woman died a few days later and the coroner's jury certified that she had died a natural death.

Another section of the laws tried to prevent masters from treating their slaves so harshly that they would be driven to revolt. The slave codes on each island laid down the minimum of clothing, food and housing that should be supplied. A Montserrat law of 1693 said that all planters should set aside one acre (just under half a hectare) of provision ground for every eight slaves. Old and useless slaves could not be turned out of the plantations. All slave codes forbade masters to kill their slaves or use cruel and unusual punishments. The Barbados law laid down a fine of £15 on the planter who killed his own slave. Yet few masters were ever found guilty as they were always tried by a jury of fellow planters.

Other controls

When there was a serious slave disturbance or revolt, the planters could call on the local militia. This was a force of part-time soldiers made up of whites and free coloureds. But they were not often called on. The greatest security from trouble came from making it difficult for the slaves to unite. Planters divided their slaves into grades with different privileges. They mixed slave gangs so that they held Africans with different backgrounds and languages. Adult males were often rotated around several plantations to prevent them thinking of themselves as leaders of a family, an age-set or a secret society. Slaves were not taught to read and write for this might mean they would pick up ideas which threatened the slave system and pass them on to other Africans.

Free coloureds and blacks

The white plantocracy also felt threatened by the increasing numbers of free coloureds. White men were allowed to free their slaves and this was sometimes done as a reward for long and obedient service. Sometimes assemblies passed legislation freeing certain slaves for help in putting down a revolt or for bravery in fighting a European invader. But most freed slaves were the coloured children of white men and slave women. As all children took the legal status of their mother such children were born-slaves even though their father was a planter, overseer or book-keeper, but many such fathers wanted their children to grow up free.

Assemblies passed many local laws to prevent freed slaves being able to rival the wealth and social position of the plantocracy. The laws were aimed at both free coloureds and blacks although the victims were more often coloured because they were more likely to own property.

Free coloureds had to register with a vestry which gave them a ticket of freedom valid for seven years. Failure to show the ticket on demand could lead to fines, imprisonment or enslavement. Free coloureds could not give evidence against a white in court, they could not vote or hold a public office. Other laws limited their chances of becoming wealthy. Most islands forbade them to own plantations and, in Jamaica, they could not inherit more than '2,000 pounds currency or worth of property'. There were less strictly kept laws against coloureds taking up certain crafts such as carpentry and masonry, or working on plantations as book-keepers and overseers.

All these limitations depended on knowing who was or was not a coloured or a white. This was carefully defined in laws which laid down that a coloured person was anyone from a full black to a quintroon, who had one part black ancestry to thirty-two parts white. The child of a quintroon and a white man, defined as an octoroon, crossed the colour line and was legally recognised as white.

Added to the laws, the coloureds suffered from social discrimination. Many had close private relationships with whites but they could not appear at white dances, racing meets, banquets and other entertainments. At the end of the eighteenth century the two groups did attend the same Baptist and Methodist churches but, according to the Reverend William Jones, the whites kept away from coloureds, 'searching for seats as distant as possible from them'. Yet, despite this, the coloureds were necessary to Caribbean society. Many of them worked as skilled artisans on the plantations or in the towns. They made up the greatest portion of the part-time soldiers in the local militias which were kept chiefly to deal with slave disturbances. They also filled positions in the towns which had been left vacant by poor whites. Coloureds were clerks, traders, tavern-keepers, butchers and higglers.

The exceptions

There were just a few who escaped all the restrictions. A coloured in Jamaica who was lucky enough to gain money or education could petition his island assembly for a private Act which granted him the same rights as a free white, apart usually from voting and holding public office. As a result of special Acts some Jamaican free coloureds rose to influential positions as newspaper editors, teachers and lawyers. Planters regularly got permission from the assemblies to allow their coloured sons to work on their plantations as book-keepers and overseers. James Swaby, the illegitimate coloured son of a planter from St Elizabeth, Jamaica, successfully petitioned the assembly for a private Act which allowed him to inherit his father's sugar plantation, 217 slaves and 337 head of cattle. Yet despite these exceptions, most coloureds remained desperately poor.

A creole society?

The plantocracy which ruled the British Caribbean was white, but this was not the same as being completely English in its life-style. But was the plantocracy so different from the upper class in England that we ought to speak of a quite separate creole way of life? This is a difficult question to answer because the people who wrote about the Caribbean in the eighteenth century gave so many different impressions.

Travellers' descriptions

Some travellers stressed how like Britain the West Indian islands were. Janet Schaw who visited Antigua in the 1770s wrote that the ladies there 'have the fashions every six weeks from London, and London itself cannot boast of more elegant shops than you meet with at St John's'. Going into the countryside, she was impressed by the homes of the planters, the many banquets and balls and by being taken on a 'charming ride through many rich and noble plantations'. The traveller Oldmixon wrote in a similar way about Bridgetown: 'a city of 1,200 houses, built of stone, the windows glazed, many of them sashed; the streets bounding the houses high, and the rents dear.' In the countryside, he declared, 'the Master Merchants and Planters live each like little sovereigns.'

To Oldmixon and Janet Schaw the islands were places where the planters could live the ideal life of leisure of English gentlemen. Yet, their writings show signs of the tension and fear which lay below the surface. Janet Schaw spoke of the Christmas holiday when the 'inhuman whip' was not being used. But it was a time when 'every man on the island is in arms and patrols go all around the different plantations as well as keeping guard in the towns'.

Fear of the African was obvious and many writings defended the use of the whip to keep them in their place. Matthew Lewis, writing from his knowledge of Jamaica, said, 'I am indeed assured by everyone around me that to manage a West Indian estate without the occasional use of a cart whip, however rarely, is impossible'. Sometimes, too, travellers were shocked by signs of immoral sexual behaviour by white men. As Janet Schaw wrote, it 'appears too plainly from the crowds of mullatoes'.

One visitor who stressed ways in which the plantocracy was creole rather than British was Lady Nugent, wife of the governor of Jamaica from 1801 to 1805. Her diary reports many times when she considered the men and women of the plantocracy to be not up to the best English ways of behaviour. She saw signs that white creole language was moving away from the English. When she mentioned a breeze blowing through a window a planter's wife replied, 'Yes, Ma-am, him rai-ly too fra-ish'. At a ball she followed the English tradition and danced just once with the oldest servant – but,

of course, he was a black slave and this horrified the whites.

Lady Nugent thought that being surrounded by black servants had a bad effect on young creole whites who quickly became little tyrants. This troubled the Reverend John Roland, a campaigner against slavery, whose parents were planters. Of his boyhood he wrote:

My parents, kind and humane as they generally were to their slaves, yet allowed me to insult, strike and hit them as I pleased. I used to think them on a level with the mules and horses on the estate.

Charles Leslie, speaking of Jamaica, was troubled by the poor education of creole whites:

Learning here is at the lowest ebb; there is no public school in the whole island . . . to read, write and cast up accounts is the education they desire.

It was far better he thought for young whites to be educated in England, but such young men came to have a dislike for the West Indies as a crude and cruel society and failed to return. By the end of the eighteenth century there were no longer enough wealthy planters to fill all the seats on the councils and assemblies in the Leeward Islands. So the property qualifications were lowered to allow managers and attorneys to stand for elections. This was done rather than have coloured property owners take a share in government and law-making. As John Waller described after a visit in the early 1800s:

No property, however considerable, can raise a man or women of colour, not even when combined with education, to the proper rank of a human being, in the proper estimation of an English or Dutch creole.

English governors and officials

In one place Lady Nugent's diary comments on a political problem. It was the case of a young boy sentenced to death whom her husband wished to save from the gallows, but 'Nugent couldn't do it without giving great offence and alarm to the white population.'

Like all British governors of the West Indian colonies, Lord Nugent had to be very careful not to offend creole opinion. In the seventeenth century several governors had suffered from trying to have their way against the wishes of the planters. The speaker, or chairman, of the Bahamas assembly had first fired a shot at the governor and then 'broke the governor's head with the butt of his pistol'. Governor Parkes in Antigua was less lucky. When the planters in the assembly failed to persuade the British government to remove him, they dragged him from Government House and beat him to death. Not surprisingly, eighteenth-century governors did not usually challenge the local power of the creole planters. Very few of them stayed long enough to understand the ways of creole society, as the average term of office was only three-and-a-half years.

Another difficulty for governors was that many other officials appointed by the government in Britain did not bother to take up their post in the colonies at all. Englishmen were given posts as island secretary, provost-marshal, surveyor-general, receiver-general and clerk of the supreme court. As was the custom with many jobs in the civil service in England, they paid a deputy to do the work and kept part of the salary for themselves. Their deputies in the Caribbean were usually planters or attorneys who were more likely to side with the other creoles than with the governor.

Slave control in French colonies

The French colonies never had a plantocracy which was so fully in control as it was in the British islands. Until 1785, there were no French local assemblies. All laws and policies were decided in France and carried out by the governor or the intendant and the many officials on the islands. Another reason was that sugar was only one of the important crops in the French islands. In the mid-eighteenth century the Abbé Raynal visited Martinique and listed four distinct classes of planters.

The first class owned 100 large sugar plantations and 12,000 slaves; the second 150 sugar estates with 9,000 slaves and the third, 30 sugar plantations with 2,000 slaves. The fourth class was much the largest. There were 1,500 planters with over 12,000 slaves who grew provisions, coffee, cocoa and cassava rather than sugar. Even St Domingue, which was by far the largest sugar producer of any European colony, had only 648 sugar plantations compared to 2,587 growing coffee, cocoa and indigo.

So the rich white class of landowners – the *grands blancs* – were divided between planters of sugar and other crops. But the French islands also had a large class of small whites or *petits blancs*. These were smallholders, craftsmen, small shopkeepers and the poorer clerks and officials.

The Code Noir

These differences in white society affected the position of slaves and free coloureds, especially in the early days when many of the Africans had been brought to the French islands not to work

Fig. 13.3 *Governor Parkes of Antigua.*

in large field gangs but to serve small farmers, craftsmen and traders. In 1685 the French government issued the *Code Noir*, or black code, to regulate the treatment of slaves. The Code was divided into three sections. The first dealt with religious questions, the next with the position of slaves and the third with the procedures for granting freedom.

The religious section was drawn up to make sure that the French colonies remained true to the Catholic faith. English planters resisted the idea of religious teaching for slaves, but the French were compelled to give instruction in the faith and to encourage baptism and legal marriage. Sundays and holy days were to be observed and slaves were to be buried in holy ground. The Code forbade concubinage between slaves and freemen, although this was usually ignored from the start.

The second part of the Code defined the slave as private property. Because they were the property of another man, slaves could not own property themselves, nor could they make contracts, hold public office or take part in trials. Other parts of the Code forbade slaves to carry arms, assemble in crowds, take up trades or use violence against free people. On the other hand, the planter was forced to have some respect for basic human rights. He was obliged to give allowances of food and clothing and to care for the disabled. Punishments were limited to whipping or putting in irons. Owners could not break up families by sale. The Code gave slaves a right unknown in the English colonies. They could go to the legal official known as the *procureur-général* (or attorney-general) and complain if a master did not carry out his obligations.

Easy procedures for freeing slaves were laid down in the final section of the Code Noir, which stated that those freed were to have the same rights as other Frenchmen. The number of free coloureds rose more rapidly in the French colonies than the British. Small owners were sometimes more willing to free slaves they knew personally than were large planters to whom slaves were just names in a stock book. Petits blancs often married slave women and thus freed them.

Restrictions on coloureds

The influence of the Code Noir in keeping some respect for human rights weakened as the number of both slaves and free coloureds rose in the eighteenth century. The French whites pressed for restrictions on the coloureds. In 1766 the French government gave in, declaring that it was wrong for the coloureds, who were still close to slavery, to expect to share in the positions held by white men. It ordered that coloureds were not to serve in the island militia or to carry arms. Coloureds were no longer to have equal rights in law and certain professions were closed to them. To mark their difference from the whites, free coloureds were forced to wear identifying clothing. Ladies were allowed to wear a scarf but not a hat; cotton petticoats were permitted but not silk, which was reserved for white women. Petticoat inspectors stood at church doors where they checked the coloured ladies as they came to mass. To save embarrassment the ladies pinned up their hems a few

Fig. 13.4 *A woman in Martinique, photographed in the 1890s, wearing a skirt hitched up so that the petticoat can be seen.*

inches to make viewing easy. This practice is still reflected in the national costume of Martinique and Guadeloupe. In 1779 the freedom of movement of coloureds was restricted by a curfew which kept them indoors at night.

Despite the many controls on the free coloureds their right to own property was never taken away. Many became wealthy and could send their children to France to be educated. Wealth and education made the French free coloureds more influential than those in the English colonies. The time would come when coloured leaders, many of them with friends in France itself, would play an important part in overthrowing the supremacy of the whites who had imposed so many restrictions and humiliations on them.

Restrictions on slaves

As the number of slaves grew in the eighteenth century the Code Noir was increasingly ignored by owners. Concubinage became common; marriages were not encouraged. Once they were baptised, slaves were not allowed to return to church. No one checked to see that food and clothing allowances were being given. Instead of acting as protectors of the slaves, the procureurs-généraux in each colony took the lead in laying down regulations which were very similar to the police laws in the English colonies. Masters were ordered to prevent meetings of slaves and not to send them out as hucksters or day workers without passes. There were efforts to force planters to buy food so that they did not give slaves provision grounds and time to work them. Shopkeepers in the towns were sometimes forbidden to buy from slaves.

These changes in the management of slaves were officially recognised in 1771 by the French government, which wrote to the governor-general of the French colonies:

It is only by leaving to the masters a power that is nearly absolute, that it will be possible to keep so large a number of men in that state of submission which is made necessary by their numerical superiority over the whites. If some masters abuse their power, they must be reproved in secret, so

that the slaves may always be kept in the belief that the master can do no wrong in his dealing with them.

In the end, it is clear that the slave societies in both the French and English colonies depended on the use of force. This was well understood by the planters. One of them, Bryan Edwards, wrote:

In countries where slavery is established, the leading principle on which the government is supported is fear . . . It is vain to deny that such actually is, and necessarily must be the case in all countries where slavery is allowed.

Slave control in Spain's colonies

Las Siete Partidas

In many ways, Spain's slave codes were similar to France's. They were laid down by the government in Europe and not by the planters. Like the French they were concerned to see that the slaves were brought into the Roman Catholic faith. One important difference is that the first Spanish code can be traced back to times before the American colonies were settled. It was written in the thirteenth century and was known as Las Siete Partidas. In its turn this was based on a code drawn up at the time of the Christian Roman Emperor Justinian. The Roman Empire contained many slaves and Justinian's code set out to find the middle way between keeping slavery which denied them civil rights and insisting that slaves should have rights as human beings protected by law.

So, Las Siete Partidas laid down that slaves could not be inhumanly treated by their master and had the right to take a complaint to the courts. It recognised that slavery was not a natural state for human beings and ruled that slaves who could buy their freedom must be emancipated, whether or not their master wished to set them free. When Las Siete Partidas was made to apply to the American colonies, great emphasis was placed on the slave's right to be taught religion and the master's duty to see that this was done. Plantation slaves had to be free from work on Sundays and Holy Days. They must have a priest to say mass for them.

The Cedula, 1789

Twice the Spanish government updated this code. The first time was in 1680 when it issued the *Recapilacion*, or summary of colonial laws. This set limits on slaves' rights to meet together, to move about and to carry weapons. At the same time it said that they must be baptised and instructed in the Christian faith and encouraged to marry.

The second time was in 1789 when the government issued the Cedula or slave code. It was possibly drawn up by a French Catholic planter living in Spain's colony in Trinidad, although it was issued by the king of Spain for his whole empire. At the time the Cedula was often said to be proof that the Spanish treated their slaves much more humanely than the British and French. If it had been followed this would have been so. The Cedula repeated the regulations about promoting Christianity among slaves and went on to lay down detailed rules for their treatment. For instance, local justices were to decide on the food and clothing they must be given. Slave owners had to provide each slave with a bed and blankets at no more than two to a room. Slaves under 17 or over 60 were not to work. No more than twenty-five lashes were to be given in punishment.

On paper the regulations gave the slaves of the Spanish far more protection than the British police laws or the French Code Noir. In practice, the differences were nothing like as great.

Planters in Spanish colonies were just as likely to ignore slave codes sent from Spain as they were the Council of the Indies' rules on trading. In fact, when the 1789 code was issued, planters in Cuba and Central America objected so strongly that the Council of the Indies agreed to withdraw it. Even in Trinidad it had little effect, partly because most of the planters there were French who had been encouraged to come to the island with their slaves. Often the slaves were put to work on clearing the forest to open new plantations. They were overworked and given poor clothing or shelter and too little food. This meant they could not stand up to the tropical diseases which killed nearly a thousand in the year 1788 alone.

Free coloureds

Spanish laws limited the rights of free coloureds just as British and French laws did. But while the treatment of plantation slaves was probably harsher than the regulations allowed, the free coloureds were generally treated more mildly. The Spanish were often less concerned about keeping a social distance from people with 'racial' differences. Free coloureds had jobs as minor officials in many Spanish colonies. They were often officers as well as soldiers in militias. Free coloureds in French colonies often praised the conditions in Trinidad but again this was for a special reason. When Chacon became governor the island had a very small population. To increase it he offered grants of land and civil rights to free coloureds and free blacks provided they were Catholic. Many of them came to Trinidad and many of them brought slaves with them.

Assignments

1 *How did slaves keep alive their African heritage and cultural life in the Caribbean? If possible give examples from your own territory.*

2 *'In Jamaica in 1774 there were only 18,420 [whites] compared to 205,261 slaves, a proportion of about 1 to 11 . . . . The result was fear of the African and strong measures to keep him under control', page 110:*
   a) Find out if you can what was the proportion of whites to slaves in your territory in about 1700. Give reasons for this proportion.

b) *Give as many reasons as you can why there was 'fear of the African' by the whites.*

c) *What 'strong measures' did the whites take to keep slaves 'under control'?*

3 *What were the advantages and disadvantages of being a free coloured or a free black in the British Caribbean?*

4 *How did the French islands of the Caribbean differ from the British Caribbean? Look at the following areas:*
i) the power of the sugar planters, ii) the laws that controlled the lives of slaves, iii) the position of the free coloureds.
  What features did both French and English societies in the Caribbean have in common?

5 *In what ways were the slave laws in the Spanish Caribbean similar to and different from the slave laws of the British and French islands?*

14 THE RISE AND FALL OF THE WEST INDIA INTEREST

Wealth from sugar

In 1763 Britain had become ruler of a world-wide empire. She had just seized Canada from France and already owned thirteen colonies on the North American coast. There was a string of British trading settlements and merchant companies in India and the Far East. To many people of the time, the leading figures in the empire were the West Indian planters who were far richer than traders and settlers in any other colony. The basis of their great wealth was the demand for sugar in Europe. As the demand had risen so had the price. In 1733 a hundred-weight (50 kilograms) could be sold for 16s 11¼d: by 1763 it would fetch 38s 6d.

Plantation profits

What this prosperity meant can be seen from the account books of an Antiguan planter in 1756. His plantation contained 202 hectares and had a labour force of 300 slaves, who produced

Fig. 14.1 *Caribbean trade was so valuable to Britain that a whole section of the London docks was built to receive West Indian goods. This eighteenth-century painting shows a London wharf, ships and warehouses.*

200 hogsheads of sugar and 120 puncheons of rum. The land, slaves, building and equipment were valued at £20,000 sterling. For the sugar and rum the planter earned £3,600 and his expenses for the year were £1,900. This left him a profit of £1,700 which equalled 8.5 per cent of the £20,000 invested in the estate. This was the account for a good year. In a bad year when a hurricane struck, or perhaps when French sugar reached Europe at a much lower price, the plantation's sales and profits could fall. At the same time the planter's expenses would be no smaller and so his profit could be cut to a few hundred pounds or nothing at all.

This is why many planters never became wealthy. On the other hand, men who became masters of several plantations could stand a bad year on one of them and still make a profit on the others. In this way a smaller number of planters became very rich. One way of becoming owner of several plantations was to marry the daughter of a planter neighbour who had no sons. But often the most successful planters were those who used their property as security to borrow money which they lent out at higher rates of interest.

Wealthy planters

In the 1740s and 1750s successful planters lent money to poorer planters, to newcomers to the Caribbean and to the local government of their islands. But much of their money was invested in Britain in sugar factories, merchant companies, new canals and some of the earliest factories.

In the seventeenth century merchants in Europe had put up the money to start plantations. The food, equipment and supplies coming across the Atlantic had been worth more than the sugar and tobacco going back. In the eighteenth century cargoes to Europe were larger and more valuable than those to the Caribbean. Instead of borrowing, the wealthiest British planters were lending. The sums were huge. It was reckoned that in 1775 nearly £11 million went to the owners of Caribbean colonies living in Europe. Another calculation is that just over two-thirds of the year's profits for the whole of Jamaica went to Britain in 1773.

Fig. 14.2 *A nineteenth-century cartoon showing a wealthy plantation owner of the eighteenth century.*

Absentees

Many of the wealthiest planters used this money to become powerful in British society. They were the absentees who left their estates in the hands of attorneys and lived in England. Absentees built some of the finest English country houses and were often famed for the number of carriages and servants they could afford with still enough left to make their way in banking, business and, most important, in politics.

In eighteenth-century England only a few voters and sometimes single landowners could elect a man to the House of Commons. Most Members of Parliament simply bought their seats by bribing the electors or paying the landowner. Here was one use for the profits made in the Caribbean. Between 1730 and 1775, seventy absentee planters became MPs. Antigua alone produced twenty-two MPs, one lord mayor of London and nine absentees who had enough wealth to buy the title of lord or knight. The Beckford family, whose wealth came from their Jamaican plantations, had three brothers in Parliament at the same time. Two members of the family also became lord mayors of London.

The West India interest

These powerful absentees made up the most important part of what was known in Britain as the West India interest. Another part was made up of merchants who traded with the sugar colonies. Finally there were the men appointed by the colonial assemblies to be their agents in England and to press for changes in British law which would benefit the West Indies. The West India interest in Parliament was often successful in seeing that laws were passed to benefit the Caribbean colonies more than other parts of the British Empire or even Britain herself.

An example was the Sugar Duties Act of 1763. It set up a special force to stop French planters smuggling their molasses into Britain's thirteen colonies in North America. In return for the molasses, the British colonists sold cheap estate supplies to the French planters. The West India interest believed that this helped the French to sell their sugar more cheaply in Europe. The Sugar Duties Act was bitterly resented by British settlers in the thirteen colonies who had made businesses from trading with the French. To them it was a sign that Britain's Parliament paid more attention to the West India interest than to their needs. One American colony objected, saying:

> This Act [concerning Sugar and Molasses] was procured by the interest of the West India planters with no other view than to enrich themselves by obliging the northern Colonies to take their whole supply from them.

Problems for sugar

Weaknesses in the plantation system

When the Sugar Duties Act was passed, the West India interest seemed at the height of its power, but this was just the time when planters began to see signs that the golden age of sugar could soon end. The plantation system on most British islands was a hundred years old and many weaknesses were beginning to show up.

Most planters earned their living from a single crop. In a year when the profits from sugar were small they could not turn to another product to make up the gap in their income. As the plantations grew older the expenses of running them rose. Buildings had to be repaired and renewed. The first fields were often exhausted from a hundred years' cropping, and planters were faced with the cost of clearing the more difficult, hilly ground.

The slave system no longer seemed so cheap. Every year the number of disabled and old slaves grew. They produced very little but they had to be fed, clothed and housed. Thousands of pounds had to be spent on buying new slaves to replace them in the fields and mills. Yet few planters thought of switching to cheaper, labour-saving devices such as harrows and ploughs. Most believed that the slaves had to be burdened with heavy work for the sake of order, even if this meant raising the price of sugar to cover the increasing costs.

Planters who became absentees and lived in England added to the costs of the estates. Attorneys and managers had to be paid in the Caribbean. Very little of the profits earned by an absentee's plantations stayed in the colony. Few absentees showed any interest in improving the conditions of life in the islands. During the colonial period hardly any public roads, schools or hospitals were built. The West Indian islands became places for Englishmen to come, make money and leave. Those who stayed permanently in the Caribbean and had few connections with England were generally the less wealthy planters.

French competition

As the English planters faced these difficulties the French sugar islands were just entering their time of greatest prosperity. The French colonies were larger: St Domingue was greater in area than all six British islands combined. French planters paid only a 1 per cent export duty compared with the $4\frac{1}{2}$ per cent paid by their English rivals. Most of the costs of local government on the French islands were paid by France; the British planters had to pay for them with local taxation.

After France lost Canada she had money, ships and men to develop her West Indian

121

colonies. The cost of shipping and insurance fell and bankers became eager to lend money to planters at low rates and merchants sold them estate supplies at lower prices. Unemployed soldiers found work in the Caribbean building roads, irrigation systems, bridges and water mills. Over 40,000 hectares were artificially irrigated in St Domingue. The French were now able to export more sugar than the English and sell it at a lower price. The result was that refiners in France could sell sugar to almost any European country while the high price of English colonial sugar meant that English refiners could not find markets outside Britain.

The British planters' reply

To meet this French challenge the British planters increased production, especially in Grenada and Tobago. In Grenada the slave population rose from 12,000 in 1756 to 30,000 in 1776. Tobago had been almost deserted in 1763; only seven years later the island held 3,093 slaves and 238 whites, who had mostly come from the overcrowded Leewards. Nearly all of them borrowed the money to pay for clearing the fields and buy their first slaves and supplies. Production in Jamaica and the Leewards was also increased by clearing cane fields in areas which earlier had not been thought worth the expense. These planters too had to borrow the money.

It was soon obvious that the extra production would not save the planters. Sugar piled up on the English market and brought prices down. The average price of 38s 6d per hundredweight (50 kilograms) in 1763 fell to 35s between 1771 and 1775. The 3s fall was not enough to undercut the French, but it was a serious blow to planters who had borrowed money. In 1770 they owed between them £16m. (Compare this with total value of a year's sugar from Jamaica, which was about £1m.) The bankers and businessmen who had lent the money were quick to see that they might do better lending to planters and traders in the new parts of the British Empire.

In 1775 the planters suffered another blow. The thirteen British colonies in America opened war for their independence from Britain. The British navy stopped estate supplies from America reaching the Caribbean colonies. When France joined in on the side of the rebels, her warships stopped much of the British sugar reaching Europe.

In 1783 the British signed peace and allowed the colonies their independence as the United States of America. But the end of the war did not end the suffering on the Caribbean plantations. Britain refused to allow planters to buy supplies from the Americans even when they were needed to save lives. It was estimated that 15,000 slaves died in Jamaica between 1784 and 1787 'of famine or of disease contracted by scanty and unwholesome diet'. Some planters tried to trade illegally with the Americans and the British navy was sent to prevent this smuggling. Horatio Nelson, then a young naval officer, came to dislike the West Indian smugglers, calling them 'vagabonds' and 'as great rebels as the Americans'. In place of trade with the Americans, British officials encouraged Caribbean planters to buy from English colonists in Canada or from merchants in England. Estate supplies from both places were more expensive because of the greater distances.

In the end the British government slowly changed the orders against trade with the Americans. In 1794, American vessels were allowed to bring supplies direct to British ports in the Caribbean and elsewhere. But although Americans did return to trading, many of them had already found better markets in the French and Spanish islands. The cheap American estate supplies were now helping the competitors of the English sugar planters.

Attempts to reorganise

During the American War of Independence the assemblies on all the island colonies set up committees to find solutions to their great difficulties. The committees recommended that costs might be cut if the islands produced their own estate supplies. Planters and small farmers were encouraged to raise cattle to supply beef and working animals for the plantations. In Jamaica and Antigua unused salt pans were

Fig. 14.3 *Botanical gardens, such as these at Castleton, Jamaica, were used to cultivate new plants.*

opened so that local turtle and fish could be salted. New food crops were planted. Ackee trees were brought from West Africa in 1778. Mangoes arrived by accident in 1782 when a French ship carrying trees from Mauritius was captured by a British frigate. Captain Bligh's ship brought the first breadfruit trees from Tahiti in 1793. Funds were set aside to open botanical gardens where the plants could be grown and then passed on to planters.

The committees also suggested ways of setting the colonies free from the risks of depending on one crop. Cinnamon, clove, nutmeg and black pepper trees were planted. New coffee plantations were opened in Jamaica. Several planters in Barbados grew cotton in part of their cane fields. To increase the profits from sugar some owners tried new varieties of canes, such as the Bourbon and Otaheita, which were richer in sucrose. Cash prizes were offered for anyone who could improve the recovery of

sugar from the boiling and curing processes.

The attempts at reform had very little success. The eastern islands had little room for large-scale cattle raising. Slaves everywhere did not welcome the new foods, but insisted on their usual rations of wheat or corn flour and salted cod. The breadfruit was thought fit only for pigs until after emancipation.

It was found that the spice crops could not compete with cheaper spices which the British and Dutch took to Europe from the Far East. Only nutmeg became an important cash crop for Grenada. Jamaican coffee was successful, but only until large-scale plantations were opened in Brazil and Central America. For a while it seemed that cotton might be a profitable alternative to sugar. By 1790 the islands were supplying about 70 per cent of all cotton imported into Britain, but then English manufacturers began to import cheaper cotton from the southern United States. The improvements in sugar production were just as disappointing; the yields went up but the extra income was taken up by the cost of dearer estate supplies and the high interest repayments on loans.

Decline of the West India interest

By the end of the eighteenth century the old British Caribbean colonies were in a desperate position. The golden age of sugar had come to an end and these islands had lost their pride of place as the most favoured part of the British Empire. The West India interest began to lose its strong position in British politics. By the late eighteenth century new powerful groups were growing, such as the men who made fortunes from trading in India. Other Britons began to question the advantages which the planters had from the Navigation Acts. They had been passed a century before but they were still in force and made it difficult for the British to buy cheaper sugar from French colonies.

As we shall see in Chapter 16, the West India interest was able to put up only a weak fight against the campaigns which began in the 1770s to end the slave trade and slavery itself.

Assignments

1 *What problems did the British West Indian sugar planters make for themselves and which were outside of their control?*

2 *What steps were taken in your territory to solve the planters' problems in the late eighteenth century?*

3 *How do you think Britain reacted to the problems facing the planters at this time?*

4 *Document, with illustrations, the absentee management of the plantations in your area. What plantations did they own and what crop was their wealth based on?*

15 SLAVE COLONIES AND EUROPEAN CONFLICT

The Caribbean and the mainland in 1700

The map on page 120 shows European ownership of the Americas in 1700. For the next 115 years there was almost constant disagreement between the three main European powers, England, France and Spain. These conflicts led to wars, which lasted altogether for 48 of the years up to 1815. The wars had their main causes in European quarrels but rivalry in the Americas played a part. The wars had little effect on the most important eighteenth-century development which was the growth of societies divided between European plantocracies and African slaves. Yet the eighteenth-century history of most territories will include a time when it was a base for European seamen or soldiers, or when it changed hands either for a few years or up to the end of colonialism.

Wars and the asiento

To the Treaty of Utrecht, 1713

In 1700 Spain had a new king, the grandson of the French king, Louis XIV. The next year the new king granted France the asiento to carry slaves to the Spanish colonies. He also arranged for French warships to guard the Spanish fleets as they crossed the Atlantic. England saw the combined French and Spanish navies as a threat to her seapower in the Caribbean. At the same time, Austria and Holland had good reasons to fear that the alliance between France and Spain meant danger to their territories in Europe. They joined with England to fight Spain in the War of Spanish Succession (1702–13).

Each side sent fleets to the Caribbean and soldiers to garrison towns in their colonies. The main French bases were at Martinique and Guadeloupe while the British fleets used Port Royal in Jamaica and English Harbour in Antigua. The fleets were sent for defence rather than attack. Their main purpose was to stop the rival power from taking an undefended base. This defensive movement displeased French and English planters who each had hoped that war would lead to a chance to destroy the other's sugar trade. But they had to act on their own without support from their governments in Europe.

Planters from Barbados organised a raid against the French part of St Kitts. The French were deported to St Domingue and Guadeloupe. Another English expedition then raided Guadeloupe where they burnt cane fields, destroyed mills and carried off many slaves. The French on Martinique replied with raids on English plantations in St Kitts, Nevis and Monserrat. A joint attack by the French and Spanish drove the few English settlers from the Bahamas. The colonists also organised their own naval warfare. Each side gave commissions to captains to turn privateer and raid the other's merchant ships. In one year, French privateers captured 163 British merchant vessels.

In 1713 the war came to an end. Little had been decided in Europe, but the Treaty of Utrecht stated three things which were important for the Caribbean. France agreed that Britain should now own the whole of St Kitts. She also recognised that Britain owned Newfoundland, Nova Scotia and Hudson Bay. All these were a threat to the safety of French Canada. Thirdly, the Spanish took the asiento from France and gave it to Britain. At the same time Britain was allowed to send one merchant ship with small supply boats known as tenders to the yearly fair at Porto Bello.

Traders and garda-costas to 1750

British merchants used these rights as cover for much wider trading. Ships carrying slaves

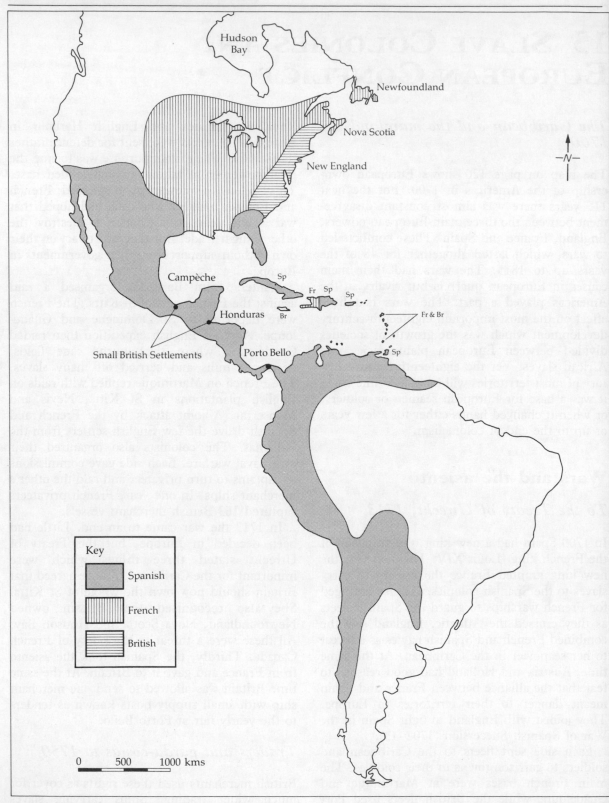

Map 25 *The Americas in 1700.*

under the asiento unloaded other goods as well. While the annual trading shop was anchored off Porto Bello it was reloaded at night from its tenders. Even more smuggling was carried out by merchants from the British islands, especially Jamaica. They took many goods to the mainland, including weak or old slaves whom they sold at cheap rates to Spanish settlers. They visited Campeche and Honduras where small settlements of English were cutting dyewoods and hardwoods which fetched good prices from British cloth and furniture makers. To the Spanish these settlements were illegal.

The Spanish fought back by allowing privately owned ships to become *garda-costas*. They could seize any British ship which was carrying produce from the Spanish colonies. Up to 1727 at least eighty-six British ships were captured and their cargoes sold as a reward for the garda-costa's crew. This led to demands in Britain for

war against Spain. For years the government tried to avoid war for fear it would damage Britain's legal trade with Spanish settlements.

In 1738 the opposition party brought Captain Jenkins to the British House of Commons to describe how his ear had been cut off by the crew of a garda-costa. He said they had told him to carry the ear, pickled in brandy, back to the English king. Captain Jenkins refused to remove his wig and it is very likely that the story was made up to swing opinion in favour of war against Spain. If so, it worked, for Britain declared war in 1739. The first five years of the war which followed were known as the 'War of Jenkins Ear'. In 1744 it widened into the War of Austrian Succession as other powers joined in. France once again fought on the Spanish side against Britain and Austria.

When peace was finally signed in the Treaty of Aix-La-Chapelle, Dominica, St Lucia, St

Fig. 15.1 *During the War of Jenkins Ear, the British fleet captured Porto Bello, 1739.*

Vincent and Tobago were all declared neutral islands and the French and English agreed not to colonise them. The first part of the Treaty was signed in 1748 and the final part in 1750. In the final part, Britain agreed to sell the slave asiento and the right to trade at Porto Bello back to Spain. It was the end of one cause of conflict in the Caribbean, although the English still smuggled goods into the Spanish Empire and their logwood settlements in Central America continued to grow slowly.

France and Britain compete for empires

The Seven Years War

After 1750 the main conflicts between European powers in the Americas were concerned more directly with rivalry between Britain and France. The first matter to be decided was ownership of North America. Here Britain had thirteen colonies on the eastern seaboard. Between 1700 and 1775 their population grew from under a third of a million to nearly two million. They had become the most important markets for goods made in Britain. In return, their products such as tobacco and timber were in great demand in Britain. In the 1750s the French began to build a line of forts starting in Canada and running behind the narrow strips of English colonies. This threat was matched by French pressure on English trading settlements in India. In 1756–63 the two countries fought the Seven Years War to decide these questions of empire.

By 1759 the British had gained the upper hand over the French on the American mainland. The British Prime Minister then ordered that the French West Indian islands should be captured so they could be kept to bargain with when the time came to make peace. The French were almost powerless to stop this. By 1761 the only French colony which Britain had not seized was St Domingue and even that was cut off from France by the British navy.

In the peace the most valuable islands were used as bargaining counters. The British handed them back in return for the whole of Canada. Britain also kept the French colony of Grenada and the Grenadines as well as three neutral islands, Tobago, St Vincent and Dominica. France took over the fourth neutral island, St Lucia.

In the Seven Years War, Britain had driven the French armies from India as well as Canada. At the peace in 1763 she ruled a world-wide empire with lands in India and the Far East as well as the Caribbean and North America. Only twenty years later this 'first British empire' had lost its thirteen colonies on the coast of America. It was a story in which the Caribbean sugar colonies could not escape being involved.

The thirteen colonies and the sugar islands

Between about 1700 and 1775 the Caribbean had many close links with the mainland British colonies, which were governed in a similar way to the islands with governors, councils and elected assemblies. But the closest connection was through trade. The mainland colonists made their living as timber-cutters, farmers, manufacturers, ship-builders, and traders. A large part of the goods they produced were sold as estate supplies to the sugar plantations in the Caribbean.

The key to the trade was the huge quantities of molasses which were left after the cane had been milled for export to Europe. On most plantations it was simply stored in large tanks. Merchant ships from the mainland toured the islands, calling in at plantations and filling hogsheads with molasses from the tank. With the money they earned by selling the molasses, planters bought goods for their estates.

In 1771 New York imported over two million litres of molasses and Boston about a million. Much of this was turned into rum and sold throughout the American colonies or exported to England. The table shows the goods exported from these two ports in the same year. Apart from Boston and New York, traders set out for

New York		Boston	
Tallow candles:	64,500 lbs (29,200 kg)	Whalefat candles:	55,710 lbs (25,230 kg)
Lard:	44,140 lbs (20,900 kg)	Bricks:	341,800
Corn:	63,319 bushels	Shook hogsheads:	12,539
Sugar:	4,362 lbs (1,975 kg)	Hoops for hogsheads:	513,580
Bread and flour:	3,250 tons (3,302,000 kg)	Dried fish:	57,472 quinals
Butter:	35,100 lbs (15,400 kg)	Pickled fish:	8,386 barrels

the Caribbean from about a dozen other important American ports.

Colonial revolt

After the Seven Years War the British government tried to make the American colonists pay a share of the costs of defeating the French. They aimed to do it by taxing legal documents. In future they were to be written on paper which had a stamp to show that the tax had been paid. The American colonists refused to pay, saying that their assemblies alone had the right to demand new taxes. On this point the Caribbean settlers agreed with the Americans. In St Kitts and Nevis, British colonists rioted against the tax duties and destroyed the stamped paper. The British government gave way over the stamp tax and tried to collect the money through import duties on all lead, paper and tea imported by the colonies.

The colonists still objected and rioted against the duties. The British withdrew them, except for the one on tea. When the British East India Company tried to unload tea at Boston, the citizens dumped the cargo into the sea. The British decided to punish the people of Boston by closing the assembly of their colony, Massachusetts, and ruling it directly. Again the Caribbean colonists supported the Americans. The Barbados and Jamaica assemblies sent protests to the English king.

Fig. 15.2 *American colonists burning paper carrying the tax stamp.*

The assemblies change sides

But in 1775 the British government sent an army to force the Americans to obey the regulations. The colonists decided to fight for independence. This move brought about a change of opinion in the Caribbean colonies. More West Indians had family or trading connections with England than with America. The planters also feared to lose their special position within the British Empire. Their prosperity would collapse if rebellion in the thirteen colonies meant they could not sell sugar to Britain.

The island colonists also faced the unpleasant fact that their white population was much smaller than the mainland's. They felt they needed British soldiers and warships to protect them from foreign invasions and from their slaves. So, instead of protests, the island assemblies rushed to send petitions to England, stating their loyalty. The Jamaican assembly's petition made their reasons clear:

129

Weak and feeble as this colony is from its very small number of white inhabitants, and its peculiar situation from the encumbrance of more than two hundred thousand slaves, it cannot be supposed that we now intend, or ever could have intended, resistance to Britain.

The planters were forced to admit that they needed the protection of the British army and navy. Yet the islands paid a heavy price for their loyalty during eight years of war that followed.

The War of American Independence, 1775–83

France, Spain and Holland joined the war on the side of the Americans. Several other European nations objected to British attempts to stop and search all ships which might be carrying arms to the Americans. They signed an agreement of 'armed neutrality' to fight back when ordered to stop by the British.

In the Caribbean these forces were joined by American privateers who attacked British shipping from bases in the Dutch, Danish and French islands. Their activities caused great hardship to the British islands. In the first year of the war the quantity of sugar shipped to Europe fell by a half. Estate supplies, which had come mostly from North America, quickly became scarce and their prices rose. The cost of grain is said to have risen by 400 per cent by the end of 1777. Insurance rates on British ships in the Caribbean rose from 7 per cent of their cargo's value to over 20 per cent. After France joined the war, it became safe only to travel in convoys.

Planters tried to grow local provisions to replace those which fell into the hands of the enemy, but most of the crops failed after hurricanes ripped through the islands in 1780 and 1781. In the Leewards there were long droughts in the periods between the hurricanes.

Several islands were captured in the war. Dominica was taken by the French in 1778. The British replied by taking St Lucia in the same year, but in 1779 they could not stop the French capture of St Vincent and Grenada. In 1780 Sir George Rodney was put in charge of British operations in the Caribbean. He had quick successes against the Dutch, capturing their poorly defended island colonies and their Guyana settlements. Then, in 1782, the British army under General Cornwallis surrendered at Yorktown. Britain was now powerless in North America, and both the Spanish and French fleets opened full-scale war in the Caribbean.

The French fleet quickly retook St Eustatius and the Guyana colonies, following this with the capture of Tobago in 1781 and St Kitts, Nevis and Montserrat in 1782. Meanwhile the Spanish had taken Florida and some of the Bahamas. The two allies were then ready for a joint expedition to capture Jamaica. The island was saved by Admiral Rodney, who caught up with the joint fleet as it passed by the Saintes Islands between Dominica and Guadeloupe. Only seven of the Spanish-French ships were taken, but the rest of the invasion fleet was scattered. The Battle of the Saintes saved the West Indies from further attack. In the following year, all who had taken part in the war signed the Treaty of Versailles (1783). The treaty recognised the independence of the thirteen colonies which

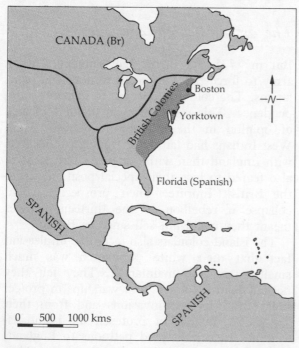

Map 26 *North America and the Caribbean at the time of the War of American Independence.*

CANADA (Br)

Boston

Yorktown

British Colonies

—N—

Florida (Spanish)

SPANISH

SPANISH

0   500   1000 kms

became known as the United States of America. In the Caribbean, all the territories were returned to their pre-war owners except that France kept Tobago and gave St Bartholomew to Sweden in return for an agreement that French ships could trade in Swedish ports.

Trinidad and Guyana

The French Wars, 1793–1815

Only six years after the Treaty of Versailles, revolution broke out in France in 1789. Two years later the country was a republic and in 1793 Britain went to war with the new government. The wars lasted until 1802 when the two countries signed a truce, which lasted only a year. Fighting started again, this time with Britain as the leader in a European coalition against the French emperor Napoleon Bonaparte. It went on until the British and Prussians defeated Napoleon at the battle of Waterloo in 1815.

The greatest change which came to the Caribbean during these French Revolutionary Wars and Napoleonic Wars was the independence of the first free black state, the French colony of St Domingue which was renamed Haiti. Chapter 17 tells that important story and how, at one stage, Britain tried to seize St Domingue at the height of the black revolt in 1793. They failed to take the island, but by 1795 Britain had captured all the other French Caribbean colonies apart from Guadeloupe. Once again, they would mostly be used as bargaining counters when peace finally came. A more important outcome of the wars was the gain of Trinidad and Guyana, along with St Lucia.

The Guyanese colonies

In 1795 the French armies occupied Holland. The Dutch government invited their English allies to take their colonies rather than see them fall into the hands of France. This is how Britain became ruler of Cape Colony which grew into the modern state of South Africa. In the Caribbean, Holland had two colonies on the coast of Guyana: Berbice and Demerara-Essequibo. In April 1796 the British General Abercomby appeared with a fleet off Stabroek and landed British troops to take over the two colonies. There was no resistance, for the Dutch governors did not wish their colonies to fall into French hands. In any case about two-thirds of the white population was British. Most of them had migrated from the sugar islands to the three tiny settlements on the Berbice, Essequibo and Demerara rivers during 1742–72 when L. van Gravesande was the Dutch governor.

Fig. 15.3 *A painting of about 1830 showing a plantation on the west coast of the Demerara estuary in British Guiana. Notice the low-lying land and the use of windmills.*

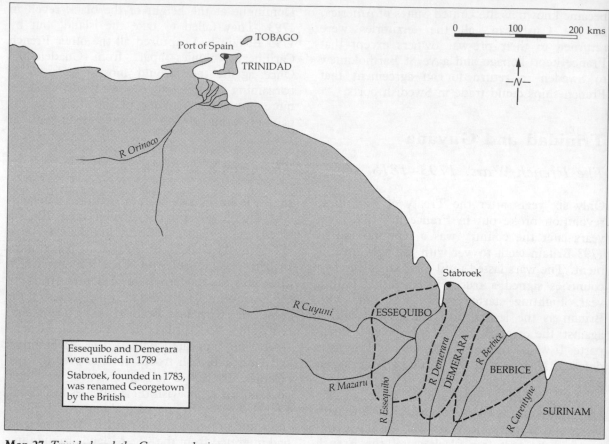

Map 27 *Trinidad and the Guyana colonies.*

Before his day the colonies had developed very slowly from the 1630s when Dutch planters had first settled there. The Dutch had been far more successful as traders than planters. Yet, the Dutch had provided the skill in drainage which made it possible to clear the long narrow plantations which ran from the bush through to the low-lying land on the estuaries of the three main rivers. The buildings of Stabroek, too, were built in the Dutch style. Stabroek had been founded in 1783 when the Dutch took their colony back after a brief French occupation in the War of American Independence. It had become the capital of the colony of Demerara-Essequibo when the two colonies were united in 1789. At the time of the Treaty of Paris, which ended the wars against Napoleon, British agreed to buy the two colonies (as well as the Cape of Good Hope) from the Dutch. They were renamed British Guiana and Stabroek became Georgetown, the new colony's capital.

Trinidad

Spain had joined the war on France's side so, after he had taken the Guyanese colonies, Abercomby was ordered to seize the Spanish colony of Trinidad. He arrived in Port of Spain with eighteen ships and landed 7,650 men. Against him, the Spanish governor, Chacon, had four ships and only 500 fit men. He surrendered the island without a shot being fired.

Like the Guyanese colonies, Trinidad had developed only very slowly. Before the arrival of Governor Don José Maria Chacon in 1784 its population, not including Amerindians, was never more than a few hundred. In that year the Spanish government issued a decree which allowed non-Spanish Roman Catholics to immigrate. This had attracted planters from the

French sugar islands and also French-speaking free coloureds. In 1797 the island's population was 17,643. Of these 10,000 were slaves. Most of the 2,086 whites were French, but for every free white there were two free coloureds.

In 1802 France and Britain signed the Peace of Amiens. Most of the Treaty was simply an agreement to have a truce in the fighting, and return all conquered colonies to their former owners, except for Trinidad which was to be kept by Britain.

The Treaty of Paris

As soon as war broke out again in 1803, the Royal Navy immediately began to re-occupy the overseas colonies of France and the countries which lay under her rule. By 1810 she had occupied all European colonies in the West Indies except those of Spain. Meanwhile the British navy was blockading all the main European ports so that France and her conquered empire were cut off from overseas trade. When the Peace of Paris was signed the British had such complete control of the seas that they could dictate which colonies they would keep. They already owned Trinidad from the Peace of Amiens. They now added Tobago as well as St Lucia from France and Demerara-Essequibo and Berbice from Holland.

Crown colony government

The British government was not ready to allow the new colonies in Trinidad and Guyana the same law-making assemblies that ruled the older sugar islands. It feared that trouble could break out in the colonies, which would involve the British in heavy costs in men and money. For instance, both colonies had white populations divided between different European peoples: Spanish, French and English in Trinidad; Dutch and English in Guyana. As well as quarrelling between Europeans, there was a fear of revolt from the 60,000 slaves in Guyana. In Trinidad there were so many free coloureds that, even if only a small proportion had been wealthy enough to claim the right to vote, they might have controlled an assembly on the island.

Another reason was that Britain abolished the slave trade in 1807. This particularly annoyed planters who had moved to the new colonies in the hope of starting plantations in the huge areas of unfarmed land. Planter assemblies would have tried hard to find ways of importing slaves illegally. So the power to make laws for Trinidad was kept in the hands of the British government. It became a crown colony, ruled by a governor who took his orders on all matters of importance from the Colonial Office in London. The colony had no assembly, only a council whose members were all appointed by the governor and which could only advise him.

Crown colony government was then forced on the Guyanese colonies but with some differences. The governor was advised by a Court of Policy which had grown up under Dutch rule. Planters in each district were allowed to elect men to sit on a *Kiezer*, or college of electors. The electors then put forward eight names and the governor chose four of them to sit on the Court of Policy with four of his senior officials.

At the end of the French Wars crown colony government was applied only to Trinidad, Guyana and St Lucia. Later in the nineteenth century the other colonial assemblies had their law-making powers replaced by crown colony government.

Assignments

1 *What effect did the wars of the eighteenth century have on:*
   i) England; ii) the planters in the British colonies; iii) the slaves in the British colonies?

2 *What changes took place in Guyana and Trinidad when they became British colonies?*

3 *What legacy for today's Caribbean was created by the events of the eighteenth and early nineteenth centuries?*

16 RESISTANCE AND REVOLT

Resistance

No one opposed slavery more than the slaves themselves. The whole period of plantation slavery in the British Caribbean is one of revolts. The first important one broke out in Barbados in 1675 only a few years after the planters there had learned about sugar from the Dutch. The last took place in Jamaica in 1831–2, just a year before the British government abolished slavery. Over the two centuries, there was daily resistance by African men and women as they tried on the one hand to keep control over their own lives and on the other to sabotage the prosperity of the Europeans.

Passive resistance

There were countless small ways in which slaves could stand up for themselves. Newly arrived Africans would simply not hear when they were given an order by a master calling them by the new name he had given. Slaves who had been longer in the Caribbean knew many more ways. They could exaggerate injuries which made them unfit for work. Tools or machinery could be damaged and cattle or horses maimed. A skilled farmer could damage the roots of crops without being found out. Perhaps above all, the Africans could prevent Europeans really understanding them.

Planters and their staff often described the slaves as unintelligent, careless, and dishonest. Of course, this showed their prejudice but it was also often a sign that the slaves had been successful in concealing their skill as farmers and mechanics or their understanding of a European's orders. Sometimes they were able to use their master's belief in their simplicity to poke fun at them even in their hearing:

Hi de Buckra, hi
Massa W-f-e de come ober de sea

Wid him rogueish heart and him tender look
And while he palaver and preach him book
At the negro girl he'll winkie hime yeye
Hi! de Buckra, hi!

Women had just as much skill as men in resistance. A favourite means was to delay weaning their children until as near their second birthday as they could. When masters or overseers tried to order them back to work they would reply that this could lead to the death of the child – which would mean one less slave in future years. Women also played a full part in concealing slaves who broke estate rules and visited other plantations.

Active resistance

At times slaves used more direct ways of fighting slavery. Some tried to poison their overseers and planters came to fear poisoning almost as much as they feared rebellion. Poison was suspected whenever a white died suddenly, although the cause was more likely to be heavy drinking or poor medical care. In his history of Jamaica, Edward Long listed over a dozen poisons which masters should be on their guard against. Monk Lewis told the story of a Jamaican attorney. He was:

> . . . brought to the doors of death by a cup of coffee and only escaped a second time by his civility, in giving the beverage, prepared for himself, to two young book-keepers, to whom it proved fatal.

Some slaves killed themselves rather than submit to slavery. Newly arrived Igbos often did this and gained a reputation for cowardliness from the Europeans. The account of Igbo society on page 86 suggests that the real reason was far more likely to be that they were used to governing themselves. Suicide was probably a way of striking back at the Europeans who had taken away this proud independence.

Marronage

Running away

Many slaves simply ran away. In the small, densely populated colonies most runaways headed for the crowded port towns and tried to get hold of false certificates of freedom which would make it possible to hide among the free coloured people. In the bigger colonies slaves could make their way to the interior where they joined other fugitives in one of the hidden runaway villages. People living in these villages had to be ready to leave their plantings and live-stock at a moment's notice if discovered by the militia or troops. But there were always slaves who chose the uncertainties of freedom to the misery of slavery. As early as 1519 slaves in Hispaniola built their first runaway villages. As late as 1819, only twelve years before emanci-pation, the militia in Trinidad was regularly called out to destroy runaway villages which had grown up since 1802 when English masters had first brought their slaves to the colony.

Runaways stood little chance in the small colonies. In 1684, the Antiguan assembly posted a reward of £2 10shillings for a live runaway and £1 for a dead one. Three years later there were fewer than fifty fugitives left to 'excite and stir up the Negroes to forsake their masters . . . and . . . to make themselves masters of the country'. In the larger colonies some runaway villages became too strong or too well hidden to be so easily destroyed. Out of this grew one of the most important forms of resistance to slavery in all the colonies – marronage.

The Maroons

The word is used to describe the life-style of runaway slaves who established their own inde-pendent communities. The most successful created something more than a simple hideout in the mountains or bush. They built perma-nent villages where they ruled themselves under their chosen leaders, grew their own food, provided their own medical care and often traded with other Maroon groups. In 1784 a recaptured runaway slave in French Guiana described the Maroon village where he had shel-tered. It was a way of life which combined African skills and traditions with some new ones learned in the Caribbean. Family life seems to have been respected. It was an alternative to slavery which Africans on plantations anywhere in the Caribbean would have understood and longed for:

> there are twenty-seven houses and three open sheds – ten in the old gardens which had been cleared several years earlier and sixteen in those cleared last year . . . . inhabited by twenty-nine strong male Negroes, twenty-two female Negroes who are also fully fit, nine Negro boys, and twelve Negro girls.
>
> Louis noted . . . Couacou takes care of wounds as does Andre and that Couachy repairs the muskets.
>
> That Sebastien and Jeanneton bleed people.
>
> That Bernard, nicknamed Couacou, baptises with holy water and recites daily prayer.
>
> That all the Negroes and Negresses are equipped with axes and machettes.
>
> That the said Andre, Louise, Remy and Felicite . . . are all being treated with herbs in their houses . . . It is Couacou who is the herbalist . . . .
>
> That whenever land has to be cleared, everyone works together and once a large area has been burned, everyone is allotted a plot according to the needs of the family . . .

Cimarrons

The first runaways to set up their own commu-nities were some of the first African slaves taken to the Spanish island of Hispaniola. They fled into the mountains and intermarried with Arawaks. The Spanish described them as *Cimarron*, the Spanish for dweller on the moun-tain top. The Cimarrons fought the Spanish until 1533 when they signed a treaty which gave them a large preserve in Hispaniola. The Span-iards promised not to attack this preserve and in return, the Cimarrons agreed to hand over any new runaway slaves.

By the end of the sixteenth century there were Cimarron groups on all the Spanish terri-tories. They were a powerful force on Puerto Rico after most whites there left to conquer the mainland. Cimarrons were even stronger on the isthmus of Panama. One of their towns there was said to have 217 houses.

Maroons in Jamaica

The French changed cimarron to 'marron' and the English version was 'maroon'. The first time that British colonists met marronage was in Jamaica. When they invaded in 1656, the Spanish released slaves and allowed them to link up with the Maroons already in the interior. Chapter 6 describes how they fought a guerilla war against the English until Juan de Bolas signed the peace treaty which allowed the maroons to settle in a small preserve in the Cockpit country. Another Maroon leader, Juan de Serras, fought on. No one knows how many slaves ran off to join him but there were certainly large numbers. In 1673 there was a slave rebellion and at least 300 slaves from St Anne's parish joined de Serras's mountain settlements.

By the 1730s Maroons had built permanent villages at Trelawney Town, Accompong and Crawford Town. Nanny Town was founded by Nanny, an Ashanti woman who was an important religious and political leader of the Maroons in the 1730s. For most of the time they had little or no contact with the European-owned plantations. But whenever planters cleared new estates near the Maroon territory the two ways of life came into conflict. Slaves on the new estates could flee more easily to join the Maroons. For their part, Maroons often raided the plantations. The Jamaica assembly sent troops to try to overrun the Maroons. This fighting of the early 1730s became known as the First Maroon War.

The war ended in 1739 when it was clear that the Maroons could not be driven from their strongholds. The English agreed to a treaty similar to the one signed by the Cimarrons and the Spanish in Hispaniola. Captain Cudjoe, leader of the Trelawney Town Maroons, was

Fig. 16.1 *Trelawney Town, in the eighteenth century, when it was the largest Maroon village in Jamaica.*

the first to sign. He and his people were given a 600-hectare preserve in which they could make their own laws and choose their own leaders. The Maroons agreed to stop raiding plantations, to return runaways and to help the militia put down slave revolts. Two white commissioners were also allowed to live in the village 'in order to maintain friendly correspondence'. Soon after, the Maroons in Accompong, Crawford Town and Nanny Town signed similar treaties.

The Second Maroon War

In 1795 the Trelawney Town Maroons had several reasons for being discontented with the British. They had sent a new commissioner, Captain Craskell, who ordered two Maroons to be flogged for stealing pigs from a white planter. Maroons did not object to the punishment but to the fact that it was carried out by a black overseer of a slave prison watched by black prisoners who were runaway slaves handed over by the Maroons. They ordered Captain Craskell to leave Trelawney Town. British officials in the parish agreed that he should be replaced by a commissioner acceptable to the Maroons. However they were overruled by the island's new governor, Lord Balcarres. He feared that giving way to the Maroons might encourage them to lead a full-scale black revolt of the sort that had broken out in St Domingue. (See Chapter 17.)

Balcarres sent troops to crush the Trelawney Town settlement. A few of the older Maroons surrendered but the rest ambushed the British forces. The Second Maroon War followed. General Walpole tried to pin the Maroons down by building a chain of army posts around their territory. He sent for hunting dogs from Cuba to help in tracking down Maroons. They were never used as the Maroons agreed to peace. Sadly, that was not the end of the story. General Walpole agreed that Maroons who surrendered in ten days would not be executed or shipped from the island. When he realised that most could not reach his forces in that time he extended the deadline. But the Jamaica assembly overruled him and said that the 500

Fig. 16.2 *A treaty between British officers and Maroons. Note how many Maroons appear to be wearing distinctive head-ties, which suggests they might be Muslim. Why do you think they are wearing so little clothing?*

latecomers should be sent to the British settlement in Nova Scotia. There they suffered greatly from the cold and refused to do much work. The Nova Scotia government did not want to pay for their upkeep and, after four years, the survivors were shipped to Sierra Leone in Africa.

After the Second Maroon War, the Maroon villages and the slave plantations existed side by side as had been agreed in the 1739 Treaty. The Maroons would not shelter runaways but this did not stop slaves fleeing and setting up new illegal villages like Me-No-Sen-You-No-Come in the Cockpits. There were always slaves willing to take the risks of freeing themselves.

The Bush Negroes in Guyana

Maroons were just as successful in the Guyanese colonies of the French, Dutch and English. Nearly all the plantations were on the coast or the banks of rivers just before they reached the sea. The wet marshes and tangled jungle behind made excellent hiding places for the Maroons' free villages. From these hiding places they got their name of 'Bush Negroes'. Today this has an offensive sound, suggesting a wild life, but most of these Maroons set up stable village communities.

The first runaways escaped from plantations set up by Lord Willoughby, the governor of Barbados who fled to Surinam in 1651. This explains why the creole spoken by the Bush Negroes and all black Surinamers had an English base, although most of the later runaways came from Dutch plantations. In the eighteenth century the death rate among slaves in Surinam was higher than even on the French and British islands. So many replacements were brought to the colony that 90 per cent of the slaves on many plantations had been born in Africa. Such recent memories of freedom led many to risk the torture given to captured runaways and try to make their way to join the free villages.

From their hidden homes the Bush Negroes raided the European plantations and forced the Dutch to send expeditions into the interior to attempt to crush them. These expeditions were costly in soldiers' lives and probably helped future runaways, for the Europeans took slaves with them who thus learned of the pathways through the bush. Rather than continue with the wars the Dutch governor made treaties in 1761 and 1767 with the two main groups of Bush Negroes. The treaties were modelled on those with the Jamaican Maroons and gave the Bush Negroes freedom in return for an agreement to return any new runaways. The Bush Negroes promised not to approach nearer the European settlements than a two-day journey by foot or ten hours by boat. A Dutch official known as 'post-holder' was to live in the village of each Bush Negro chief.

The treaties closed the south of Surinam to further runaways, but this did not stop slaves making their way to the east towards the borders with French Guiana. Others fled from the Dutch plantations in Demerara-Essequibo and Berbice in modern Guyana. Their new villages in the interior were built on circular pieces of ground cleared of bush. The huts were hidden by planting fruit trees, yams and plantains and the whole area was then defended by a wide ditch filled with water which covered sharpened stakes. False tracks were laid to lead enemies away from the underwater firm paths into the village.

Revolts

The first slave revolt took place in Hispaniola in 1522, only very shortly after the first Africans were brought to the island. From that time until emancipation there were revolts against slavery at least every few years. The most common were desperate protests against harsh conditions and often affected only small areas in a colony. For example, Barbados had revolts in 1675, 1686, 1692 and 1702. The most important reason was that planters failed to provide food, clothing and other supplies for their fast growing numbers. The 1754 rising in Crawford Town, Jamaica, was another protest against harsh treatment. Some revolts took place simply because slaves were given a chance to make their protest. Africans on one plantation in Jamaica revolted when the estate was cut off by flood waters and they knew troops could not reach them.

Such revolts had little chance of success. All European colonies kept militia forces to deal with slave risings. When slaves controlled the whole Danish island of St John for ten months they were finally defeated by troops sent from French Martinique. Sooner or later, and generally sooner, there would be enough trained men, some of them on horseback and all with muskets, to deal with a rising. This could happen even when a slave leader aimed to take over the whole colony. In 1760 an African chief, Tacky, planned a rising carefully with Ashanti slaves. Their aim was said to be a total massacre of the whites and to make Jamaica a black colony.

Tacky's rebellion began when a small party stole into a fort, seized muskets and set off across the estates killing white colonists and adding hundreds of slaves to their band. They might have gone on to further successes if a slave had not spread the alarm. Within hours, militia were riding to meet them. The rebels fought bravely but most of them soon gave up and tried to slip back to their estates. Tacky and some followers fought on until they were killed by Maroons.

There were clear signs that Tacky was not alone in his desire to overthrow European rule. While he was being hunted in the mountains, other groups of Coramantines (as Europeans called the Ashanti Africans) were rebelling in different parts of the island. It was months before all slave resistance was put down. By that time 300–400 Africans and 60 Europeans were dead.

Cuffy's rebellion

Even more serious was the 1763 rebellion led by the slave Cuffy in the Dutch colony of Berbice. Like Tacky, Cuffy was an Ashanti and his revolt strengthened the European belief that the Ashanti were natural rebels. Its background may have been the harsh treatment of slaves. Their owners saved money by not importing enough supplies to feed them properly. Many estates had absentee owners who left cruel overseers in charge. However, many of Cuffy's followers aimed at far more than protest at bad conditions. They wanted freedom and the chance to rule themselves in all or part of the colony.

Fig. 16.3 *Cuffy, Guyana's national hero, appears on a commemorative coin in 1970.*

The rebellion began in February 1763, when Cuffy led his followers to seize plantations along the Canje river. A month later they had reached the Berbice river (see Map 27, page 132). Cuffy began to call himself Governor of the Slaves and it seemed as if he might soon rule the whole colony. Some Europeans were then ready to abandon Berbice. They forced the Dutch governor to agree to this but he delayed, hoping that re-inforcements would come. In April a British ship arrived with 100 soldiers and the governor was able to take over a plantation on the Berbice river and turn it into a stronghold.

Cuffy then wrote to the governor suggesting that they divided the colony. The Dutch could keep the coast while the Africans would have the interior. Again the governor delayed by saying that he would ask the government in Holland to agree. In the meantime help came from the next-door colony of Demerara. The governor there, Van Gravesande, organised a counter-attack. Two ships came from Holland and another ship with a hundred soldiers from Barbados. At the same time Van Gravesande sent officers to lead an Indian force to attack Cuffy's troops from the rear.

Cuffy tried to regain the upper hand by attacking the plantation stronghold on the Berbice river. The attack failed and Cuffy faced a challenge to his leadership from one of his deputies. In May he committed suicide. It was the beginning of the end. The Europeans and their Indian allies were closing in. By the end of October 1763 the main revolt had been crushed as the rebel slaves were either killed or fled for their lives into the forest.

Revolts after Cuffy

Like Tacky in Jamaica, Cuffy was a recently captured African. Some Europeans drew from this fact the message that the greatest danger of revolt came from such Africans rather than 'creole' slaves who had been born in the Caribbean. There might be some truth in that. Some creole slaves remained loyal to the planters during Cuffy's rebellion and it was possibly a creole who betrayed Tacky. However, it may be just as likely that Cuffy failed because he tried to negotiate with the governor rather than leading the all-out war to take the whole colony that some of his followers wanted.

Whatever the truth, it was certainly the case that the main nineteenth-century rebellions were led by creoles. The three most important were in Barbados in 1816, Demerara in 1823 and Jamaica in 1831. All took place after Britain abolished the slave trade so that no new Africans were brought to her colonies. They also had a different aim from Cuffy. He fought for a colony with a separate homeland for the Africans. The nineteenth-century rebels wanted to hasten the day when they and all slaves in British colonies would be given their freedom by the government in England.

Assignments

1 *In what ways did the slaves show themselves to be the most militant opponents of slavery?* or: *'No one opposed slavery more than the slaves themselves.' Discuss.*

2 *Read the section in this chapter sub-headed Marronage and answer the following questions:*
   a) *Give examples of as many independent communities of runaway slaves as you can.*
   b) *In what ways would these communities be 'independent'?.*
   c) *Suggest reasons why 'all the Negroes and Negresses are equipped with axes and machettes.'*

3 *In what ways were the Maroons in Jamaica and the Bush Negroes in Guyana similar?*

4 *Select any one slave revolt: i) analyse its causes; ii) describe the course of the revolt; iii) examine the repercussions and consequences of the revolt.*

5 *Look at Fig. 16.1. What does it suggest about Maroon life? In which ways would this be different from the lives of the slaves on the plantation? How does the picture give a different impression than Fig. 16.2?*

17 THE HAITIAN REVOLUTION

1789 in St Domingue and France

The French islands, like the British, were shaped most of all by the sugar plantations. Yet there were some differences. One was that sugar and slavery had developed a little later than in the British islands. In 1789 French planters were making much more profit than their British competitors. They were shipping slaves in much larger numbers. In some years as many as 40,000 were taken to St Domingue. Most went to large plantations. Big estates, with many new slaves to be 'broken in', meant that conditions for Africans were harsher than on the British islands.

The main wealth of the French islands was in the hands of its plantocracy, which had many absentees like the British. Yet the French planters had less control over the government of their islands. They had no assemblies until 1787. Then they were set up with the power only to advise, not to make laws. On the British islands the few colonial officials were often resisted by the settlers. In the French colonies there were many royal officials to enforce the countless regulations made in France. They were in endless disagreement with the planters who continually pressed for the right to govern themselves. Sometimes the officials had the support of the poor whites, or petits blancs, the shopkeepers and craftsmen who made up a much larger group than on the British islands. These poor whites often resented the great wealth of the planters.

Many of the free people of colour on the French islands were far wealthier than those in the British colonies. French laws allowed them to own unlimited amounts of property and a large number actually became masters of plantations and slaves. Yet, however wealthy, the French free coloureds resented the fact that they were denied equality with whites. They were not allowed to join the colonial militias, wear European dress, play European games or meet together for feasts or wedding celebrations. Nor could they use the European titles of Monsieur and Madame.

Each group on the French islands felt the others to be its enemy. The planters hated the officials, despised the poor whites, distrusted the growing wealth of coloureds and feared the slaves. The coloureds and poor whites wanted the privileges of the planters. The slaves, especially on St Domingue, had revolted several times and were ready to do so again. This was the uneasy situation when revolution broke out in France in 1789.

The French Revolution

The background to the French Revolution lay in the sharp social divisions of the country. The noble families and the leaders of the powerful and wealthy Church had many privileges. They paid no taxes and yet often gave little service to the State. Their wealth and privileges were resented by the millions of French peasants and by middle-class lawyers, officials and merchants. When the French government became bankrupt an ancient form of parliament, known as

Fig. 17.1 *On 14 July 1789 the people of Paris broke into the Bastille, a tower which was said to be used by the king as a gaol for political prisoners.*

141

the 'Estates-General', was called in 1789, its first meeting for 175 years. At the meeting, the middle-class leaders demanded changes in the government of the country and the abolition of the privileges of the nobility and Church. The king gave way and the revolutionary members of the Estates-General turned themselves into a National Assembly, the real rulers of France.

By 1791 the king and queen were prisoners, many noblemen had fled the country, the city of Paris was in revolutionary hands and the Church's lands and other properties had been seized. The National Assembly issued the Declaration of Rights of Man which stated that 'men are born free and equal in rights'. The watchwords of France's new revolutionary leaders were 'Liberty! Equality! and Fraternity!' (brotherhood).

The French Wars

To many people in Europe the idea of Liberty, Equality and Fraternity brought hope of a better and more just life; to blacks and coloureds in America it gave the hope of freedom. But the kings and ruling families of other European countries feared the spread of revolution to their lands. In 1792 war broke out between France and her European neighbours and these 'Revolutionary Wars' lasted until 1802.

For the first period of the wars the most important French revolutionary leaders were the Jacobins. Led by Robespierre, the Jacobins were fanatical in trying to build a new society based on Liberty, Equality and Fraternity. At the same time they had their rivals executed at the guillotine in what their enemies called a 'reign of terror'. Eventually other French leaders sickened of this and overthrew the Jacobins. Power then passed step by step into the hands of the French army, and especially to one of its most successful generals, Napoleon Bonaparte.

In 1799, Napoleon Bonaparte seized control of the government of France and until 1814 he was the sole ruler of France, first as consul then as emperor. At the beginning of his rule he needed time to strengthen his position at home.

After defeating most of his enemies, he made peace with them in 1801 and 1802. War broke out again in 1803 and the 'Napoleonic Wars' continued until 1814. In that year, and again in 1815, Napoleon was defeated in battle and his empire came to an end. The events which took place in Europe between 1789 and 1814 had a profound influence upon the Caribbean region in general, and upon the French Caribbean islands in particular.

Three revolts

The planters' revolt

In the Caribbean the planters were the first to revolt. The governors of St Domingue and the other French islands ordered them not to send representatives to the Estates-General. But the planters disobeyed and sent six delegates to the meeting in Paris. In the Estates-General they demanded that the colonial assemblies set up in 1787 be granted the power to make laws like those in the British islands. The royal government refused to listen to this request and the planters joined with other members of the Estates-General who took part in the overthrow of the French government. They became members of the new governing body of France, the National Assembly. On 2 March 1790, the National Assembly granted the West Indian assemblies the right to make their own laws.

The coloured revolt on St Domingue

The planters had scored a victory over the old royal government of France and its officials in the Caribbean. But the free coloureds feared that the planters would use their new powers to pass even more repressive racist laws. They began to organise their own protection. In Paris they were helped by an abolitionist society, *Les Amis des Noirs* – the Friends of Black People. Members of Les Amis des Noirs argued that the revolutionary slogans of Liberty, Equality and Fraternity should apply to black just as much as white men. But, in 1790, the National Assembly was not prepared to listen to this plea. A young coloured living in Paris, Vincent

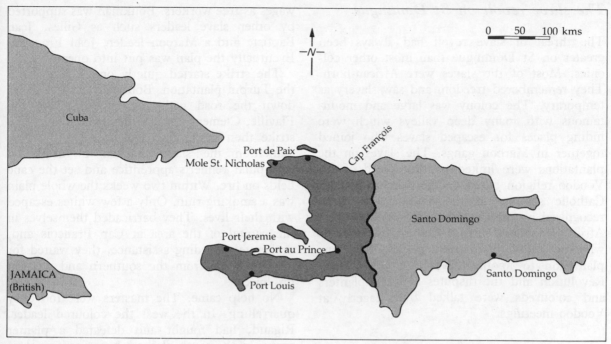

Map 28 *St Domingue.*

Ogé, petitioned members of the National Assembly asking them to grant free coloureds the right to be represented in the colonial assemblies.

The National Assembly refused and Ogé left France to lead a coloured revolt against the planters in St Domingue. He stopped first in England where he was given help and money by the abolitionist, Thomas Clarkson. From England he sailed to the USA where he bought guns and ammunition, which he unloaded on the north coast of St Domingue in October 1790. He appointed his two brothers and a friend, Marc Chavannes, as his chief lieutenants. But the free coloureds in St Domingue were not yet ready to fight for their rights and only a few joined the young revolutionaries. A planter militia was hastily called together and succeeded in defeating the small band with very little difficulty. Ogé and Chavannes were captured and brutally executed.

The slaves are armed

News of the executions weakened support for the planters in the National Assembly. The French members were shocked at the cruel deaths of men who had fought for the cause of Liberty, Equality and Fraternity. Les Amis des Noirs again asked for free coloureds to be given the right to join the island assemblies. On 15 May 1791 the National Assembly agreed to a law allowing 'persons of colour, born of free parents' to have the right to vote for members of the colonial assemblies. Unfortunately they left it up to the planter-controlled assemblies to put the law into effect. They refused, even though only the wealthiest coloureds would have qualified, and instead talked about leaving the French Empire and joining the British.

In desperation the coloureds on St Domingue began to form their own militias and arm their slaves. The planters did likewise. These were dangerous steps to take as it was unlikely that slaves would fight for planter or coloured masters in a war which would bring them nothing. The petits blancs supported neither side: they would gain nothing from a planter victory and did not wish to see the coloureds gain equality with whites. Instead, they followed the example of Paris workers and formed their own separate revolutionary councils.

The slave revolt on St Domingue

The threat of slave revolt had always been greater on St Domingue than most other colonies. Most of the slaves were African-born. They remembered freedom and saw slavery as temporary. The colony was large and mountainous with many deep valleys which were hiding places for escaped slaves who joined together in Maroon gangs. The slaves on the plantations were linked by the spread of the Voodoo religion based on the worship of both Catholic saints and the Voduns, or gods, recognised by the people of Dahomey in West Africa. Voodoism already had its own priests who met regularly to pass on news from one plantation to another. News of the French Revolution and the disputes between planters and coloureds were talked over eagerly at Voodoo meetings.

Mackandal

The St Domingue slaves also shared a number of common myths and heroes. Among the most popular was the story of François Mackandal who, in 1757, devised a plan to destroy the whites by dumping arsenic in their water supplies. At the last minute he was betrayed by the jealous husband of his lover. Mackandal was chained and burned alive, but a legend grew among the slaves that he had escaped the flames by changing into a mosquito and flying away. Many believed he would return to lead them to freedom. (Both the English and French later discovered that, after the black armies, the mosquito was indeed their most deadly enemy in St Domingue.)

Boukman

In 1790 and early 1791 Boukman, a creole slave who had been born in Jamaica, was quietly moving from plantation to plantation in the rich northern plain of St Domingue. At each place he explained his simple plan: all slaves should stop work until the planters agreed to pay them wages as free workers. Boukman was supported by other slave leaders such as Gilles, Jean Baptiste and a Maroon leader, Jean François. Eventually the plan was put into operation.

The strike started quietly on 22 August on the Turpin plantation. Boukman led the slaves down the road gathering support from the Flaville, Clement and Termes plantations. The strike then broke into violence. On the Noe plantation the slaves hacked to death an unpopular refiner's apprentice and set the cane fields on fire. Within two weeks the whole plain was a smoking ruin. Only a few whites escaped with their lives. They barricaded themselves in the capital of the area at Cap François and, desperately needing assistance, they waited for help to come from the southern and western provinces.

No help came. The masters were too busy quarrelling. In the west the coloured leader, Rigaud, had fought and defeated a planter army. In the south planters began to arm their slaves, who were still loyal, for war against the coloureds. The petits blancs had no love for either side; to protect themselves they revolted in the capital, Port au Prince, and set up a revolutionary council. Two-thirds of the city had been burned to the ground.

France supports the slaves

Not one of the warring groups had enough arms or trained troops to defeat the others completely. For more than a year the looting, burning and killing went on. The planters held on to their strongholds and called on the French government to send an army to restore order. But the National Assembly had come under the control of politicians who had little sympathy for the planters and their slave system. Besides they were facing a war in Europe and could hardly spare troops and arms for St Domingue. Finally an army was sent in September 1792. Its commander, Sonthonax, was a supporter of the Jacobins, the group which most strongly believed that 'Liberty, Equality and Fraternity' should apply to all, not just to the more prosperous whites.

Emancipation, 1793

Sonthonax refused to help the planters unless they first agreed to allow the coloureds places in their assembly. When they refused he offered his support to the coloureds; but they would not accept his demand that there should be no reprisals against the rebellious slaves. Finally he decided that order would come to the colony only if his forces had the support of the slaves. In August 1793 he granted emancipation to the slaves of St Domingue. It was a year before the French government made the emancipation legal, but by then it had had a deep effect on St Domingue. Sonthonax's emancipation decree had united the planters and coloureds against him, but it had won him the support of many slave generals.

Britain and Spain intervene

Attacks on French islands

In February 1793 England had gone to war with revolutionary France. One of her reasons had been alarm at the execution of the French king and the fear that the revolutionary movement would spread to other European countries. The emancipation of the slaves of St Domingue made them fearful, too, about the spread of black freedom movements across the Caribbean. So it was decided to send troops to the French islands, where they could join forces with the planters. If successful they would both put an end to slave emancipation and destroy the power of revolutionary France's forces in the Caribbean.

In 1794, British forces made landings on St Domingue, Martinique, Guadeloupe and St Lucia. The most successful was on Martinique where the French planters willingly helped the British to take over the island. The same happened on Guadeloupe and St Lucia but then the Jacobin government in France sent a commissioner and an armed fleet. He turned the tables on the British and French planters by announcing emancipation, and he was then able to recapture the islands with black support.

The British invade St Domingue

The British hopes for success in St Domingue were high. The French planters had sent messages to Jamaica in which they agreed to surrender the colony to the British for as long as the war lasted. The British also had the support of the Spanish who ruled the eastern half of the island. They, too, feared the results of slave emancipation.

In September 1793 a force of 900 British soldiers left Jamaica and landed at Port Jérémie on the south-west of St Domingue. At the same time Spanish troops crossed the border from the east. The invasion had one effect which had not been expected. The free coloureds were quick to join the side of Sonthonax and the ex-slaves. They feared that a British victory would lead to the introduction of the British colonies' laws that restricted the freedom of the coloureds.

Despite this, the British and Spanish troops were very successsful for the first few months. The French planters greeted them as allies. By March the whole southern province was in British hands and they were making plans to move north to help the Spaniards. But further successes depended on more troops being sent from Jamaica, and in 1795 no reinforcements came. The reason was a Maroon revolt in Jamaica. The British commander there needed every soldier on the island to put down the rising and hunt for the French agents who were thought to have landed to encourage the Maroons. New recruits for St Domingue were sent from England but they were not seasoned for the Caribbean. They quickly died in thousands from yellow fever. In the same year the British lost their ally when Spain made peace with France and handed over Santo Domingo to her. The British invasion might yet have succeeded but for the new commander of the black armies, Toussaint L'Ouverture.

Toussaint L'Ouverture

The black general

Toussaint was born a slave on the Breda plantation in the northern plain. Before the revol-

Fig. 17.2 *Toussaint L'Ouverture.*

ution he had a privileged position as steward of the livestock. When Boukman, Jean Baptiste and the other slave generals had started the revolt in 1791 Toussaint had held back. He was then 45 and had his wife and two young sons to think about. When he did join, it was not as a soldier but as a physician in Jean Baptiste's regiment. But before long he had proved himself to be a very able army commander because of his excellent horsemanship and ability to lead men. He quarrelled with Jean Baptiste and led part of the regiment away to fight as a paid band with the Spanish army in Santo Domingo. Then came the news of the British and Spanish plan to invade St Domingue and bring back slavery. Toussaint took his regiment back to fight with Sonthonax's forces. His real aim was to make St Domingue safe not for the French but for ex-slaves.

Toussaint defeats the French and British

By 1797 Toussaint had risen to be commander of the united French revolutionary and black army which was made up of 20,000 armed men. He then began to suspect that the government in France was weakening in its support for the cause of freeing the slaves. So Toussaint ordered Sonthanax and his soldiers to leave St Domingue. He was now in sole charge of the fight for black freedom.

In just a year Toussaint's armies completed the defeat of the British. By October 1798 the enemy could hold no more than a tiny stronghold at Mole St Nicholas. The British then withdrew to Jamaica.

The coloured war

Toussaint now turned against the coloureds. The coloured commanders, Rigaud and Alexander Pétion, had no love for the ex-slaves. They wanted to set up their own coloured republic in the south of St Domingue. Toussaint immediately sent two of his generals, Jacques Dessalines and Henri Christophe, to crush this move to divide St Domingue. In a brutal campaign Dessalines' forces massacred over 10,000 coloureds. Rigaud and Pétion fled to France.

Santo Domingo captured

The coloured defeat left Toussaint as master of St Domingue. In 1799 the French government reluctantly recognised this and made him governor-general. Two years later Toussaint invaded and conquered the once Spanish Santo Domingo.

The independent colony

But France was now ruled by Napoleon Bonaparte who intended to restore slavery in St Domingue and hand the plantations back to their French owners. Toussaint knew that it would not be long before Napoleon sent a strong force to the Caribbean. Before that day he had to make his position as strong as possible. He had a constitution drawn up for the island declaring it to be self-governing. Most of the power was in his own hands and he shortly had himself declared governor for life. Yet he also tried not to offend France too greatly, so the constitution described St Domingue as an 'independent colony of France'.

More important than the constitution were Toussaint's efforts to build up the prosperity of the island. Only if they could grow crops for export could the ex-slaves buy the guns and ammunition they would need when the day came to fight to keep their freedom. So Toussaint ordered his followers back to the plantations and insisted that they worked long, hard hours in return for a quarter of all they grew. At the same time he persuaded many of the planters to return, knowing that they had the skill needed to manage sugar production. It was meant as a sign that the new government of St Domingue wanted the goodwill of her neighbours, especially the United States. President Adams had already helped with arms and supplies needed to defeat the British. He now agreed to a trading treaty with Toussaint's new state.

The French return

The invasion Toussaint feared came in January 1803. It was ordered by Napoleon as a first step in his 'American Scheme' to rebuild a French empire in the Americas. He sent his brother-in-law, General Leclerc, with secret orders to remove Toussaint and then restore slavery and the old plantation system. France would then have a base for the reconquest of the other sugar islands.

Leclerc's force had 54 ships and 23,000 troops. He landed at Cap François in January 1803 and quickly occupied most of the larger towns including Santo Domingo and Port au Prince. But he found it impossible to defeat the main black armies which moved swiftly from one mountain stronghold to the next. When the April rains came to slow down the fighting, Leclerc had already lost 5,000 men killed and another 5,000 in hospital. But he eventually succeeded by deceit. He kept his orders to reintroduce slavery secret and negotiated with Toussaint's generals. Dessalines and Christophe both agreed to accept a pardon, provided that they were given good pensions. Leclerc allowed them to keep command of their troops which were made part of the French army. Disheartened by his generals' actions, Toussaint himself negotiated. Leclerc promised that his soldiers would not be disbanded, and Toussaint agreed to give up his leadership and retire to the plantation where he had been born.

Toussaint exiled

Leclerc dare not carry out Napoleon's orders to reintroduce slavery while Toussaint remained on the island for fear that he would once again lead the people against the French. Christophe and Dessalines made it clear they no longer supported Toussaint, so Leclerc felt safe in removing him by trickery. He invited Toussaint to his camp with the greeting, 'You will not find a more sincere friend than myself'. But Toussaint was arrested and shipped off to France where he was imprisoned in the icy Fort de Joux high in the mountains near the Swiss border. He died in solitary confinement late in 1803. His body was buried in the basement of the castle's chapel. In the late nineteenth century the chapel and graves were destroyed to make way for a new wall.

Haiti

Revolt of the generals

The arrest of Toussaint did not help Leclerc. As the news spread, groups of ex-slaves formed armed bands in the hills. The only thing which stopped them breaking out into general revolt was the fact that Christophe and Dessalines remained loyal to Leclerc. But this lasted only as long as Napoleon's orders to restore slavery remained secret.

Just a few weeks after Toussaint was seized, some slaves escaped from a ship in Le Cap harbour and swam ashore to bring the news that the French had restored slavery in Guadeloupe. Napoleon's plans for the Caribbean were now in the open. Shortly afterwards Christophe, Dessalines and some of the coloured generals deserted Leclerc and took their men into the hills.

Like the British before him, Leclerc found it impossible to defeat armies who knew every trail through the mountains. Threatened by famine, his army had to buy food from American traders at extremely high prices. Yellow fever killed the new French troops in thousands. Leclerc himself died in August 1803. He was replaced by General Rochambeau who found the task of defeating the blacks impossible. The British blockaded the coast of France preventing supplies from getting through to the Caribbean. In December the last of the French troops surrendered to the British in Jamaica rather than to the victorious black generals. Thus armies made up of former slaves who had no regular training had beaten troops of the great Napoleon's army many years before any European soldiers did the same.

Independence 1804

General Jean-Jacques Dessalines declared that the colony was independent and was to be called Haiti. This was the Arawak word for mountainous, so the first free country in the Caribbean has an Amerindian rather than African or European name.

Haiti was more than an independent country. It was a country without slavery and where the majority of the population, the blacks, was free. This fact made Haitian independence quite different from other anti-colonial movements of the age. In 1783 the American colonies had won their freedom from Britain; around 1820 most states in South America were gaining independence from Spain. But the newly independent countries kept slavery; their struggle for freedom had been one of white against white.

The Haitian revolution began that way when the French Revolution broke out. It then became a struggle between whites and coloureds. But from 1791 to 1804 the main story is of the black achievement in first winning their

freedom and then defending it until they won a country as well. Haiti was only the second independent state in the New World and the first black-ruled state outside Africa. It would always be a beacon of freedom for blacks everywhere.

For slaves in other European colonies the message of the achievement of the Haiti blacks was that Europeans were not unbeatable. For whites it often led to even firmer resistance to privileges for coloureds or easier lives for slaves. Their fears were fanned by refugees from St Domingue who settled mostly in Jamaica, Cuba and Puerto Rico, while smaller numbers went to Trinidad. There were French planters and free coloureds, some of whom took slaves. The planters' stories fanned the fears that led to the harsh treatment of Jamaica's Maroons after the Second Maroon War. Later planters said that Haiti posed twin threats to their position. It encouraged the idea of black freedom; at the same time it proved that Africans, slave or free, would not work on plantations unless they were forced.

After independence

Jean-Jacques Dessalines declared himself emperor of the new state. This was a remarkable step for a man who was born a slave, and was uneducated and illiterate. He was a shrewd and ruthless leader, quite prepared to break his word or change sides if he thought it necessary. After independence he set out to rebuild the strength of the country which had suffered so much. Haiti's population had fallen from 500,000 to 350,000, her agriculture was in ruins and most other countries were refusing to trade with her. Dessalines took a high-handed approach to the problems. He took over much of the land on behalf of the State which meant that he was in a position to insist that workers continued at their tasks as before.

Dessalines claimed that he wanted good relations with the coloureds but at the same time he had plans for breaking up their large estates in the south. This may have been the reason why he was assassinated in 1806.

Following Dessalines' death Henri Christophe

claimed the right to rule Haiti. He had grown up as a free black who had been a hotel waiter. Before the Haitian revolution he had learned soldiering when he had fought with French forces who had gone to help the American colonists in their struggle against Britain. This experience had helped him to become one of Toussaint's most important military commanders.

The coloureds in the south refused to accept Christophe as president or as King Henri I as he declared himself in 1811. They set up a separate southern republic under a coloured president, Alexandre Pétion. The two countries now followed different policies on agriculture. In the south Pétion broke up the land that had been taken over by Dessalines' government and handed it out in small plots to farmers, who were mostly ex-soldiers. At the same time the owners of other large estates were breaking them up into plots which they leased to labourers.

In the north, Christophe tried to build up large plantations which could produce coffee and sugar for export. This meant firm control of the labourers who had to work for two-thirds of the time they had as slaves. By the end of Christophe's life the large plantation was becoming unworkable. Labourers did not like them, and European countries and America were refusing to buy Haitian sugar.

Alexandre Pétion died in 1818 and was followed as President of the South by Jean-Pierre Boyer. In 1820 Christophe committed suicide after a stroke and in 1821 Boyer united the two halves of the country. Haiti now finally became a land of small free peasant cultivators working smallholdings producing coffee for export alongside crops for the farmer's family or the local market. As well as being the first state to combine independence with freeing the slaves, Haiti became the first Caribbean island to look for alternatives to the large sugar plantation.

Fig. 17.3 *President Pétion.*

Assignments

1 *How did the French Revolution give some blacks and coloureds in the French Caribbean the hope of freedom?*

2 *Make a chart listing the main dates associated with the Haitian Revolution and outline the events associated with the dates you have selected.*

3 *Document and compare the contribution of each of the following to the Haitian Revolution:*
   i) Toussaint; ii) Christophe; iii) Dessalines; iv) Pétion.

18 ABOLITION OF THE SLAVE TRADE

Humanitarians

A humanitarian is someone who believes in improving conditions in which men spend their lives. Today we take humanitarianism for granted, but until the eighteenth century it was rare to find men who argued that human life could be improved. It was more usual to believe that the state of the world was laid down by fate or the will of God. In the eighteenth century men with humanitarian ideas began to appear in many professions: in politics, writing, economics, industry. They believed that slavery was unnecessary and evil, and some of them made their views sharply clear.

The poet William Cowper wrote in *The Negroes' Complaint*:

Why did all-creating Nature
Make the plant for which we toil?
Sighs must fan it, tears must water,
Sweat of ours must dress the soil.
Think ye masters iron-hearted,
Lolling at your groaning boards,
Think, how many backs have smarted
For the sweets your cane affords.

Samuel Johnson, who wrote the first English dictionary, got a round of applause when he proposed a toast to 'the next insurrection of the Negroes in the West Indies'. People who had a humanitarian outlook began to show an interest in travel books, and descriptions of the cultures of other peoples. Here they could find evidence that Africans were not the ignorant savages that the slavers described but people from well-organised societies. One widely read travel book described one of the African peoples: 'They never suffer any of their own nation to want but support the old, the blind, and the lame equally with the others.' The disabled and old were certainly not as well cared for in Britain at that time, and men began to wonder whether the Africans did not come from societies which were more noble than their own.

Quakers

Not all humanitarians were religious, but many were, and from them came leadership for a fifty-year campaign against the slave trade and slavery. Perhaps the most important group of religious humanitarians were the Quakers, sometimes known as the Society of Friends. This non-conformist sect had been founded in the seventeenth century by George Fox. Members of the Society of Friends believed in holding religious meetings in ordinary buildings without the rituals of a church service. They were taught to avoid any kind of amusement or elaborate dress, to live lives based on love and never to use violence. Many Quakers went to Pennsylvania and Barbados. George Fox instructed them to welcome their slaves to religious services, to treat them kindly and to free them after a number of years of faithful service.

In 1676 the Quakers in Pennsylvania became the first English colonists to emancipate their slaves. The Quakers in Barbados had to be more cautious because they were few in number. Their meeting houses were torn down by angry planter neighbours. Magistrates jailed and fined them for their religious beliefs which forbade them to take oaths or join the militia. The Anglican clergy urged the assembly to expel 'this base sort of fanatic people commonly termed . . . Quakers'. In 1695 the Barbadian magistrates fined the Quakers over £7,000 for ignoring the colony's laws by allowing slaves to attend religious meetings. At least one Quaker was executed. In face of this opposition the Quakers gave up their open opposition to slavery in Barbados.

In England they became the first campaigners against the slave trade and in 1727 passed a proposal against the trade. In 1761, Quakers who still took part in it were expelled. This was just four years before Granville Sharp had the experience which led to the beginnings of the anti-slavery movement in Britain.

The Somerset case

As a young man, Granville Sharp was apprenticed to a tailor and then became a clerk in the Ordnance (or Supplies) department of the British government. He was a devout Christian and also worked hard to improve his knowledge; he taught himself Greek and Hebrew in his spare time. He never gave up working for a cause in which he believed. When the American War of Independence broke out, Sharp resigned from his government post because he was in sympathy with the Americans.

In 1765 his interest turned to the abolition movement when he met an African stumbling down a London street. Jonathan Strong had just been beaten and turned out of the house of his master, a Barbadian lawyer living in England. Sharp took the wounded man to his brother who was a doctor and looked after him until he was fit. The brothers then found him work as a messenger for a nearby pharmacy. Two years later Strong was spied by his master, seized and sold to a Jamaican planter for £30. He was put in prison to wait until a ship was ready to sail. Sharp took the case to court and managed to have Jonathan Strong set free, but the judge refused to give a judgement on whether the English law allowed a man to be bought and sold as a slave.

Granville Sharp was determined to get a clear ruling against slavery in England. He set to work studying the law and the condition of slaves in the country. In 1765 there were in Britain 14,000 slaves worth over £700,000; most of them had been brought to England from the Caribbean colonies by absentee planters. The absentees had had no worries about taking slaves since in 1749 a judge, Lord Hardwicke, had ruled that a slave running away in England could be legally recovered. They even sold them openly. Advertisements like that in the *Gazette* for April 1769 became common:

For sale at the Bull and Gate Inn, Holborn, a chestnut gelding, a tin whistle, and a well made, good tempered Black Boy.

Sharp believed that Hardwicke's ruling would be overturned if the question of slavery were taken before another English court. In 1770 he took the case of Thomas Lewis to court. Lewis was a slave who had been seized and put on board a ship bound for the Caribbean. The jury freed Lewis, but this was because his master could not prove ownership. Once again the court managed to avoid ruling on the question of whether slavery was illegal. In 1772 Granville Sharp tried again with the case of James Somerset who, like Strong, had been turned out by his master, a Virginian planter, and then seized again. This time the master had clear proof of ownership.

Somerset's case came before the Chief Justice, Lord Mansfield, on 7 February 1772. For four months Sharp tried to force Lord Mansfield to give a ruling. Mansfield was not an abolitionist and wanted to avoid a judgement. He even approached Parliament to pass a special Act declaring slavery legal in England. When Parliament refused, Mansfield proved that he was a great judge who put the law higher than his own feelings. On 22 June 1772 he ruled that his study of the laws of England found that the power of a master to use force on a slave was 'unknown to the laws of England'.

Somerset was set free. Mansfield's judgement did not say slavery itself was against the English law but it did make it impossible for owners to use force. In that way it opened the door for the end of slavery in Britain itself.

Campaigning for abolition

Committee for the Abolition of the Slave Trade

English opponents of slavery then turned to the much larger number of slaves in the colonies and the Quakers formed an anti-slavery society. In 1787 it renamed itself the Committee for the Abolition of the Slave Trade. The members

Fig. 18.1 *British humanitarian opponents of slavery.*

believed that slavery could be forced to collapse once planters could not acquire new slaves. Ending the trade, rather than slavery itself, would avoid the question of whether the planters should be compensated for the loss of their slave property. Another advantage was that the laws affecting trade were made by the English Parliament, whereas to end slavery itself would mean interfering with laws made by the colonial assemblies.

Most members of the Committee were Quakers or belonged to the Evangelical movement which was trying to make the Church of England show as much concern about spreading religious ideas as the Baptists and Methodists. Their enemies mockingly called them 'the Saints'. The leading Saints were also nicknamed the 'Clapham Sect' after the fashionable district of London where some of them lived. The Clapham Sect included Granville Sharp, Thomas Clarkson, who gave his life to investigating

slavery, and William Wilberforce, a wealthy politician. Other abolitionists were Henry Thornton, a wealthy banker who spent his fortune setting up a home in Sierra Leone for slaves liberated by the Mansfield judgement, and John Newton, who had been a slave captain until he had been converted to religion and become a clergyman. There was also Zachary Macaulay, a former book-keeper in Jamaica, and James Ramsay, who had served as a surgeon on a warship bound for St Kitts. There he had been called to attend an epidemic on a slave ship and never forgot the horrors he saw in the middle decks. He became an Anglican priest and served in St Kitts for fourteen years, making out-spoken attacks on slavery. In 1781 he returned to England and joined the abolitionists.

The campaign

The committee had the support of the Prime Minister, William Pitt the Younger, who suggested that William Wilberforce should be the Committee's spokesman in Parliament. Thomas Clarkson was sent to collect the information Wilberforce would need. He travelled to Liverpool and Bristol where he carefully checked all the information about slaving ships. As evidence about the trade's horrors he collected shackles, thumb screws, teeth chisels and branding irons. The ship's captains kept clear of him 'as if I had been a mad dog' but Clarkson wrote down the names and stories of 20,000 seamen. He ended with more information on the slave trade than the slavers had themselves.

Economic arguments for abolition

The evidence showed up the weaknesses of two arguments that slavers put forward in defence of their trade. They claimed that it was important for training seamen who could work on warships in times of war. Clarkson proved that a higher proportion of seamen than slaves died on the middle passage. Slave traders argued that they were essential to the prosperity

Fig. 18.2 *An illustration of evidence collected by the abolitionists. The words at the bottom read, 'Mr Francis relates, "Among numberless other acts of Cruelty daily practised, an English Negro Driver, because a young Negro thro' sickness was unable to work, threw him into a Copper of Boiling-Sugar-juice, & after keeping him steeped over head & Ears for Above Three quarters of an hour in the boiling liquid, whipt him with such severity, that it was near Six Months before he recovered of his Wounds & Scalding." '*

of the two greatest slaving ports, Liverpool and Bristol. Clarkson had no difficulty in showing that each port had more ships engaged in other trades. The government earned more from customs, duties and taxes on imported cotton and exports of manufactured goods than it did on the slave trade.

This was even more true as the British trading empire began to grow in new parts of the world, especially India and the far east. Britain's merchants and seamen as well as industrialists and their workers knew that their prosperity and their jobs depended on trading with these new settlements and trading posts. In 1782 one in twelve ships sailing from Liverpool was a slaver trading with Africa and going on across the middle passage. In 1807 only one

in twenty-four ships followed this route.

The growth of the British Empire in India led to the growth of a powerful 'East India interest' in British politics. Merchants who imported food goods from India and industrialists who needed Indian cotton objected to the favoured treatment given to the West Indian interest for two reasons. One was that the tea and cotton from India were not produced by slave labour. The other was that the West Indian planters' profits were boosted by the price of sugar which was high because they were protected from foreign competition by the Navigation Acts.

To back these objections to slavery they often used the ideas of an economist, Adam Smith. In 1776 he had written *The Wealth of Nations* which said that laws which stood in the way of free trade were bad for the prosperity of a country as a whole. If Britain allowed in sugar from other countries they, in turn, would drop their laws against importing goods made by British people. In any case, Adam Smith wrote, 'the work of freemen comes cheaper in the end than that performed by slaves.' He believed that forced labour was done less well than paid work. Slavery was expensive when you added up the costs of buying and keeping slaves and paying towards the forces needed to prevent revolts.

Final steps to abolition

The evidence collected by Thomas Clarkson convinced William Wilberforce and many other MPs that the slave trade was 'an affront to God and below the dignity of a civilised people'. Outside Parliament the movement gathered support from missionary societies and humanitarians. It was also backed by many industrialists. One was Josiah Wedgwood who owned Britain's largest pottery business. He produced china decorated with the famous plaque which had the words which became the symbol of the anti-slavery movement:

Am I not a man and a brother?

Success did not come quickly for Wilberforce and the other abolitionists in the English Parliament. The West India interest still held many seats in the House of Commons, and they were backed by MPs who had their election expenses paid by the slavers in London, Bristol and Liverpool. Twice, in 1789 and 1791, Wilberforce put forward a proposal to abolish the trade only to have it turned down. In 1792, however, he was successful and the House of Commons agreed that the trade should be abolished by stages by 1796.

But in 1793 England went to war with France and Prime Minister Pitt withdrew his support for abolition. His argument was that he did not want Parliament to be quarrelling over other questions while England was fighting a war. The abolitionists believed that his real reason

was his hope of capturing St Domingue for Britain. If this happened England would be able to flood Europe with cheap sugar. But to grow sugar on St Domingue required thousands of slaves each year. Certainly Pitt would not support abolition while British troops were fighting on the side of the planters in St Domingue.

Many times in the next fourteen years Wilberforce put forward a proposal to end the trade, but on each occasion it was turned down. The first signs that success might soon come appeared in 1804 when Haiti won her freedom. There was now no chance that French sugar would rival British. Some abolitionists pointed out that the black victory showed that slaves did desire freedom just as much as a European would. It even brought some racist thinkers over to the side of abolition. *The Times* newspaper of London, for instance, said that it would be dangerous to increase the number of blacks in British colonies in case they followed the example of Haiti.

Some West Indian planters themselves were coming to favour abolition. In 1806 so much sugar was sent to Britain that the price slumped and the average planter made no profit. These planters believed their losses would become greater if the new conquests of Trinidad and Guyana were turned over to sugar. This could be prevented if they were not able to import slaves.

Abolition

The abolitionist movement was helped by the death of Pitt in 1806. The new Prime Minister was Charles James Fox who was a keen supporter of abolition. In the spring of 1807 the English Parliament passed the Abolition Act. The slave trade was to end on 1 January 1808.

British warships were sent to hunt down captains who ignored the law. They also stopped the ships of any nation at war with England and freed their slave cargo. Several nations followed the British example and passed laws against the trade: the United States in 1808, Holland in 1814, France in 1818 and Spain in 1820. However, the Spanish and

United States governments took no really serious action to stop the trade until the middle of the nineteenth century. Each year thousands of Africans were still carried to the southern states of the United States, to Cuba and Puerto Rico, and to Brazil. A small proportion were freed by the British naval patrols sent to stop and search ships suspected of carrying slaves. Up to 1834 most of the Africans they liberated were taken to Sierra Leone to join slaves freed in England after Lord Mansfield's judgement.

Assignments

1   *Explain why there was a large increase of English opponents to slavery by the end of the eighteenth century.*

2   *Make a list of poems, articles, or other material used in Britain in the campaign against slavery.*
    a)   *Give examples from the pieces you find.*
    b)   *How did the abolitionists hope these works would bring slavery to an end?*
    c)   *Describe other methods used by the abolitionists in their campaign against slavery.*

19 THE CHURCHES AND THE SLAVES

The European churches

The Church of England

In the early days of the British colonies only one church, the Church of England, or Anglican Church, had any importance. This matched the position in Britain where in many ways the Church of England played an important part in British government. Bishops were members of the House of Lords. The whole land was divided into parishes and each parish had its vestry committee which was responsible for local tasks such as road repairs and the care of the poor. Eighteenth-century Anglican vicars were often accused of having little interest in religion and being more concerned with living like landowning gentlemen. Many built themselves large houses, and joined the local landowner in his amusements such as fox-hunting. In many parishes they became magistrates, often dealing out harsh punishments to poor people accused of begging or poaching animals for food.

Most Anglican priests in the Caribbean were very little different. They were connected with the plantocracy, by marriage, by sitting in the assembly or being a magistrate. In most cases the priests accepted slavery and the police laws that went with it. A few clergymen wanted to convert slaves to Christianity, but they were quickly stopped. In 1680 a Barbadian clergyman, the Reverend Godwyn Morgan, wrote a pamphlet in favour of bringing slaves into the Christian Church. The island assembly immediately protested to the Board of Trade in London. The protest said that 'converted negroes' would be harder to manage and less valuable for 'labour and sale'. Besides, it went on: 'The Negroes' savage brutishness renders them wholly uncapable of conversion to Christianity.'

Fig. 19.1 *The seal of the Society for the Propagation of the Gospel. Note the figure in clergyman's dress and the black people shown rushing to hear him. Was this ever the reality?*

Fig. 19.2 *Codrington College, Barbados.*

A few years later, the Anglican Church started the Society for the Propagation of the Gospel with the idea of making Bibles available to 'heathens'. The Society was given three plantations by a Barbadian planter, Christopher Codrington, and built Codrington College as a missionary training school. But graduates from the college did little work among the slaves until after emancipation. Until then the college's plantations were worked by slaves, branded with an 'S' for Society.

The Moravians

The first group to make a serious effort to bring slaves to Christianity were the Moravians. They had suffered 300 years of persecution from both Catholic and Protestant Churches in Europe for their faith. Moravian brethren believed they should lead simple lives and spread the word of God from person to person without the rituals of the churches. Many Moravians moved from their homeland in modern Czechoslovakia to Saxony in modern Germany. From there, they sent missionaries to the Danish islands in 1732. Later missions were opened in Jamaica in 1754, in Antigua in 1756, Barbados in 1765 and St Kitts in 1775.

Many planters would not accept the Moravians on their estates. They believed that it was dangerous to teach Christianity to slaves. Church services would bring them together in large crowds. The slaves might learn too much of their masters' language, politics and way of life. But the Moravians were careful to teach the slaves that Christianity meant accepting suffering on earth in return for rewards in heaven. So a few planters, especially in Antigua and St Kitts, came to believe that Christianity would encourage hard work and obedience in slaves.

The English non-conformists

Non-conformists were Englishmen who refused to conform to the rules and practices of the Church of England. Their numbers swelled in the eighteenth century as a result of the great social changes which were taking place in Britain. The population began to rise rapidly and new classes of workers grew up in the new manufacturing industries. Many Christians became alarmed at the disorder, drunkenness, violence and ignorance in the industrial districts. So non-conformists, such as the Baptists and Presbyterians, began to send preachers into these areas to persuade people to accept religion as the starting point for a better and more moral life.

The most successful non-conformists actually started within the Anglican Church and then broke away. These were the Methodists. The movement started with John Wesley and a group of students who formed a 'Holy Club' at Oxford University. They were nicknamed Methodists because they methodically set about regular worship, charity and preaching. John Wesley spent his life travelling in the poorer districts of England and the new American colonies, and preached more than 40,000 sermons. He began as a Church of England clergyman but ended as leader of a separate organisation which was the largest non-conformist church in Britain.

The missionary societies

Non-conformists started with missionary work among British people who lived immoral lives. Many believed there was similar work to be done in the Caribbean. They were told that the slaves had never heard of God and Christ, and were immoral in the way they dressed, by not being properly married, and by breaking the Sabbath by going to market or drinking and dancing on Sundays. So missionaries began to arrive from England in the 1780s and then in large numbers when collections were made in the 1790s to start missionary societies. The Baptist Missionary Society began in 1792, the London Missionary Society in 1795, the Scottish Missionary Society in 1800 and the Methodist Missionary Society in 1813.

In most cases the planters tried to hinder the missionaries. Some assemblies passed regulations which said that missionaries must have a licence from the parish magistrates to preach. The fees for the licences were high. St Vincent tried to head off the missionaries by passing a

Fig. 19.3 *Buildings of a mission at St John's, Antigua. What does the illustration suggest about the life-style the missionaries wanted blacks to follow?*

law which forbade anyone to preach who had not lived in the colony for a year. Most assemblies made laws forbidding religious services between sunset and sunrise. Some made it illegal for missionaries to use converted slaves to teach others. Occasionally planters threatened slaves attending services or even tore down meeting houses. In 1789 the Methodist chapel in Barbados was stoned, and slaves caught at the services were publicly whipped.

The societies took great care to avoid trouble with the planters. The London Missionary Society's instructions stated: 'Not a word must escape you, in public or private, which might render the slaves displeased with their masters or dissatisfied with their station.' It chose its missionaries from men who did humble work as carpenters, gardeners, weavers, small shopkeepers and so on. This was so the missionaries would work humbly among the slaves and not challenge the white leaders of colonial society.

By taking such care not to offend the planters the new missionaries were able to get permission to enter some plantations. Soon each island had a small number of Christian slaves. On the small islands some planters welcomed the work of the missionaries in making blacks more loyal. When Antigua was threatened by invasion in the French wars, troops of blacks were raised to defend the islands. One was made up of Methodist slaves and the other had a large number of Moravians.

The slaves and Christianity

Religious ideas come together

By the 1830s Christianity was far more widely spread among slaves and much more likely to lead them to resist slavery than to support their masters. In 1834, there were 150 non-conformist missionaries in the British West Indies. About 47,000 slaves were full members of their churches and another 86,000 were counted as 'hearers and enquirers' who were keen to learn more about Christianity. Altogether these two groups made up one in nine of all the slaves in Britain's Caribbean colonies.

What was the reason so many slaves turned to Christianity in the first part of the nineteenth century? Some missionaries believed that they were being converted to a more 'civilised' and European way of life. The truth is more likely to be that many Africans felt a close connection between their world view and the ideas of Christianity. Chapter 12 shows that most Africans believed in a creator god and so did Christians. The African spirit world was not very different from Christian ideas about the special powers of saints. Both Africans and Christians believed that their spirit or soul lived on after death.

Many ceremonies had very similar meanings. Christian children were often named when they were baptised as small infants into the church. This was very close to the African tradition of outdooring when a child was presented to the world and named. Christians often swore sacred oaths on the Bible and oath-taking was very common in some African secret societies. Africans knew their history through stories and folk sayings and these were not very different from the Old Testament history or the parables in the New Testament.

Even more important to the slaves was the strength that many said they gained when they were converted. After they or their ancestors had been torn from their African roots, slaves may have found it difficult to be sure that their religious ideas were not sometimes a cause of their captivity and weakness. Because they could not follow through their religious ideas in the open they must have felt less than full human beings. Christianity could change that. People who declared that they were converted and then were baptised in public could have a new pride in their beliefs and in themselves.

Black Baptists

That new strength was strongest in the churches with all black congregations. Here they could sing hymns in their own way, and express their faith through drumming and dancing. No one thought them ridiculous if they called out when the spirit moved them or if they said that they had seen visions of a better world or of heaven.

In these early black churches the missionary was usually white but many preachers and leaders of services were black deacons. In Jamaica and the Bahamas black leadership was even firmer. Many' slaves there had been converted to Christianity by black Baptists. In Jamaica the two leading black preachers were George Lisle, a black American, and Moses Baker, a black Bahamian.

Slaves, planters and missionaries

Revolts 1816, 1823 and 1831

Black self-confidence alarmed the planters especially in the years from 1807 onwards when they were facing demands in Britain that they should emancipate their slaves. As we shall see in Chapter 20, there were slave revolts in Barbados in 1816, Demerara in 1823 and Jamaica in 1831. Black Christians played an important part in both the last two. The governor of Demerara reported that the slaves had told him that 'God had made them of the same flesh and blood as the whites'. The Jamaica revolt was led by a black Baptist deacon, Samuel Sharpe.

Violence against missionaries

Planters put the blame for these revolts on the white non-conformist missionaries. In Demerara the Congregationalist minister, John Smith, was sentenced to hang at a court-martial for encouraging slaves to revolt. It was later proved that he had preached to his congregations against joining the revolt but he died in prison while waiting for the king's pardon. In Barbados, the

Demerara revolt led some planters to take the law into their own hands. They burned the Methodist chapel in Bridgetown and forced its missionary, William Shrewsbury, to leave the colony. In Jamaica, leading Baptist missionaries such as William Knibb, Thomas Burchell and James Alsopp were also harassed for encouraging revolt. Again it was proved that they had pleaded with their congregations not to join the war and they were acquitted.

The most reactionary planters in Jamaica then followed the example of the Barbados planters. They formed the Colonial Church Union. Its aim was to prevent slaves being preached any doctrines except those of the Church of England. The main organiser is believed to have been an Anglican clergyman, William Bridges. Their methods were not unlike those of the Ku Klux Klan which grew up later in the southern United States. In a few months they destroyed sixteen non-conformist churches in Jamaica. Early in 1833 the Colonial Church Union was outlawed by the governor.

The planters had misunderstood the position. It was true that non-conformists had brought a form of Christianity to the Caribbean which the slaves could accept because it related to their African religious ideas. But it was the slaves themselves who had developed the confidence to join the revolts. In any case, none of the revolts happened simply because the slaves had become Christian. In the Barbados revolt of 1816, Christians had played a very small part. In Jamaica and Demerara they had been important but what united all the rebel slaves was the desire to hurry along emancipation.

Assignments

1 *With reference to any one British Caribbean territory, research the history of the Church of England in that territory from the time of the British occupation up to emancipation. Use the following headings (or supply four headings of your own):*
   a) *Why the Church of England came to . . .*
   b) *The Church of England and the planters.*
   c) *The Church of England and the slaves.*
   d) *Problems facing the Church of England in this period.*

2 *Describe the work of either the Moravians or one of the non-conformist groups in one British Caribbean territory before emancipation.*

3 *Suggest reasons why there were so many Christian slaves in the British Caribbean up to the time of emancipation.*
   Did slaves who were not Christian have any other religious beliefs?

20 EMANCIPATION

Plantations after abolition

The slaves

English abolitionists believed that slavery would soon disappear after the trade was ended. They thought the planters would have to protect their remaining slaves and encourage settled family life to increase numbers. As the slaves increased the planters would gradually free them and hire the fittest as labourers. The missionaries would be welcomed to teach the ex-slaves how to live as honest, hard-working freemen. Unfortunately, the abolitionists were wrong. Ill-health, overwork and the lack of proper family life pushed up the death rate, especially for babies

and infants. The slave population began to fall. Those remaining had to work harder and many field gangs soon had more women than men. Hard, grinding toil, combined with a poor diet, meant fewer pregnancies, more miscarriages and more dead babies.

The planters

Plantation profits continued to fall in the face of competition from new areas. Although there was a labour shortage in the new colonies in Guyana and Trinidad, sugar production there was growing. Worse from the West Indian point of view was that England began to import East Indian sugar. This strengthened the East India

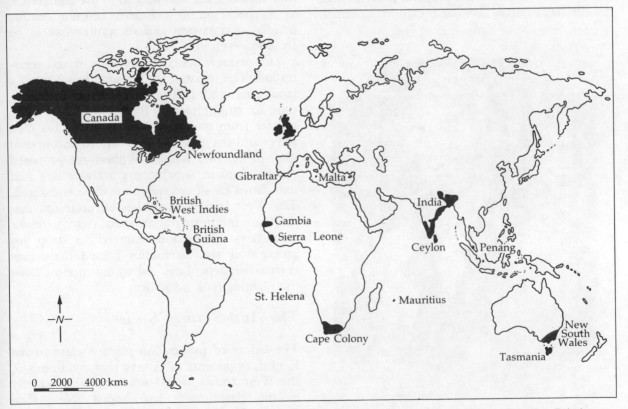

Map 29 *The British Empire in 1815. The colonies in the West Indies became much less important now that Britain had possessions in Africa, Asia and Australasia.*

interest in the British Parliament. At the same time more sugar from Cuba and Brazil was passing on to the world market. Faced with these difficulties the planters were in no mood to improve the conditions of their slaves or welcome new missionaries.

The attitude of the planters often turned public opinion in Britain against them. In 1808 the Jamaica assembly passed the Consolidated Slave Act which forbade Methodists and other non-conformists to teach slaves or have them in their chapels. Reports of this reached Britain and the abolitionists and the missionary societies protested strongly. The British Parliament then disallowed the Jamaica law.

However, the abolitionists could not stop planters giving cruel and sadistic punishments to slaves. In 1812 Arthur Hodge, a slave-driver in Tortola, was tried for murdering sixty slaves under his care. He was found guilty but the jury recommended mercy. The magistrates, however, decided he should be hanged; the governor had to declare martial law and call in a British

Fig. 20.1 *Arthur Hodge, murderer of slaves.*

warship to keep order among the planters while the sentence was carried out.

Illegal trading and registration

The abolitionists soon had evidence that the planters were breaking the law against the slave trade. The navy stopped shipments from Africa but it was much harder to block the trade between different islands. Most of this was carried out by planters in Trinidad and Guyana who bought slaves from the older colonies owned by Britain or other European countries.

In 1812, the abolitionist MP, James Stephen, persuaded Parliament to agree to a scheme for registration. All slaves in Trinidad and Guyana were to have their names entered on a register. It would be illegal to own an unregistered slave. Stephen hoped that it would be possible to spot which slaves had been illegally shipped into the new colonies. He also wanted to use registration as a check on ill-treatment because deaths, accidents, runaways and recaptures had to be recorded each year.

The planters found many ways round registration. The registrar in Trinidad was himself a landowner and helped them by giving extra time to import slaves. It was still legal for a planter from another island to bring his own slaves and the governor of Trinidad encouraged this. In Britain, William Wilberforce proposed that Parliament should pass a law which said that slaves in all colonies should be registered. The West Indian assemblies all protested that this was interfering with their right to make local laws. Wilberforce agreed to drop his proposal if the assemblies passed their own registration acts. They did so but in most cases the planters took no notice.

The Anti-Slavery Society

The failure of registration made it clear to the English opponents of slavery that conditions in the West Indies would not improve gradually as the abolitionists had hoped. New men entered the struggle. In Parliament Wilberforce was replaced as the main spokesman on slavery

Fig. 20.2 *One of the motifs of the Anti-Slavery Society.*

by Thomas Buxton. He was supported by young anti-slavery campaigners. Unlike the older abolitionists, they were not prepared to avoid awkward questions such as whether planters should be compensated if their slaves were freed. They wanted a British Act of Parliament to end slavery once and for all. In 1823 they formed the London Society for the Mitigation and Gradual Abolition of Slavery. Within a year 220 branch societies were opened in cities and towns throughout Britain, and a newspaper, *The Anti-Slavery Monthly Reporter*, was started. The Society's president was the king's brother, and among its many vice-presidents were five lords and fourteen Members of Parliament. The most outspoken of them all was the leader of the East India sugar interests in Parliament.

Amelioration

Faced with such a strong anti-slavery movement, the West India Committee tried to head off the attacks. They told the Colonial Secretary that they would support some proposals for improving the condition of slaves. The Foreign Minister, George Canning, raised these 'Amelioration Proposals' in Parliament in March 1823, and promised that his government would, sometime in the future, ask Parliament to agree to emancipation. With this promise the abolitionists supported the amelioration proposals which were agreed in May 1823.

The proposals said that the government should write to each of the colonial governors suggesting that the assemblies should pass local laws to improve the condition of slaves. The laws would state that female slaves should not be whipped and that overseers and drivers should not carry a whip in the fields. Records should be kept of all lashes given to male slaves and all punishments should be put off for at least twenty-four hours. Religious instruction and church marriages were to be encouraged. Slaves should have time off on Saturday to go to market so that they would be free to attend church on Sunday morning. The proposals asked the assemblies to pass laws against selling slaves for debt and breaking up families. The colonies should set up schemes to help slaves save money and buy their own freedom. The most daring proposal was that a slave could testify in court against a free man provided that a minister supplied him with a character reference.

The failure of amelioration

The proposals met with fierce resistance in the colonies. In the crown colonies the governors were ordered to carry them out, but the governor of Demerara refused to publish them right away for fear of rioting. In Trinidad the planters immediately asked for them to be withdrawn. The assemblies on the older islands greeted the proposals with outbursts of anger. They ignored warnings from the West India Committee that the only way to stop the anti-slavery movement in Britain was 'by doing of ourselves, all that is right to be done – and doing it speedily and effectively'. In Dominica the planters talked about independence; in Jamaica the assembly discussed joining the United States; in Barbados the assembly said that their slave laws were already 'a catalogue of indulgencies to the Blacks'. In the end most of the assemblies passed only a few of the least important amelioration proposals.

The amelioration proposals failed, but they were an important landmark in the struggle for emancipation. The British government had promised that emancipation would come one day. The refusal of the planters to accept amelioration meant that the anti-slavery campaign was given a stronger case. It split the West India interest between those in England who had tried to delay emancipation by amelioration, and those in the Caribbean who clung desperately to a passing way of life.

The free coloureds

The planters seek support

The planters turned to the free coloureds for support in their struggle against the abolitionists. They also needed to prevent them joining with the slaves – as happened in Haiti. In 1795 the Jamaican assembly had granted pensions to such families of free coloureds' as shall be killed or disabled in the public service'. In 1813 it allowed free coloureds to give evidence in court, to inherit unlimited amounts of property, and to take up trades such as owning and renting boats. The free coloured leaders were aware that the assemblies were trying to buy their support against the slaves. The most active of them wanted to make the most of their opportunity. Throughout the colonies they formed associations to demand that the assemblies remove all their disabilities.

In 1823 the Grenada assembly gave in and removed all but a few unimportant restrictions. Free coloureds in other colonies immediately pressed for the same changes. In Trinidad they sent a petition to the governor demanding the freedom of assembly, the removal of special seats for coloureds at places of amusement, and an end to all 'impediments in the way of marriage between white and free coloured'. Free coloureds in Jamaica threatened to withdraw from service in the militia unless granted full equality with whites.

The assemblies had not planned that the free coloureds should take up the improvements they offered in such an outspoken way. In most cases they replied in insulting terms. The Barbadian assembly gave a definite 'no' to the coloureds and reminded them that keeping the rights they had been granted in the past depended 'entirely on their good conduct'. The Jamaican assembly was just as insulting, although it did agree to pass more special acts granting full rights to individual coloureds.

The free coloureds support emancipation

In the years after 1823 most free coloureds became convinced that their position would improve only after the entire slave system was brought down. They sided with British officials over the question of amelioration. In return the British officials supported the free coloureds' struggle with the assemblies. In 1823 the governor of Barbados described the free coloureds as 'by far the most loyal subjects His Majesty has'. In 1829 the Colonial Secretary issued an order removing all disabilities from free coloureds in Trinidad. In Jamaica, governors protected the two outspoken coloured leaders, Edward Jordan and Robert Osborn. The two men published a newspaper, The Watchman, in which they poked fun at the assembly and published the debates on emancipation which were taking place in England. Jordan was arrested in 1831 for urging in The Watchman that the free coloureds 'bring down the system by the run, knock off the fetters, and let the oppressed go free'. Such attacks forced many assemblies to remove the disabilities at last, but by then it was too late. The refusal to help the free coloureds in the 1820s had turned them into strong supporters of the anti-slavery movement.

The emancipation revolts

Eighteenth- and nineteenth-century revolts

Chapter 16 described the most important revolts in the eighteenth century. In the years between abolition and emancipation there were three more major revolts, in Demerara, Barbados and Jamaica. They were different from Cuffy's and Tacky's rebellions in several important ways. Their main cause was the belief that the planters were obstructing schemes for better conditions or emancipation. The blacks' goal was to to win the right to become free farmers or labourers, not to take over the colony in the way that Cuffy's and Tacky's supporters wanted. The emancipation revolts led to attacks on Europeans' property but not their lives, while Cuffy and Tacky had started out to fight wars against the whites.

Finally, all the nineteenth-century revolts had something to do with religion, which the eighteenth-century ones had not. Christian slaves and their Baptist deacons were important leaders in Demerara and Jamaica, although not in Barbados. For their part, the planters unfairly blamed non-conformist missionaries for encouraging rebellion in Barbados as well as the two other colonies.

Slaves learned about the abolition of the slave trade when no more Africans arrived in the ports. After that there were the registration schemes and amelioration proposals. Pamphlets from the Anti-Slavery Society arrived in the Caribbean. Local newspapers carried reports of anti-slavery meetings and debates in Parliament. Slaves who could read passed on the news to their fellows. Higglers and jobbers picked up gossip in market places. Domestics heard their masters grumbling about the latest schemes for changing or ending slavery.

It is not surprising that slaves began to believe that the planters were obstructing the improvements or freedom itself which the British intended them to have. Their mood was summed up in a Jamaican song noted down by Matthew Monk Lewis in 1816:

Oh me good friend, Mr. Wilberforce, make me free!
God Almighty thank ye! God Almighty thank ye!
Buckra in this country no make we free:
What Negro for to do? What Negro for to do?
Take force by force! Take force by force!

Barbados, 1816

In 1815 the British government wrote to all assemblies asking them to pass a Registration Act. The Barbados assembly refused. The news passed quickly round the slaves and the first emancipation revolt began on Easter Sunday, 1816.

It started in the parish of St Philip on Bayley's plantation. On one plantation after another first the trash piles and then hated cane fields were fired. By Sunday evening cane fields were burning in the neighbouring parishes of St John and St George: '. . . mill after mill on the revolted estates was turned into the wind to fly untended, and bell after bell was rung to announce that the slaves on such plantation had joined the revolt.' News of the disturbances reached Bridgetown early on Monday morning. Martial law was immediately proclaimed. Troops of militia and regulars marched to the parishes. The slaves scarcely resisted the troops, mainly because many were not yet ready to seek violently what they believed the abolitionists might achieve peacefully. Most had not taken up arms at all, a fact which the governor, Sir James Leith, honestly admitted. Not a single planter had been hurt and only one militia man killed.

The planters showed no such humanity. Several slaves caught off their estates were murdered on the spot. Others were rounded up and put in front of a makeshift court of inquiry. They were sentenced to death and returned to their owner's plantation where the execution was carried out as an example. Several were deported to British Honduras but local officials refused to allow them on shore so they were trans-shipped to Sierra Leone. Several months later the assembly set up a Select Committee to investigate the cause of the revolt. They tried to use their investigation to discredit the emancipation movement in Britain. They laid the whole blame on the shoulders of a free coloured man, Washington Franklin, who they reported had read newspaper reports of the anti-slavery debates to the slaves and discussed emancipation with them.

Demerara, 1823

In 1823 the rumour spread among slaves in the Demerara plantations that the king had sent a 'free paper' but that the governor would not issue it. A revolt quickly broke out and within two days 13,000 slaves had joined in. Like the Barbados revolt, it was not a violent affair. The slaves spoke to the governor under a flag of truce and told him that 'their good King had sent Orders that they should be set free and that they would work no more.' They went on to say that they wanted land for themselves with three days in the week to farm it as well as time to go to chapel on Sunday. When the slaves refused to go back to their plantations they were mown down with musket fire. More than a hundred slaves were killed and only one white. After that, the troops marched up and down the coast holding courts-martial and then shooting the rebel leaders.

As we saw in Chapter 19, non-conformist missionaries suffered too. In Demerara the Congregationalist John Smith was condemned to hang and died in prison. When news of the Demerara revolt reached Barbados a mob of planters forced the Methodist William Shrewsbury to leave. These reprisals against missionaries had the opposite effect from the one the planters wanted. They enraged people in England and strengthened support for the emancipationists.

Jamaica, 1831

In Jamaica, Samuel Sharpe, a slave Baptist deacon, was well placed to have news about English politics and about the arguments in the island assembly. He could read and he had a relative who worked in a printery in Kingston. In 1831 it was clear that the British Parliament would emancipate the slaves soon and that the planters would try to find ways of keeping their unpaid forced labour.

Christmas Day and Boxing Day were holidays. Sharpe planned a strike to begin on the day after. His followers agreed they would refuse to work unless they were paid wages.

Their plans were a well-kept secret and most planters and overseers were taken completely by surprise. Missionaries who worked with the slaves like the Baptist, Thomas Burchell, and the Methodist, the Reverend H. Bleby, were just as ignorant of the planned strike.

It began quietly in St James when the slaves on several plantations peacefully but firmly refused to go back to work after the Christmas holidays. The first violence happened when the great house and sugar works at Kensington estate in St James were burnt. The fire at Kensington was the first of many. As in Barbados the cane fields, symbols of bondage and toil, were burned on one estate after another. The militia sent out from Montego Bay were driven back and the revolt spread to Trelawney parish. At the same time minor disturbances broke out in St Elizabeth, Manchester, St Thomas and Portland. These were quickly put down, but the main trouble areas in the north-west remained in turmoil until after the New Year when additional militia troops and a detachment of regulars were sent from Kingston. Over 400 slaves were killed and Sharpe was executed with about 100 followers before the 'Baptist War', as the slaves called it, was put down.

As in Barbados and Demerara, the planters and assembly refused to believe that the slaves on their own were capable of joining together in the name of emancipation. The assembly set up a Commission of Inquiry which blamed the revolt on: 'the unceasing . . . interference of his Majesty's ministers','. . . the false and wicked reports of the Anti-Slavery Society', and '. . . the teaching and preaching of religious sects called Baptists, Wesleyan, Methodist and Moravians'.

Just as in Barbados and Demerara the planters turned their anger against the non-conformist missionaries. Three leading Baptists, William Knibb, Thomas Burchell and James Alsopp, were threatened with trial for encouraging rebellion. All were released because it was shown that there was clear evidence that they had pleaded with their congregations not to join the war. Then followed the organised attacks on non-conformist churches (see page 160).

The missionaries in England

Once again the planters had miscalculated. In the summer of 1832 William Knibb and Thomas Burchell were giving evidence to the committee which the House of Commons had set up to consider emancipation as soon as possible. Then they went on speaking tours to Baptist chapels and anti-slavery meetings throughout Britain.

By this time the anti-slavery movement was reaching a peak of activity. In 1830 a few young active members such as the Quaker brothers, Joseph and Emmanuel Cooper, had set up the Agency Committee. Its aim was to win public opinion over to immediate emancipation. The Agency Committee divided the country into five districts and put a paid lecturer in charge of each. Within a year they had set up over a thousand new anti-slavery groups. The flood of support was described by one absentee planter living in south-west England:

> In this neighbourhood we have anti-slavery clubs, and anti-slavery needle parties and anti-slavery tea parties and anti-slavery in so many shapes and ways that even if your enemies do not in the end destroy you by assault, those that side with you must give up for very weariness.

Knibb and Burchell gave the Agency Committee's work a further boost. Their stories of the brutality used against the slaves was bad enough. In the three emancipation revolts a thousand slaves had been killed against thirteen whites. But their accounts of the persecution of white missionaries in the largest and best-known colony enraged English opinion even more. The abolitionist, Zachary Macaulay, was amazed. He wrote:

> The religious persecutions in Jamaica has roused the immense body of Methodists and Dissenters throughout the land to a feeling of the most intense and ardent description . . . I stand astonished myself at the result.

For the first time the missionary societies came out into the open and joined with the abolitionists in calling for an immediate end to slavery.

Fig. 20.3 *A handbag carried by an anti-slavery Englishwoman.*

Emancipation

The Reform Act, 1832 for Plantocracy

Samuel Sharpe's last words in May 1832 were: 'I would rather die on yonder gallows than live in slavery.' Only a month after he died the last British obstacle to emancipation was overthrown. In June 1832 the British House of Commons was reformed.

MPs in the old Parliament mostly sat for small towns or country districts with very few voters. Often a single landowner controlled all the voters so he could sell the seat in Parliament. Many members of the West India interest bought their place in the House of Commons in this way. This old House of Commons had matched social conditions in the eighteenth century when Britain's wealth came from agriculture and overseas trade. It was quite unsuitable now that she had become the world's leading industrial power. After a long campaign and many riots, Parliament agreed to change the system by the 1832 Reform Act. Many of the old country seats were taken away and given to

Fig. 20.4 *An English cartoon of 1833. The black man has the features of the famous British soldier and politician, the Duke of Wellington, who opposed emancipation on the grounds that the slaves had not been prepared for freedom. In the picture he is protesting at being forced in the water before he has been taught to swim. William Wilberforce is mocking at the Duke's argument and saying that going into the water is the only possible way to learn.*

industrial towns which before had no MP. The number of people with the right to vote was increased so that buying a seat in Parliament was usually impossible.

When the new reformed House of Commons first met in January 1833 a clear majority of MPs were in favour of the immediate end of slavery. MPs and voters in the new manufacturing areas were opposed to the Navigation Acts which gave the colonies protected markets in Britain. They wanted free trade, without import and export duties, so they could sell their goods abroad cheaply and so cheap food could be imported for the new factory workers. They had no sympathy with the planters' struggle to keep their slaves if this meant that Britain had to pay more for her sugar. Many of the MPs, too, were strengthened in their view by religious feelings that slavery was evil.

The Emancipation Act, 1834

In August 1833 the debates were over and MPs passed the Emancipation Act. The planters and assemblies were told there would be £16.5 million compensation if they passed their own emancipation laws. But it was made clear that whatever the colonies decided to do, slavery in the whole British Empire was to end sharp, on midnight 1 August 1834. The Act arranged for the compensation to be paid to slave owners in the West Indies. Compensation was only to be paid if the colonial assemblies passed their own laws to make certain a smooth changeover to freedom. All children under 6 years old were to be freed immediately. Everyone else could be made to serve an apprenticeship if assemblies thought it necessary. Apprentices would have to work 40½-hours a week without pay for their

Fig. 20.5 *Emancipation day as it was illustrated in a nineteenth-century history book in England. What impression about the West Indies did the artist mean to give English schoolchildren?*

former masters, but beyond that they could demand a wage or hire themselves to another planter. Apprentices could not be sold unless the estate to which they belonged was sold. To settle all disputes between masters and apprentices a number of special magistrates were to be sent out from England. An apprentice could buy his complete freedom at a price agreed between the special magistrate and the master.

Assignments

1 *'The attitude of the planters often turned public opinion in Britain against them', page 162:*
   a) *What was the attitude of the planters in the British Caribbean in 1808, after the abolition of the slave trade?*
   b) *Give examples of how public opinion in Britain turned against the planters.*
   c) *What do you think was the main result of the attitude of the planters after 1808?*

2 *Explain the meaning of the word* amelioration.
   a) *What was the purpose of the 'Amelioration Proposals' of 1823?*
   b) *Why did the 'Amelioration Proposals' fail?*

3 *Study the major revolts in Barbados 1816, Demerara 1823 and Jamaica 1831:*
   a) *What features did these revolts have in common?*
   b) *What were the main consequences of these revolts?*

4 *Try and obtain a copy of the Emancipation Act or an abridged version. What do you think were the main features of the Act?*

21 APPRENTICES

Apprenticeship

August 1 1834, the date laid down by the British Parliament for emancipation, was a great day in the history of the Caribbean, and 668,000 people became free. But, as it drew near, they saw that only their young children would be completely free. For the others there was to be a time of apprenticeship. The praedials, or fieldworkers, would serve six years and the non-praedials four years. The Emancipation Act had laid down the period of apprenticeship for the crown colonies in Trinidad and British Guiana and allowed the assemblies to decide whether or not to introduce it in the other islands. Only Antigua and Bermuda decided on immediate emancipation without apprenticeship.

What was the purpose of apprenticeship? While officials in the Colonial Office were drawing up the Emancipation Act they were guided by a paper, written by the minister in charge, which said:

> The great problem to be solved in drawing up any plan for the emancipation of the Slaves in our Colonies, is to devise some mode of inducing them when relieved of the fear of the Driver and his whip, to undergo the regular and continuous labour which is indispensable in carrying on the production of Sugar.

In other words, the British wished to see the slaves free but with as little risk as possible to sugar producers. They feared that the ex-slaves would simply leave the plantations after emancipation and the sugar trade would be ruined. This same fear led the planter assemblies in every colony except Antigua to pass a set of police laws to create an apprenticeship system as laid down in the Emancipation Act. These laws forced the ex-slaves to work without payment for $40\frac{1}{2}$ hours a week. Any overtime had to be paid for and the masters had to allow apprentices to keep their homes and collect their rations as before.

On the heavily populated islands, the assemblies made their decision entirely on the grounds of cost. Because there was hardly any unused land the ex-slaves and their families would have to live on the estates. Except in Antigua, planters reckoned they would gain more from the $40\frac{1}{2}$ hours free labour than they would lose by still having to support the children, the old and the unfit. In the less crowded colonies the planters wanted apprenticeship to stop a mass movement off the plantations. In Nevis, Montserrat and the Windwards they had encouraged slaves to grow provisions on marginal lands away from the cane fields. Now they worried that these lands might make the ex-slaves independent. Masters in Trinidad, British Guiana and Jamaica were even more reluctant to give full freedom lest there was a mass movement to the interiors where Maroons and Bush Negroes had already made their homes.

The Colonial Office view

To be fair to the officials of the Colonial Office, apprenticeship seemed the only way to prevent the colonies falling into miserable poverty. More than a century of domination by the plantocracies had left them without the services needed in a free society. There were very few roads and hardly any schools, hospitals and orphanages. The officials believed that these could be provided only if the colonies continued to earn money by exporting plantation crops. They thought there was just a faint hope that in the four or six years of apprenticeship the ex-slaves would learn to turn themselves into wage-earning plantation workers. The Colonial Office also believed that a few years of control over the lives of ex-slaves would prevent outbreaks of violence against the owners and give assemblies time to make new laws on public order to replace the old police laws.

The ex-slaves object

To the ex-slaves the idea of being apprenticed to their masters to learn about freedom was ridiculous. In Trinidad they marched into Port of Spain to hear the governor read out the Emancipation Act. When he got to the sections on apprenticeship they called out 'dam tief' and 'old rogue'. For five days they hooted and shouted every time the governor appeared in public. The Riot Act was read and the militia called out to restore order. Apprentices rioted also in Montserrat and St Kitts. In Jamaica the militia was called out to round up unwilling apprentices and return them to the plantations for their first lesson in freedom. In British Guiana, officials avoided serious trouble by appointing a few apprentices as special constables and leaving them to persuade the rest to return to work.

Enforcing apprenticeship

Special magistrates

The Colonial Office made an attempt to see that apprenticeship was carried out fairly by sending special magistrates to the Caribbean. Most were retired British army officers and civil servants. One official described them as 'architects of freedom' and 'untainted by slavery'. But this was only half the picture. He should have added that their main purpose was to see that the plantation system continued even though many tried to give justice to the ex-slaves. The laws they had to enforce were the Apprenticeship Acts passed in each colony. Naturally the planter assemblies made them to suit their own needs and to make it difficult for ex-slaves to move freely. In Trinidad and British Guiana, where there were no assemblies, the planters put pressure on the governors to pass the regulations they wanted.

Important among the new acts were the vagrancy laws. They made it illegal for apprentices to leave the plantation during their free time without written permission from their master or overseer. Other laws made it difficult for apprentices to buy their freedom, and fixed high charges for licences to carry out trade as carpenters, coopers, masons and blacksmiths. Small retail shops and fishing boats were heavily taxed. Higgling was discouraged by high fees for the use of local markets and by laws which laid down that a different trading licence was needed for every parish.

Magistrates and planters

The special magistrates had to enforce laws which were weighted against the interests of the apprentices. Another difficulty was that governors had appointed local planters as temporary special magistrates until the posts could be filled by men sent from London. Governor Hill had appointed 92 in Trinidad following the disturbances in Port of Spain. Most were soon dismissed but their close connection with planter interests meant that the newly arrived British magistrates were suspected of being biased against the apprentices in the same way. There were, in any case, too few special magistrates at first to handle all the grievances between masters and apprentices.

	Special magistrates originally allotted	Present in 1834	Finally allotted
Jamaica	33	28	63
British Guiana	13	5	15
Trinidad	6	2	11
Bahamas	3	0	6
Barbados	6	6	8
St Kitts and Anguilla	4	2	5
Tobago	2	0	4
Grenada and Cariacou	3	1	5
St Vincent and Grenadines	3	3	3
Nevis	1	0	2
Montserrat	1	0	2
Dominica	3	1	5
Virgin Islands	1	0	1
British Honduras	1	1	2

The pay of a special magistrate was only £400 a year and, out of this, he had to provide his own housing, food and travelling expenses. No arrangements were made for leave or retirement

Fig. 21.1 *Nineteenth-century English people were often critical of planters. A magazine cartoon mocks at their way of life.*

pensions. The low pay and poor conditions made it all too easy for special magistrates to accept meals and lodgings from a planter the night before listening to an apprentice's complaint against him.

Workhouses

One common form of punishment ordered by special magistrates was to send apprentices to the parish workhouse. The Emancipation Act had forbidden physical punishment on the plantation, but each colony had set up workhouses where it could be carried out. The workhouses were not controlled by the special magistrates but by the parish vestries which were dominated by planters. The most usual form of punishment was the treadmill. Victims were tied to a bar hanging over a large wooden cylinder with a series of steps cut into its circumference. When the brake was taken off, the cylinder began to spin and everyone had to run quickly to catch the downcoming step. The idea came from England where it was used to drive simple machinery in prisons; in the Caribbean it became an instrument of torture.

In Jamaica apprentices sentenced to hard labour in the workhouse were forced to wear chains and iron collars which had rarely been used in the last days of slavery. In Barbados, females sentenced to the workhouse had their heads shaved. The punishment did not end when the apprentice was freed from the workhouse. In most colonies they had to use their free time to repay the hours of work they had missed while serving their time.

These extracts from the journal of a special magistrate in Barbados show how the workhouse was used to control apprentices who dared to work less hard than their masters demanded or who challenged a planter.

Miss N. Seals (*Complainant*) vs Sarah Francis (*Defendant*)

Fig. 21.2 *Apprentices on the treadmill in Jamaica. It was later forbidden as a punishment for females.*

Complaint: Inattention to work and disobedience.
Decision: Ten days hard labour.

John Myers (*Complainant*) vs seven pregnant
females (*Defendants*)
Complaint: Indolent performance of duty.
Decision: Three days solitary confinement. Medical
certificate said they could do some work.

J. T. Hutchinson (*Complainant*) vs Matty
(*Defendant*)
Complaint: Disobedience of the Driver's orders
and telling her she lies.
Decision: Seven days confinement and hard labour.

R. W. Harding (*Complainant*) vs twenty-four
women, four men and Alick and Dutchess
(*Defendants*)
Complaint: Alick and Dutchess encouraging the
others to be idle.
Decision: Alick and Dutchess one month's
confinement each. The rest to work six free
Saturdays.

Blossom (*Complainant*) vs her master, William
Adamson (*Defendant*)
Complaint: For not providing wholesome lodging.
Decision: Blossom ordered to serve three days
confinement for not proving charge.

Controlling apprentices on the plantation

Planters did not always need the special magistrates to control their apprentices. Those who
became too independent, or resisted the
master's demands for overtime work, had their
rations cut or their customary handouts of rum,
sugar and saltfish stopped altogether. Planters
had the right to decide if the apprentice's work
was satisfactory. They often found fault and the
apprentice was then 'fined in time' by being
sent to finish a task in the time they would
normally be working for wages. A common
form of punishment was for a planter to have
an apprentice placed in the lock-up on a
trumped-up charge to wait for the arrival of the
special magistrate. Just before he came the
charges were dropped and the apprentice was
released.

Many apprentices tried hard to find some
means of earning money after they finished their
$40\frac{1}{2}$ hours unpaid work. They hoped to save
enough to buy land, tools or perhaps a cart so
they could set up as small farmers, craftsmen

173

or traders when apprenticeship ended. Ways of earning cash included selling produce from provision grounds or working for higher wages on another property.

Planters soon discovered means of hindering an apprentice's chances of earning enough to save. In Barbados and St Kitts, many owners stopped importing most of their labourers' food as they had done in the days of slavery. Instead, they gave apprentices provision grounds in the fallow cane fields. This saved money and tied apprentices more closely to the plantations. In colonies where the slaves had always worked provision grounds masters attempted to make it difficult to earn money from them. Some cut down fruit trees, others forbade apprentices to keep livestock.

Many owners rearranged the 40½ hours work so that it was spread over five days, rather than the usual four. This left apprentices with little time to go to their provision grounds on Fridays to prepare for Saturday market. Apprentices needed a licence in order to be able to work away and they had to have a ticket from their master before they could sell in the market. It was easy for the planter to find an excuse for withdrawing the licence or ticket on the grounds that the apprentice had not carried out the 40½ hours work satisfactorily.

Honest magistrates

Those magistrates who did honestly try to carry out their work without favouring the masters were soon marked out and avoided. This could be done easily in colonies such as Jamaica where the magistrates were not required to visit a plantation with less than forty slaves unless they were specially summoned. Magistrates who went out of their way to investigate complaints from apprentices sometimes risked their lives. At the least, they were harassed by the masters and their friends who crowded into the court room to shout insults. The Englishman, Thomas Harvey, was shocked at the proceedings in the court of Richard Chamberlaine, one of the two coloured special magistrates in Jamaica. He wrote:

At this court, we could not but observe the very great difficulties the magistrate had to contend with, nor sufficiently admire the manner in which he discharged his duties. The room was filled with planters and overseers, some of whom were spectators only; and when any low, vulgar abuse of the magistrate was stated in evidence . . . it created a general laugh.

Every colony had some honest magistrates such as Richard Chamberlaine. Their efforts at least were worthwhile. Apprentices learned that legal proceedings could offer a little protection against their masters. The number of complaints brought by apprentices against planters increased steadily throughout the apprenticeship period. If this had not been so there would have certainly been serious trouble in many colonies. Even although flogging and punishment on the treadmills went on, it had to be ordered by the magistrate and took place in the workhouse where there was less chance of excessive punishment, or the death of an apprentice, going unnoticed.

The end of apprenticeship

Each month the special magistrates sent a report to the Colonial Office. From the reports, officials and members of the anti-slavery movement built up a picture of the sufferings of the apprentices and soon became convinced that the only way to protect them was by changing the system. In 1837 a British Parliamentary Committee read the evidence and recommended that the workhouses be taken away from the local magistrates and placed under the orders of the colonial governors. Flogging was prohibited and use of the treadmill forbidden for female prisoners. Even these small improvements roused the opposition of the planters who complained of British interference in their affairs. Rather than accept them, they favoured the end of apprenticeship itself.

Many planters, in any case, felt that apprenticeship was no longer useful. A licensing and ticketing system could still control the movement of labourers, while the planters would be free of the trouble and cost of providing homes

Fig. 21.3 *A painting of 1838. It shows members of the Baptist Church in Jamaica listening to the island's governor read the proclamation of the end of apprenticeship in the square at Spanish Town.*

and rations. There was also the fact that the non-praedials were due to become fully free in 1838. If they chose to leave the plantations there was little point in keeping the field-workers.

In early 1838 the planters were telling the colonial assemblies that they were ready to accept the end of apprenticeship. Laws were then passed which ended apprenticeship in all colonies on 1 August 1838, two years earlier than the date set by the Emancipation Act.

Assignments

1 Write a description of the reading of the Emancipation Act in your area. Your account should include: i) where the reading took place; ii) who were present; iii) the response of different groups to the main clauses of the Act.

2 Why did the Colonial Office think that apprenticeship was the first step in creating a free society? Did the planters see apprenticeship in the same way?

3 Outline the main difficulties of the apprenticeship period:
i) for the apprentices; ii) for the planters; iii) for the special magistrates.

4 Why did Antigua not have a period of apprenticeship? Why did apprenticeship end in 1838 in the other British Caribbean colonies?

22 THE END OF FRENCH, SPANISH AND DUTCH SLAVERY

Freedom in French colonies

The story of abolition in the French colonies starts in St Domingue. As we saw in Chapter 17, the success of the black revolt led by Boukman encouraged the French revolutionary commander to emancipate the slaves in August 1793. A year later the revolutionary government in France decided that its slogan of 'Liberty, Equality and Fraternity' applied to all people of whatever colour. The slaves in the other French colonies were declared free. That meant emancipation for the black people of Guadeloupe, French Guyana and St Lucia as well as St Domingue. The slaves on Martinique and Tobago could not be freed because the islands had been taken by Britain. Those on St Lucia had only the briefest taste of full freedom because Britain seized the island in 1794. The slaves across the whole island immediately revolted and it was two years before they were finally crushed.

In 1802, France's revolutionary movement had been destroyed by the soldier Napoleon Bonaparte who made himself emperor. He sent forces to the Caribbean to end the eight years of freedom. Toussaint's black armies were too strong for them in St Domingue and the French lost the colony for ever. In Guyana, Guadeloupe and Martinique the blacks put up a hard fight. Hundreds, and maybe thousands, died in Guadeloupe before the French were able to restore slavery.

There is a lesson in the contrast between the revolutionaries freeing the slaves in 1794 and the emperor using force to bring slavery back in 1802. Slavery was not likely to end in French colonies while the emperor or one of the kings who followed him in 1815 was on the throne. Emancipation needed another revolutionary government to support the rights of the slaves. The contrast also shows us that the emancipation movement in France had much more to do with political ideas than with religious groups like those which were important in England. The French supporters of emancipation were people who demanded more democracy and equality in their own country. This also meant they opposed the strong position of the Catholic Church in France. So the French emancipation movement was mostly 'secular' – which means the belief that progress would come when religion had less hold over people's minds and priests had less power in society.

POOR CONSOLATION.

PARISIAN.—"COURAGE, MON AMI; 'AM I NOT A MAN AND A BROTHER?'"

Fig. 22.1 *A cartoon from an English magazine showing a French working man comparing his lack of freedom with a slave's.*

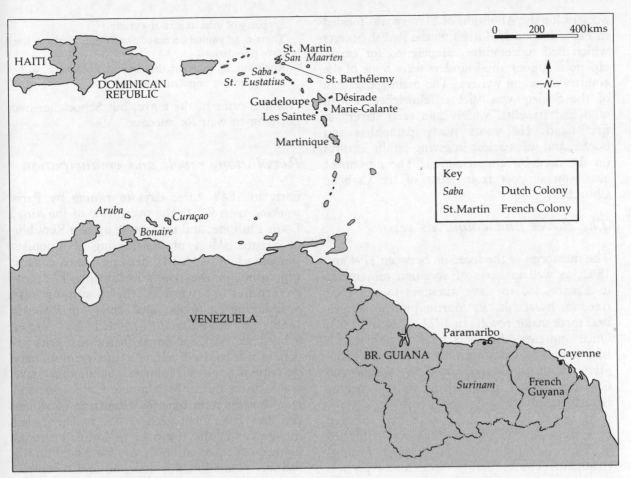

Map 30 *The Dutch and French colonies in the nineteenth century.*

Weakening of the French West India interest

In 1815 the French Wars ended and a peace treaty was signed in Vienna. In the treaty France agreed to end the slave trade. To planters in Martinique and Guadeloupe this seemed a great opportunity. They had about a quarter of a million slaves between them and no rivals who wanted to send sugar to France. Haiti was turning over to small-scale farming. French Guyana was crippled by the abolition of the slave trade mainly because the colony had only 15,000 slaves and the planters could get no more.

However, the hopes of the Martinique and Guadeloupe planters were soon dashed by the growth of sugar beet farming in France. The French were the first Europeans to develop the crop on a large scale. As early as 1839 there were some 550 sugar beet factories producing about 48 million kilograms of sugar. This cut the demand for French Caribbean cane sugar. It also meant that there was a large beet farming interest in French politics. In Britain the East India interest became more powerful than the West India interest in Parliament. In the French assembly, representatives from the sugar beet districts outnumbered those with connections with trading or planting in the Caribbean.

The emancipation movement

The weakening of the West India interest in French politics helped the rapid growth of an abolition movement in the 1830s. In 1834 a new

Society for the Abolition of Slavery was formed in Paris. It modelled itself on the British Society which had successfully campaigned for emancipation. Among the founders were some of the country's leading writers. The main spokesman of the Society was Victor Schoelcher, a man who had travelled widely and seen slavery at first hand. He wrote many pamphlets and books, and was tireless in giving public lectures on the need for emancipation. The movement also won support from parts of the Catholic Church.

The slaves and coloureds resist

The memories of the freedom between 1794 and 1802, as well as news of abolition movements in France, led to slave attempts to win their freedom by revolt. In Martinique they organised three major revolts in 1822, 1824 and 1833. Once apprenticeship was over in the British islands they had another form of protest. Thousands of slaves escaped from Martinique and Guadeloupe and made their way to nearby British islands.

At the same time there were free coloured campaigns. In 1823 a pamphlet was published in Paris drawing attention to their unequal treatment. The French government's reply was to deport thirty Martiniquans to Senegal in French West Africa.

Amelioration

Slave resistance and emancipationist pressure led the French government to try measures for amelioration just as the British had done. In 1833 the branding and mutilation of slaves were forbidden, and free coloureds were allowed full civil rights. In 1845, regulations further limited physical punishment and insisted on elementary education and religious instruction for slaves. These measures only drove Victor Schoelcher into frequent demands for immediate emancipation. His society grew so that it had a committee in every department in France and, in 1847, he put forward sixteen points in favour of the abolition of slavery to the French National Assembly. Among them were:

Property of man in man is a crime.
There is an annual excess of deaths over births in the slave population.
Abolition, by rehabilitating agricultural labour, will attach the free population to it.

Nothing came of the move, but Schoelcher had not long to wait for success.

Revolution, revolt and emancipation

Early in 1848, three days of rioting by Paris working men led to the overthrow of the king, Louis Philippe, and the setting up of a Republic in France. Most of the leading abolitionists welcomed this and became enthusiastic supporters of the new government. The new government rewarded their support by proclaiming the abolition of slavery on 3 March 1868. A commission, headed by Victor Schoelcher, was appointed to see that emancipation was carried out. As the revolutionary movement grew in France, yet another slave revolt broke out in Martinique. Cane fields and great houses were burned. Hundreds of whites fled the colony altogether, others barricaded themselves in the towns or in fortified strongholds on the plantations. One stronghold on the Sannois plantation was attacked and destroyed and all thirty-seven whites inside were killed. Meanwhile in French Guyana it was reckoned that three-quarters of the slaves had simply left the plantations.

The bitter resistance of the slaves, and the fear that the French colonies might follow the path of Haiti, meant that most plantation owners accepted the emancipation decree with a sigh of relief. In any case they did not have assemblies like those in the British islands which organised a long campaign against emancipation. Planters were relieved to have compensation money for slaves they might not have been able to hold down much longer. Six million francs was set aside by Schloecher's Commission as an immediate payment, as well as 120 million francs in government bonds which paid interest of 5 per cent. No compensation was paid for slaves bought after 1831, for children under 5 or adults over 60.

No apprenticeship

The ex-slaves received no compensation in land or money. But they were not forced to serve an apprenticeship. The fact that there was no apprenticeship was one reason why the movement from the plantations in Martinique and Guadeloupe was not as widespread as in the British colonies after 1838. The ex-slaves were just as anxious to show their contempt for field labour but there was not the opportunity of saving when they had to buy their own food and pay rent from the first day of freedom.

Freedom in Spanish colonies

The Spanish islands

In the last years of the French Wars, the Spanish Empire in the Americas began to break up. By 1821 the creole Spanish-speaking people of Central and South America had set up independent states. Spain's only remaining colonies were Cuba, Puerto Rico and Santo Domingo. In 1822 she lost Santo Domingo when it was occupied by Haiti. The Haitians ruled Santo Domingo until 1844. During that time they emancipated the few slaves left.

Emancipation came to Santo Domingo far earlier than it did to Cuba and Puerto Rico. One of the reasons for that was that plantation slavery was not important on these islands until about a hundred years after it developed in the British and French colonies. It was only from the 1760s that slaves were brought to Cuba and Puerto Rico in large numbers. Before that the islands' main settlers had been cattle ranchers and small farmers. With the slaves came the change over to plantations growing sugar, tobacco and coffee.

Trading the slaves

Cuban and Puerto Rican slavery grew just at the time that French and British slavery was weakening or being abolished. For this to happen meant that the Cubans and Puerto Ricans had to find ways to import slaves when all European countries had abolished the trade. Spain herself had agreed to abolition in treaties with Britain in 1817 and 1820. But at the time Spain had no intention of enforcing the abolition. The agreement was easy to get round because few slaves were carried to her colonies in Spanish ships. Most were taken in American vessels or ships of other countries flying the American flag. The United States refused to recognise the right of British patrol ships to stop her vessels and free any slaves on board.

The Spanish government did not give its officials orders to prevent the trade. The British consul in Havana reported that slaves were landed there quite openly. It merely cost an extra doubloon in bribes per slave. A quarter of this went to each of the captain-general, the customs controller, the harbour master and the local customs officer.

With so much money to be earned, the slave trade continued to grow through the 1820s, when the average number landed was 6,250 a year, up to the peak year of 1837 when more than 12,000 Africans were sold in Cuban auctions. Conditions on the slave ships were no better than they had been in earlier times and at least one in ten died on the voyage.

Slaves and sugar

Most slaves were bought to work on new cane fields carved out of the virgin lands on the west of the island. The labour of these slaves made possible the great Cuban sugar revolution. In 1815 Cuba produced about half the amount of sugar exported from Jamaica. By 1882, when Cuban slavery was drawing to an end, this one island produced nearly twice as much sugar as the whole of the English-speaking Caribbean.

By then, too, Cuban sugar factories were mechanised and usually worked by free labourers. The slaves were cut off from skilled factory work and laboured only in field gangs or domestic service. Most of them lacked even the primitive protection given on British slave plantations. Masters sometimes emancipated slaves, but usually only because it saved the costs of providing rations and huts in the compound. Unless they were the coloured chil-

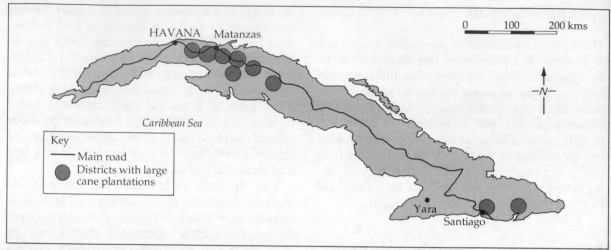

Map 31 *Cuba in the mid-nineteenth century.*

dren of whites, most emancipated slaves ended up with ever worse working conditions as parts of gangs doing contract work.

The slaves suffered under harsh police laws. They were neglected by the Church which supported slavery and would not marry slaves. Health conditions were dreadful and the death rate was high; it was reckoned that between 8 and 10 per cent of the slaves had to be replaced by new captives each year.

The sugar revolution divided the Cuban planters into two groups. The large plantations were on the west of the island. Here were many planters, merchants and businessmen who became very wealthy on the profits from sugar. In the east the farmers were less successful producers of cattle, tobacco and coffee. They used the labour of 300,000 people but only one in ten were slaves. The rest were a mixture of free coloureds and whites from many countries.

There were similar conditions in Puerto Rico. In the mid-nineteenth century the island had only 31,000 slaves which was an average of 15 for each owner. There were few large sugar plantations and most farmers produced a range of crops which included maize, cotton, rice and tobacco, as well as cattle and sheep. Only a third of the slaves were farm labourers and altogether on the island there were twice as many white labourers as there were coloured and black, whether slave or free. The smaller farmers and planters in east Cuba and in Puerto

Rico were more ready to accept emancipation than the large estate owners in the west of Cuba.

The end of the slave trade

In 1838, the Spanish government signed another treaty with Britain agreeing to end the trade. Again she took no action but this time the slaves protested. In 1843, slaves in the area around Mantanzas began a wide-spread revolt and demanded freedom. They were backed by some free coloureds. The revolt was put down with great harshness and many slaves and free coloureds were executed. But it marked the first important change of mind among some large plantation owners. They began to fear that the island might become a black republic like Haiti. Some began to use indentured labourers from the Canary Islands, Mexico and China rather than importing more slaves. But the revolt also stiffened the fear of what would follow if slaves already in Cuba were emancipated.

In 1855 Spain took its first serious steps to end the trade. Some planters were so enraged by this that they spoke of joining Cuba to the USA. The island would then become one of the group of American states where slavery was allowed. This idea broke down when the North defeated the American slave states in the American Civil War of 1861–5. During the war, President Lincoln emancipated all American slaves on 1 January 1863. The end of American slavery meant that United States ships would no longer carry slaves to Cuba and Puerto Rico.

The Spanish government again decided to end the trade in 1863. In 1866 the last slave was brought to Cuba and the government in Spain declared that slavery was to end. The larger planters resisted this because of the losses they would suffer. The smaller planters of coffee and sugar on the east of Cuba and in Puerto Rico were now ready to accept emancipation.

Politics and emancipation

The question of emancipation now became bound up with island politics. In Cuba many 'liberals' wanted to follow the example of Latin America and become independent from Spain. In the 1840s and 1850s many of these liberals had been forced to shelter in New York and the cities of Latin America. Now in the 1860s they began to win support from the small planters. A movement for independence grew up led by Carlos Manuel de Céspedes, a lawyer and eastern landowner. Arms were smuggled in from America. In 1868 de Céspedes emancipated his own slaves and then opened a revolutionary war for Cuban independence with the declaration of Yara – or *grito de Yara* – which called for freedom from Spain, a republican government and the abolition of slavery.

The war which followed lasted for ten years. Most of the fighting took place on the eastern end of the island and the rebels had little chance of success against the Spanish commander, Martinez Campos. But their struggle did help to bring emancipation forward. In 1870, the Spanish government ordered that all slaves over 60 should be freed and the newborn children of slaves should be freed on their eighteenth birthday. Until then they had to serve a form of apprenticeship known as the *patranato*. But Campos feared that unless he emancipated all adult slaves, they would join the rebels. So he quickly brought the fighting to an end and, in 1878, signed the Treaty of Zanjon with the revolutionaries. They agreed to end the war in return for an amnesty for their rebellion while the Spanish promised to abolish all slavery.

In 1878, all slaves who had fought for the revolution, as well as those who had helped the Spanish troops, were freed. In 1880 it was announced that the patranato would be ended in 1888. In fact it was given up in 1886, the year which marked the final end of slavery in Cuba. Even after this, most of the half-million Africans were denied the chance to own land, to become educated or find work which would give them the same standard of living as most of the non-African population of Cuba.

Puerto Rico, too, had its liberals who wanted independence. They opened revolution in 1868 but were soon crushed by Spanish troops. But the failed revolution had played its part in bringing emancipation earlier than in Cuba. The 30,000 slaves on Puerto Rico were freed on 22 March 1873, although they then had to enter a period of apprenticeship for three years.

Freedom in Dutch colonies

The colonies and their slaves after 1815

After the French Wars, the Dutch were left with three groups of Caribbean colonies. In the Windwards there were the islands of Aruba, Bonaire and Curaçao. In the Leewards there were St Eustatius, Saba and San Maarten where the Dutch owned half the island and the French the other half. On the mainland, squeezed between the French and British Guyanese colonies there was Dutch Surinam.

The island colonies were poorly suited to sugar, although planters tried hard to make a success of it on Curaçao. For twenty years they drove slaves hard to set and crop new canes on irrigated fields. In the end they failed. San Maarten had 92 small plantations divided between cane cultivation and cattle ranching. But the colony's main earnings came from the labour of hundreds of slaves who raked and dried salt from huge salt ponds. Surinam was a sugar-growing colony but its planters were seriously short of labour. During the Wars it had been occupied by Britain so no more slaves

Fig. 22.2 *A photograph of a Dutch settler's house in Willemstad, Curaçao.*

were carried there after Britain ended the trade.

When the war ended Surinam was returned to Holland. The Dutch started slave trading again and some Africans were taken to Surinam. But, in 1821, Holland gave way to British pressure and ended the slave trade for good. The Surinam planters faced a permanent shortage of labour along with other problems.

Emancipation

The slaves in British colonies were emancipated in 1834 and the French freed their Africans for a second and final time in 1848. In Holland, debates over the emancipation of Dutch slaves dragged on for a further fifteen years. During these years the Dutch planters were able to make use of forced labour but, for them as well as the slaves, it might have been better if freedom had come earlier. Some compensation money would have been available to pay off debts and to start again with free labour. Instead, the planters waited. Mortgages went unpaid, plantations were abandoned and the slaves, who sensed that freedom was near, increased their resistance.

As in the British and French colonies, emancipation was preceded by slave revolts. The planters in San Maarten soon realised that it was impossible to control their slaves. After 1848, there was little they could do to prevent them walking the few kilometres into the French half of the island, where they would become freemen. The planters petitioned the Dutch government to emancipate the slaves, realising it would be beter to receive some compensation rather than steadily lose slaves across the French border. The Dutch government replied that it would be impossible to free the slaves in one part of the empire and not in others. The planters then 'informally' freed their slaves but took care to keep their legal proof of ownership against the day when official emancipation might bring them some compensation.

The emancipation debates dragged on throughout the 1850s. Much time was wasted in arguing about how much compensation was to be paid and whether the slaves would have to pass through a period of apprenticeship. The Surinam planters saw labour shortages as their greatest problem and pressed for a long apprenticeship. Slaveholders in the island colonies wanted immediate freedom but higher compensation. In the end, the decision went in favour of a long period of apprenticeship.

Emancipation became law on 1 July 1863. On that day 45,275 people became free. But those between the ages of 15 and 60 had to continue working for their former masters at a minimum wage for ten years. In addition to cheap labour, the owners also received compensation at a rate of 300 guilders per slave. This rate was eventually reduced for the islands, where it was felt the slaves had been less valuable as labourers than in Surinam. Most of the owners in the island colonies had to settle for 200 guilders per slave. In San Maarten the rate was cut to 30 guilders. Only after loud protests was it raised to 100. Of course, as in the British colonies, the ex-slaves received no compensation.

Assignments

1 *Draw a map of the Caribbean and show the territories which were colonies of France, Spain and the Dutch after 1815. Indicate the date of the ending of slavery in each of these groups of colonies.*

2 *Describe the similarities between the emancipation of slaves in the Dutch, French and British West Indian colonies.*

3 *How was the ending of slavery in the Spanish colonies different from the ending of slavery in the British colonies?*

4 *What challenge did Haiti present to the rulers of European colonies?*

GUIDELINES FOR THE CXC EXAMINATION

Form of the examinations

The examinations each consist of a multiple-choice paper, an open response paper and a course work component, worth respectively 14, 56 and 30 per cent of the total marks.

Paper 1

1 hour 15 minutes. This paper is common to the Basic and General Proficiency examinations. There are sixty multiple-choice questions on the Overview. Five items will be set on each of the ten listed topics: the remaining ten items will not be identified with a specific theme, but will be concerned with general trends and overall chronology.

Paper 2

Separate papers will be set for Basic Proficiency (1 hour 40 minutes) and General Proficiency (2 hours 10 minutes). Each paper will be set on the thirteen themes detailed in the syllabus. Two questions will be set on each theme. Each question will take the form of an essay or stimulus material to which the candidate is invited to respond. The stimulus material may include extracts from documents, pictures, cartoons, maps, statistical tables and graphs and the response called for may be a single sentence, a short paragraph or an essay. Candidates must answer one question from each of the four sections of the syllabus. (Where CXC has accepted an alternative theme from a school, the candidates from that school must answer one of the two questions set on that theme as their response to the section in which it is located.)

Paper 3

(Over three terms). Nine pieces of work set and marked in the school, three per term, for three terms, with the option of substituting a project for the course work of one term. (The pieces submitted should be the exercises which a teacher would normally give and should be treated as an examination in itself.) Teachers should begin recording in the Course Work Record Book by the beginning of Term 3.

The teacher is at liberty to use a wide variety of assignments for this paper. All the questions following each chapter in this book could be used, but the teacher is also encouraged to create assignments of his or her own.

There is also the option of using a project instead of three pieces of course work. Projects usually cover *an entire theme* of the syllabus. Further details are outlined on page 19 of the CXC syllabus.

The project as course work

A project may be substituted for all or part of the course work assignments for ONE TERM ONLY. A project may therefore be allocated all the marks for the term's work. However, if the teacher feels that the project does not merit a total weight of 60 marks, one additional course work assignment may be set in the term to bring the total assignment weight up to 60 marks.

The written report of a project will normally call for 25–30 sides of letter-sized paper (8.5″ × 11″). Such a report must have the following features:

1 a specific title;
2 a list of contents which shows the material in the report arranged in chapters or sections;
3 a bibliography and a list of all other sources used, e.g. museums, personal interviews, visits to historical locations;
4 illustrations and diagrams wherever appropriate;
5 an interpretation and evaluation of the information gathered;
6 a clear indication of the work for which each student was responsible, in the case of group projects.

In addition, there should normally be:

1 a clearly and briefly stated aim;
2 a brief statement by the candidate of what was achieved in relation to the stated aim, and some indication of any difficulties encountered.

FURTHER READING

General

Student sources

P. Ashdown, **Caribbean History in Maps**, Longman, 1980.
F. R. Augier et al., **The Making of the West Indies**, Longman, 1960.
Isaac Dookhan, **A Pre-Emancipation History of the West Indies**, Longman, 1988.
Isaac Dookhan, **A Post-Emancipation History of the West Indies**, Longman, 1988.
A. Garcia, **A History of the West Indies**, Harrap, 1965.
S. C. Gordon, **Caribbean Generations**, Longman, 1984.
D. G. Waddell, **The West Indies and the Guianas**, Prentice-Hall, 1967.

Easier books

R. N. Murray, **Nelson's West Indian History**, Nelson, 1971.
A. Norman, P. Patterson, and J. Carnegie, **The People Who Came**, Books 1 and 2, Longman, 1986, 1989.
P. Sherlock, **West Indian Nations**, Jamaica Publishing House, 1973.

For teachers

C. Hampshire, **The British in the Caribbean**, Weidenfeld & Nicolson, 1972.
J. Parry and P. Sherlock, **Short History of the West Indies**, Macmillan, 1971.
W. A. Roberts, **The French in the West Indies**, Cooper Square Publishers (New York), 1971.
E. Williams, **From Columbus to Castro**, Deutsch, 1970.

Student sources on particular states

B. Brereton, **A History of Modern Trinidad**, Heinemann, 1981.
C. V. Black, **History of Jamaica**, Longman, 1983.
V. T. Daly, **The Making of Guyana**, Macmillan, 1974.
F. A. Hoyos, **History of Barbados**, Macmillan, 1976.
E. Williams, **History of the People of Trinidad and Tobago**, PNM Publishing, 1962.

Early history and European settlement

Student sources

E. Jones, **Protector of the Indians: the Life of de las Casas**, Longman, 1973.
A. Kendall, **Everyday Life of the Incas**, Batsford, 1973.

E. Newarth, **They Lived Like This in Ancient Maya**, Man Parrish, 1966.
D. O'Sullivan, **The Age of Discovery**, Longman, 1984.

For teachers

A. Calder, **Revolutionary Empire**, Dutton, 1981.
N. Davies, **The Aztecs**, University of Oklahoma Press, 1980.
A. P. Newton, **The European Nations in the West Indies**, Black, 1966.
R. B. Sheridan, **The Development of the Plantations to 1750**, Caribbean University Press, 1970.

African background and slavery

Student sources

M. Crowder, **West Africa: an introduction to its history**, Longman, 1978.
B. Davidson, **Discovering Africa's Past**, Longman, 1978.
B. Davidson, **A History of West Africa 1000–1800**, Longman, 1977.
P. Edwards, **The Life of Olaudah Equiano**, Longman, 1989.
C. McEvedy, **The Penguin Atlas of African History**, Penguin, 1980.
J. R. Milsome, **Olaudah Equiano**, Makers of African History Series, Longman, 1969.
G. T. Stride and C. Ifeka, **Peoples and Empires of West Africa**, Nelson, 1969.
J. Walvin, **Slavery and the Slave Trade**, Macmillan, 1983.

For teachers

B. Davidson, **Black Mother**, Gollancz, 1980.
R. S. Dunn, **Sugar and Slaves**, Norton (New York), 1972.
P. D. Curtin, **The African Slave Trade: A Census**, University of Wisconsin Press, 1969.
J. G. Fage, **A History of West Africa**, Cambridge University Press, 1969.
J. Inikori (ed.), **Forced Migration: Impact of the Export Slave Trade on African Societies**, Hutchinson, 1982.
R. Oliver and J. C. Fage, **A Short History of Africa**, Penguin, 1988.

Slave societies: resistance and revolt

Student sources

J. D. Bentley, **Toussaint L'Ouverture**, Hulton, 1969.
E. Brathwaite, **Folk Culture of the Slaves in Jamaica**, New Beacon Books, 1970.
L. Mathurin, **The Rebel Woman in the British West Indies during Slavery**, African-Caribbean Publications (Kingston), 1975.
G. F. Tyson, **Toussaint L'Ouverture**, Prentice-Hall, 1973.

For teachers

E. Brathwaite, **The Development of Creole Society in Jamaica 1770–1820**, Clarendon Press, 1971.
M. Craton and J. Walvin, **A Jamaican Plantation**, University of Toronto Press, 1970.

E. Goveia, **Slave Society in the British Leeward Islands at the End of the 18th Century**, Caribbean University Press, 1970.

C. L. R. James, **A History of Negro Revolt**, Race Today Publications, 1985.

C. L. R. James, **Black Jacobins**, Random House (New York), 1963.

O. Patterson, **The Sociology of Slavery**, Farleigh Dickinson, 1967.

R. B. Sheridan, **An Era of West Indian Prosperity 1750–1775**, Caribbean University Press, 1970.

Abolition and Emancipation

T. Brady and E. Jones, **The Fight Against Slavery**, BBC, 1975.

R. Coupland, **The British Anti-Slavery Movement**, Cass, 1974.

M. Craton, **Slavery, Abolition and Emancipation**, Longman, 1974.

E. Williams, **Capitalism and Slavery**, Deutsch, 1972.

P. Wright, **Knibb the Notorious**, Sidgwick & Jackson, 1973.

INDEX

Note: Figures in *italics* refer to the illustrations, figures in **bold** to the maps.